Bliss Perry

The Broughton House

Bliss Perry

The Broughton House

ISBN/EAN: 9783743305410

Manufactured in Europe, USA, Canada, Australia, Japa

Cover: Foto ©ninafisch / pixelio.de

Manufactured and distributed by brebook publishing software (www.brebook.com)

Bliss Perry

The Broughton House

THE BROUGHTON HOUSE

THE BROUGHTON HOUSE

BY

BLISS PERRY

NEW YORK
CHARLES SCRIBNER'S SONS
1890

COPYRIGHT, 1890,

BY CHARLES SCRIBNER'S SONS.

THE BROUGHTON HOUSE.

I.

"Do you suppose Mr. Sonderby will come, my dear? It would be just like him not to appear, after all. You never can tell anything about that man."

Mrs. Ellerton hardly looked at her husband as she spoke, for she was taking a last rapid survey of the tiny tea-table, and as she uttered the words "anything about that man," she bent over and made a more accurate right angle of the tea knife and spoon at the visitor's plate. She was a trifle heated, — the result of overseeing a half-trained girl in the kitchen, — and she wore, albeit somewhat lightly, that anxiety of the young housekeeper which finds in over-accuracy a compensation for the lack of experience. Arthur Ellerton was standing by the door of the dining-room, arrayed in a gray flannel study-gown and slippers. Behind him could be seen the desk he had just left, and the stained pine shelves that contained his scanty library. It was late Saturday afternoon, and the ink was still wet upon what he considered a rather satisfactory ending to his sermon for the morrow.

He looked across the room at his wife, amused at her preoccupied air, and with an admiration which extended itself even to the huge white apron that almost hid her dotted muslin gown. He watched her fine, tall figure bending over the table, the swift movement of her fingers among the glass and silver, and the gravity of her serious face as she laid a napkin for the expected guest. Then he broke into a low, contented laugh.

"Well?" she demanded, suspiciously, turning toward him.

"Nothing, Ruth; only it is such fun to see you go at things."

She straightened herself, with a whimsical affectation of displeasure, and her gray eyes danced. "You are always making fun of me, when you don't realize at all the important things I have to decide," she said.

He leaned against the door and smiled at her, without answering.

"But do you suppose he is coming?" she asked.

"I'm sure I don't know," said Ellerton. "I don't pretend to know anything about Sonderby. It isn't I who see in him some — what did you call it? — some germ — "

"You're too bad, sir," cried Mrs. Ellerton, the color rising to her cheeks, but her eyes dancing still. "You know you're just as much interested in him as I am; and he must be lonely this vacation, and we have never had him here, and—"

"And therefore if it doesn't rain and give him the excuse he had when he stayed away from Deacon Starling's, we may hope to see him, you mean. But he has five minutes more, anyway, and I'm not exactly ready myself," he added, looking down on his study-gown and slippers, and pointing ruefully to an ink-spot on his white but sinewy hand. "Let's go and see if he isn't in sight. Will you take my arm, Mrs. Ellerton?" and with mock formality, which changed an instant afterward into as decided a freedom, these high-spirited young people crossed the hall and the parlor, to the window that commanded a view of the long street of Broughton.

The parsonage was at the east end of the village. Broughton's main street had been the pride of the men who laid it out, early in the century, and it was beautiful enough still to be the admiration of the summer visitors, whose verdict upon this matter of taste, at least, was considered by the natives to be decisive. Terminating at the east in a gentle rise, upon which stood the great white Orthodox church, on either side of which roads diverged, one to South Broughton, the other to East Part, the street ended on the west at the academy building, a low brown structure with Corinthian columns and a portico. Between the academy and the church stretched a level half-mile of elm-arched street, broad and quiet. The narrow sidewalks, hardly more than foot-paths, followed the elm-tree trunks closely, curving a little every few yards for the sake of avoiding an unusually large or irregularly planted tree. The country road, with an abundant margin of grass on either side, widened into broad gravelled spaces before the hotel, the post-office, and Parkinson's store. However ample the width of the street might appear, it did not discourage the huge elms from throwing their lean branches across it towards one another, even the tiniest twigs seeming to stretch out eagerly, so that when the evening breezes began to move the dusty leaves, the rustle went equally all through the dark green canopy, and one could not tell where the northern elm branches ceased and the southern ones began, such was the inextricable soft tangle.

The parsonage, separated from the church only by the road to South Broughton, was so near the street that from the parlor window one could see almost the whole length of it. The Ellertons stood a few moments gazing down the long vista at the end of which stood the low academy, dark now against the deep gold of the sunset. The street was empty save for the afternoon stage from the Center, whose driver was throwing off the mail-bag in front of the post-office.

He was three hours late that day. Soon one white gate after another opened, here and there along the street, and a child, or a woman, or an old man, would move leisurely toward the office, knowing that the postmistress would require a quarter of an hour more to distribute the mail, but unable to deprive themselves of the pleasure of waiting and watching. But while the minister and his wife were scanning the street for John Sonderby, the academy teacher, they suddenly recognized his short figure and heavy walk as he came out from the space in front of the hotel, beyond the post-office, half-way down the street, and turned eastward towards the parsonage.

"Well, I declare. there he is!" cried Ellerton.

"Didn't I tell you I knew he would be here?" asserted the minister's wife, triumphantly, forgetting the doubt which had possessed her but a few moments previously. "Hurry, Arthur! I want you to be here when he comes in."

Ellerton disappeared up the front stairs to make a hasty toilet, while his wife took off her big white apron, and carrying it into the sitting-room, threw it somewhat unceremoniously into a closet. Then with a glance at her hair in the gilt-framed mirror hanging over the sewing-machine, and a deft stroke or two at its gold-brown masses with her quick fingers, she came through the dining-room again, took a final look at the table, hurried to the kitchen to tell Mary Jane to put the tea steeping, and then, closing the folding-doors that shut the dining-room from the parlor, sat down in her best plush chair to await the sound of the door-bell.

There was a click at the front gate, and John Sonderby came up the straight gravelled path to the piazza. He glanced at the flower-beds, with their plentiful sprinkling of new shingles stuck firmly into the soil, and pencilled with Latin names; but the flowers to be seen were few. The grass was cut as neatly as scythe could cut it, lawn-mowers being a rare luxury in Broughton. The Virginia creeper was thick upon the white posts of the piazza, and even climbed along the roof, hanging down here and there in waving pendants, scarcely stirring in the quiet evening air. The parsonage was an attractive place, nestling there under the side of the knoll, and Sonderby found himself struck with its homelikeness and charm. He had never been there before — except once in the evening — since the Ellertons came to Broughton the previous autumn. The school-teacher made few calls, at best, being fertile in excuses to himself, while to those who invited him he was exasperatingly non-committal in his formulation of acceptances and regrets.

"I don't know why I'm here," he thought, as he passed under the fringe of Virginia creeper, and hesitating a moment between the old-fashioned brass knocker upon the centre panel of the door and the brand-new bell-handle at the side, pulled the latter, slowly at first, and then with a powerful jerk. The tinkling had not ceased when the door opened. Sonderby had expected to see Mary

Jane, a pupil of his during the winter months, who acted as "help" for the minister's wife out of school hours and in vacations. But instead of the awkward figure and bashful smile of Mary Jane, Ruth Ellerton's tall form, graceful head, and shining gray eyes confronted him. He was a trifle embarrassed, and half missed the frankly outstretched hand, but collected himself as their fingers righted and she gave his hand a cordial pressure, smiling her welcome as she did so.

They stood a moment in the narrow hall, while she hung up his straw hat, remembering as she glanced at it that her brother had worn a hat of that model two seasons before. Then she ushered her guest into the parlor.

"We are very glad to see you at last, Mr. Sonderby," she began. Then it occurred to her that that was not a particularly happy opening; it implied too much as to his previous discourtesy.

"You are very kind," he replied, somewhat helplessly. She sat in her plush chair, her hands playing with the handkerchief in her lap. Sonderby had taken a cane rocking-chair, much too low for him, and sat with his knees high, looking uncomfortable.

"What do you find to do all these long summer days?" she asked, busying her brain meanwhile to discover an excuse for getting him to change his seat.

"Well," he answered, "not much of anything

in particular. I have never loafed a summer vacation before — that is, since I left college."

"No?"

"No. I can't tell yet whether I shall like it. Last year I was down at Calvin Johnson's."

"Were you? I suppose that is a pleasant place to board, isn't it?" The minister's wife spoke rapidly, as if the conversation were now successfully started. "Some friends of mine were there once, years ago. It is such a beautiful farm."

"It is probably the best farm in town," said the school-teacher. "But you see, I wasn't a boarder; that is, not exactly of the summer kind."

Mrs. Ellerton looked puzzled.

Sonderby seemed to study her. "I was haying it," he explained, looking her directly in the eyes; "haying and harvesting with the Johnson boys."

"Oh," she said.

He had apparently exhausted the topic, and sat gazing at her.

"Did you like it?" she asked.

"The haying? Well, there is some satisfaction in it."

"Oh, there must be," she broke in, with an eager vagueness. "It is such clean work, and the odor of new-mown hay is so delicious; and then these beautiful June and July days, and —"

She hesitated, seeing him smile grimly. "I used to ride on the hay-cart at my grandfather's, in the country," she went on, plunging in deeper. "My brother used to follow the cart, and what do you call it — rake after?"

"Yes," replied Sonderby, lifting himself a trifle in his low chair, and continuing to observe her. Her reminiscences failed. She was conscious of being vexed, and of the color in her cheeks. She began to see how it was that people came to think John Sonderby a difficult person to entertain. She must try some other topic, clearly.

"Are there many people at the hotel?" she inquired.

"There are not so very many."

She was exceedingly glad to see her husband, who ran down the front stairs and appeared at the parlor door at this juncture.

"Oh, how do you do, Mr. Sonderby?" Ellerton cried. "We are very glad to see you here at last." It occurred to Ruth Ellerton that her husband began much as she had done, but she had confidence in his easy way with people. Ellerton crossed the room swiftly to meet the guest: Sonderby rose a trifle awkwardly from his low chair, and the two shook hands. The minister was the taller, and his frock coat added to his apparent height; straight, athletic, with a boyish, smoothly shaven face, blue eyes, and light brown hair. Sonderby stooped slightly, but his shoulders were powerful, and his whole frame was solidly put together: his full beard made him seem older than Ellerton, though he was really three years younger.

"Glad to see you," Ellerton repeated, dropping the school-teacher's hand.

"You are very kind," said Sonderby. As the latter turned to his cane chair, he saw that his hostess had laid a possessing hand upon it.

"Won't you try that other one?" she suggested.

Before the teacher could seat himself, Ellerton began, in his high, clear, fluent voice, a rapid stream of talk, — cheery nothings: the weather, the roads, the crops, the influx of summer visitors, — in all of which Sonderby took his share briefly, but cordially and easily enough, while Mrs. Ellerton listened to her husband, half in amusement and half in admiration. Arthur had such a frank, confident manner of approaching people, as if he could discern beforehand that they would like him.

In a few minutes Mary Jane, inserting her red fingers between the white folding-doors that led to the dining-room, pushed them apart, and revealed her bashful, smiling countenance. She did not know whether it was proper to bow to her school-teacher first, or to announce that tea was served, so she made an ineffective compromise by doing both at once. Mrs. Ellerton bit her lips; then rose and led the way to the table. It was a square little table, covered with her best Irish linen cloth, and her treasured Vienna plates. On the unoccupied side, opposite Sonderby's chair, stood a wide-mouthed pitcher filled with sweet-peas. There was a pause as the three took their places; then they bowed their heads, and the minister said grace. The moment it was finished Mary Jane emerged from the kitchen door, behind which she had been listening, and proceeded to pour the water.

Ellerton passed Sonderby the cold tongue, while the hostess arranged the fragile cups and saucers.

"One lump, if you please," said Sonderby, in answer to her question; "yes, with cream."

So opened the conversation. It was really very agreeable in the parsonage, and Sonderby wondered why he had so long excused himself from coming. He faced the parlor as he sat, and across the sweetpeas he could see the open parlor window, with the Virginia creeper swaying in the breeze upon the piazza post outside, while the cool dusk gathered everywhere. There were a couple of candles upon the table in tall bronze candlesticks, but they were not lighted.

Sonderby sipped his tea, and began to feel, for him, exceedingly at home in a strange house.

"You haven't asked me anything about the school," he found himself saying, with a smile; "I have learned to expect questions about that the first thing now, everywhere I go."

"Perhaps you would like a little relief," replied Mrs. Ellerton. "I think you might be excused in vacation, anyway. I know my husband gets tired of being asked about church work, sometimes, though he doesn't like to own it."

"Take care, my dear," cried Ellerton.

"It was too bad," she persisted, looking half at her husband and half at Sonderby, "to see how you turned the subject when that old gentleman at the last conference wanted to talk about the decline of Unitarianism in the hill towns, and you insisted on talking politics."

Ellerton laughed at the reminiscence. "I couldn't help it," he said; "he was getting material for a quarrelsome article, I knew, and so I tried to steer him towards civil-service reform, instead."

It occurred to Sonderby that there were some things very unministerial about Arthur Ellerton, and he recalled mentally some of the widely varying comments he had heard upon him, during the ten months of Ellerton's Broughton pastorate.

"Is there much discussion about civil-service reform at church conferences?" he asked.

"No, I can't say there is," answered Ellerton; "perhaps it wouldn't do any harm if there were a little more. But then, you see, I haven't been attending them so very long," he added, gaily. "Perhaps one learns to be less critical in time."

"You'd better not confess what you did last April at one of them," said the minister's wife. "Did you ever hear of such a thing, Mr. Sonderby, as two young ministers sitting out on the church steps talking boating, while the conference was going on inside?"

She did not know why the school-teacher's small blue eyes brightened so suddenly.

"I plead extenuating circumstances," broke in Ellerton. "You see," turning to Sonderby, "there is a classmate of mine over in Brockville, who was a delegate at that meeting in the Center last spring. I didn't know he was there till half-way through the meeting, when I looked around and there he was. There was a paper on 'Divorce' being read at the time,— good paper too, only the man who wrote it can't write nor think of anything else."

"Perhaps that is why he writes so well about it," interrupted Mrs. Ellerton, seriously.

"My wife reads all his articles," explained Ellerton, parenthetically. "Well, I don't know which of us winked first, but we started for the door at about the same time. Why, that fellow and I had pulled in the same boat for two years, and it was nearly four since I had seen him. We stood there on the church steps, talking about the boys, and the sun came down warm and spring-like — gracious! — after that long, dragging winter up here, and we could see the ice breaking up down on the river, and the first thing I knew something was said about our crew this year, and then off we went into old times." The minister drew a long breath of satisfaction. "But the conference was almost over when we went in again," he added, contritely.

"And you are not shocked?" said Mrs. Ellerton to Sonderby.

"No," he said, simply; "I was on the crew myself."

"Were you? Well, well!" exclaimed Ellerton. "Let's see, your college — was — ?"

Sonderby named a small Maine college. "We never rowed you but once," he said. "That was my Sophomore year."

Ellerton looked hard at him. "Where were you in the boat?" he asked.

"Bow," replied Sonderby. "Do you remember the finish?"

"I should say I did," cried Ellerton.

The July day, five summers before, came back to him in an instant. The countrymen from Maine had come down to New London to win, and nearly did it. They had pulled a dogged race, were not to be shaken off, and quickened into a desperate spurt at the finish that made them lap the champions as the boats shot over the line. Ellerton remembered as if it were yesterday that supreme moment when every pound of his weight was already on the oar and the helpless terror was at his heart as their stroke increased the pace and yet the Maine boat lapped them. He had never forgotten his glimpse of the Maine bow oarsman, who was glancing over a bare wet shoulder, the jaw set, the face white, and the eyes aflame. Ellerton had heard afterward that the fellow had pulled the race with a felon on his hand. He searched the school-teacher's reticent face for a sign of recognition. The figure was the same, though clad in a black cutaway — growing shiny, it must be said — instead of its brown bareness of five years before; the jaw was heavy, to be sure, though bearded now; the eyes were like.

"Didn't you have a bad hand?" Ellerton asked.

"Yes," said Sonderby, with a smile. The men understood each other.

"My dear," said the minister, "Mr. Sonderby and I are old antagonists. It is a great pity we never found it out before."

"Isn't it!" she exclaimed. "But you expect to be here for another winter, do you not, Mr. Sonderby?"

"I don't know," the school-teacher answered.

"Oh, I hope you will," said Mrs. Ellerton, so sincerely that she even surprised herself by the unexpected emphasis. "It would be such a pity to lose you, — from the academy, — and we should be so sorry."

"Yes," interrupted Ellerton, in his hearty voice, "I wish you might stay. But, my dear, you must remember that Broughton isn't exactly a metropolis, and that Mr. Sonderby wouldn't think of staying here forever, probably."

Mrs. Ellerton smiled to herself: perhaps her husband was not planning to spend his days in a country town either.

"Let's see, you have been here — isn't it three years, Sonderby?" the minister went on.

"Three years," replied Sonderby.

"I had forgotten," said Ellerton. "I wish I knew every one in town as well as you — ought to know them." He had hesitated a moment before the "ought," because he understood that people complained that John Sonderby did not seem to care much about getting acquainted with Broughton folks.

Sonderby raised his eyebrows a little, having understood the covert reference to his social shortcomings. "No, I don't know many people here; that is, I don't know them well, though of course a school-teacher gets so that he can tell everybody's name. But do you think," he asked, hesitatingly, "that it does any good to try to be on intimate terms with so many — in that way? It seems to me that the people are simply curious: they want to find out all they can about you, and in return for the information they are willing to tell you about themselves. I can't say that I care for it," he added, apologetically. He was not used to talking about himself in this way.

"I know what you mean," said Ruth Ellerton, slowly. "I remember how it was when we first came here." She looked across at her husband, and they both laughed. She was thinking how, at the first church sociable in their house, the women of the parish had fingered the curtains, the bureau-covers, even the pillow-cases, in her own room, to determine their quality and probable price; how they had interrogated her as to her father and family, her old home, her marriage, her husband, and herself,—all with a hard, undisguised curiosity, that had made her sick at heart.

"Mrs. Ellerton thinks that people are too kind, that they really take too much personal interest in you; don't you, my dear?" laughed the minister. He was not sensitive himself to such trifles, and rather enjoyed his wife's occasional desperation.

"Oh, I suppose the minister's family belong fairly to the public," she sighed: "but perhaps, Mr. Sonderby, it is the same way with the school-teachers. But one must surely know people well, if one hopes to influence them."

"Yes," remarked Sonderby, "if it is necessary to influence them — or, what I mean is, if one can influence them. It seems to me that people are going to do about what they have grown up to do. Perhaps that isn't a very high way of looking at it, not ideal enough for a school-teacher."

"Oh," she cried, "how hard it is to know just what is right to do here!"

"Any harder than it is down at the Center, or over in Brockville, or anywhere else?" questioned Ellerton, buoyantly.

She did not answer; then, somewhat inconsequentially, she said, "I hope you will stay another winter, Mr. Sonderby."

Mary Jane came in at this point with a fresh plate of hot biscuit. It was growing quite dim now in the dining-room, and at a motion from her mistress the girl lighted the tall candles. The three talked awhile on indifferent subjects, and then Mary Jane changed the plates and refilled the gentlemen's glasses with ice-water. The hostess served her strawberries and cream, the girl passed the sponge cake, to which much of her attention that day had been devoted, and regretfully left the room. She would have so much liked to hear what Mr. Sonderby was saying about the academy.

It was so quiet and cool here in the parsonage, Sonderby kept thinking. Mrs. Ellerton was a charming woman, after all; her husband was a good fellow; it was too bad that he had kept himself so aloof from them. There was a different atmosphere here from that which he was used to at the hotel: it was more restful, yet more strenuous. Was it preferable?

"How do you like staying at the Broughton House?" Mrs. Ellerton asked. "I believe you are there this vacation."

"Yes; I have been there since the middle of June." He did not really answer her question.

"Do they set a good table?" inquired Ellerton. "They used to be famous for it, I believe."

"That was more on account of the suppers they used to get up for fishing-parties from the Center,"

Sonderby explained. "There isn't so much of that nowadays. Why, I don't know; I suppose it is a very fair country hotel. Collins seems to like it; this is the fifth year he has been here. But," he added, with a deprecatory look, "I haven't anything to compare it with. I never stayed at a hotel before, except two or three times for a night or so. You see I'm a good deal of a countryman. The town I came from, up in Maine, is smaller than this."

"So is the one I came from, down in Pennsylvania," laughed Ellerton. "There is nothing like being born in the country, is there?"

"Who is Mr. Collins?" asked the hostess, coming back to the Broughton House.

"Mr. Collins?" replied Sonderby. "I thought you knew him. He is a woollen manufacturer,— Bruce D. Collins. His mills are down near Springfield, I believe."

"Is he dark?" said the minister's wife.

"Why, yes," Sonderby answered, judicially. It was clear he had never before classified his acquaintances according to their complexions.

"I often see him," said Ellerton, "but had forgotten his name. It must have been he whom I met down on the Johnson brook a while ago. He was fishing up, and I down, and I imagine each of us was rather sorry to see the other."

"It was very likely he," Sonderby remarked. "He came up here for the fishing, in the first place, he told me. He doesn't seem to have much to do nowadays."

"Well, Broughton isn't the place for a very busy man," was the minister's reply: "he wouldn't get into the spirit of things here. Still, I have wondered a good deal what the people at the hotel manage to find to fill up the time with. One must have some variety, you know, even in summer holidays."

"Variety! I wish they would do more to help the people here, and get variety in that way. If they had the variety of some of your pastoral work, for instance," exclaimed his wife, who knew the constant and often unappreciated work that filled her husband's days.

"Well, I don't know much about pastoral work," said the school-teacher. "Perhaps we need some down at the Broughton House. But speaking of filling up the time, why, the days go fast enough. We don't do anything, either; that is, not most of us down there. Mr. Floyd — he's the artist, you know — goes out to sketch almost every morning; but he doesn't go far, and we sort of hang round and watch him."

"Oh, do you?" broke in Mrs. Ellerton, enthusiastically. "How very interesting! It must be perfectly fascinating."

She was as eager as a schoolgirl to know more. Her husband smiled at her zeal; he left pictures and poetry to Mrs. Ellerton, for the most part.

Sonderby smiled too: he was thinking how vain Floyd would be if he knew this superb-looking woman took an interest in him.

"Mrs. Floyd was a Broughton girl, wasn't she?" asked the hostess.

"Yes." Sonderby paused somewhat awkwardly, as if he had meant to say more, but he hesitated, playing with the spoon in his empty strawberry-dish. "Do you know her?" he said at last, with his small blue eyes fixed keenly upon Mrs. Ellerton.

"No," was the answer. "I am very sorry. We saw her in church one day."

"Yes, we all went one morning," said Sonderby, turning to the minister. "Collins and the Floyds and I. Did you see us?"

"I am pretty sure to see everybody," replied Ellerton, who remembered well the quartette that had been in one of the back pews two weeks previously. "In fact, I wouldn't mind seeing some of you there oftener."

A day before, John Sonderby would have resented an allusion to his non-church-going habits, especially if it had come from the parson himself. But it was impossible to be angry with this cheery, frank young fellow — an old oarsman at that.

"I don't know but I'm getting into bad habits," he confessed; "and the rest are not exactly what you would call regular — that is, not regular attendants in the school record sense," he added, somewhat feebly.

Ruth Ellerton looked grave. She liked Sonderby, and she had seen more of him this evening than ever before; but there was a something non-committal about him that distressed her. He did not take sides vigorously enough. The summer visitors harmed Broughton more than they helped it, she was sure; and she did not like to see the school-teacher walking in their easy-going Sabbathless ways.

They had already been sitting long over their fruit, and Mary Jane appeared once or twice unsummoned, at the kitchen door, to reconnoitre. It was quite dark outside. Ellerton had given the conversation a new turn by describing the universal church-going of a hundred years ago in New England, with much humor, and from a perfectly non-professional point of view; Sonderby was listening with some curiosity.

"My dear," suggested Mrs. Ellerton, folding her napkin and touching the bell. As they rose and walked into the parlor again, Mrs. Ellerton was at Sonderby's side.

"I must call on Mrs. Floyd," she said.

"Yes?" he answered. He presumed it would have been proper to say, "She will be very glad to have you," but as he doubted the truth of this sentiment, he had no recourse but his blunt "Yes?"

Ruth Ellerton was a trifle hurt by it. "I have so little time for any except parish calls," she said, rapidly, ashamed that she should notice his brusqueness.

"Yes, I suppose you are very busy," he answered, looking straight at her — "busy doing good."

She was embarrassed now; her husband was watching her, interested at Sonderby's outspokenness, — Sonderby, usually so reticent.

"But if you can come down," Sonderby went on, "I'll see that Floyd gets out all he has to show. He likes to talk about it."

"Won't you come into the library?" interrupted Ellerton. "Perhaps you may like to look over my books." They crossed the hall to the diminutive library. The minister gave his guest an easy-chair by the table, while Mrs. Ellerton excused herself in order to give some encouragement and assistance to Mary Jane. When she came back, fifteen minutes later, the two men were talking boating. Sonderby had not been greatly interested, apparently, in the minister's books of quotation and illustration, divinity lectures, and volumes of the latest systematic theology.

Their boating talk ran out after a little, however, and they did not quite return to the freedom of the tea-table conversation. Mrs. Ellerton made an effort to start her guest upon several topics. The newest books he seemed either not to have read or not to think worth reading. She tried etching, and here he surprised her by his accurate knowledge of the mechanical processes involved; but his appreciation of "states" was very meagre, and he showed so little enthusiasm over her half-dozen treasures, — a Palmer, an Appian, and a Jacque or two, — that she felt disappointed in him again. He grew restless after a while, looked at his watch, then, after some delay in which the talk on all sides grew more aimless, and the pauses longer, rose to go, explaining that he was expected to make the fourth hand at whist that night, and that the others were waiting.

Both Ellerton and his wife went to the door with him. When he had fairly got his hat in his hand he won their hearts again by the few words of laconic cordiality with which he thanked his hostess, looking at her a moment almost with reverence as she stood in the half-light, with the library lamp making gleams through her hair and bringing out the strong, grave lines upon her face; then turning to Ellerton and giving him that silent grip of which only strong men understand the meaning. He reached the front gate before the friendly door was closed, and he was alone.

He turned down the silent street, with his straw hat pushed back upon his head, his old cut-away coat unbuttoned, his hands behind him. He walked slowly. Overhead, the elms met in huge black arches; the foliage seemed solid, impenetrable. There was scarcely any moon, but now and then, through some gap in that dusky roof, a star appeared, large and brilliant. The night would have been sultry anywhere else than up among these hills; but here it was fresh, restful.

Sonderby stopped more than once to listen to the soft noises of the night, to lean against the rough bark of one of the elms and gaze upward through the black boughs and the blacker foliage to the dark blue spaces of sky.

He had had a happy three hours, a social experience quite unknown to him before, shut up as he had been these three years to Broughton ways. He was hardly ready yet for the whist at the hotel, though, after all, as he remembered, he had made that an excuse for leaving the parsonage.

Down the quiet, deeply shadowed street was a yellow glare made by the lamps of the hotel. His pace grew slower as he neared it; he hated to leave the silence, the coolness. Almost unconsciously he crossed to the other side of the street; he meant to steal by, unobserved, and take a leisurely walk down to the academy and back. There was a murmur of voices on the hotel piazza. How well he knew them all! Was it not better to be out under the elms alone, saying nothing, thinking nothing, scarcely, only with the consciousness awake?

As he stole from the shadow of one tree to another, just opposite the hotel, but the width of the broad street away from it, a rich bass voice called out from the piazza, —

"Hullo!"

Sonderby stood motionless a moment, hesitating, then walked carelessly out into the lamp-light, and crossing the dusty grass, wet with dew, turned in at the Broughton House.

II.

THE hotel stood a few feet back from the main street, leaving in front an open space, grassy once, but now gravelled. This plot was neither beautiful nor large, but it was sufficient for the evolutions of the stage, which swung up to the hotel in impressive style and with much rattling of springs every morning, to take passengers for the Center. Late in the afternoon it turned in at the hotel again, on its return, but more quietly this time, for the horses were usually tired with their ten miles of up-hill travelling. In the afternoon, too, the post-office seemed to be the end of the trip, and the hotel was only an incident; whereas, in the morning, the driver pulled up his horses at the post-office only long enough to let the sallow postmistress hand to him the mail-bag, — it was rarely too heavy, — and then cracked his whip and gathered his reins for the main performance, the circling up to the Broughton House piazza.

For thirty years, ever since the railroad was first built through the Center, the Broughton stage had made this daily trip. Once or twice, back in the war-times, the severity of the winter storms had forced the driver to leave his horses at a half-way point, and push through on foot, shouldering the mail. But he always got through somehow. During most of the thirty years there had been the same driver, a burly, jovial fellow, with a quick wit, a kind heart, and a fondness for hard cider which degenerated in time into a liking for the whiskey at the Center. He was dead now, though his jokes and witticisms were still repeated all along the road; and people never tired of giving instances of his marvellous memory — he did shopping in the Center for all the farmers' wives along his circuit, and prided himself on never forgetting an errand nor making a mistake in change — and of the rare yarns with which this accomplished liar was said to favor strangers. His successor was a lanky, taciturn young farmer, a hard driver — beginning in his turn, too, to drink down at the Center, but never missing a train nor a trip.

In July and August he brought a good many visitors up to Broughton in the afternoon stage, and most of them went to the hotel. The Broughton House had once been famous through all that section of country as "Trumbull's," and its trout for fishing-parties, its oyster-suppers and country dances in the winter for sleighing-parties, were unrivalled. What fish stories had been told, first and last, around the huge fireplace in the office! How many couples had thumbed the photograph albums in the musty little parlor, while waiting for the dining-room to be thrown open for the hot supper that followed the sleigh-ride, or while the tables were being cleared away for dancing!

Bill Trumbull was the most obliging of hosts, though he performed his active duties mainly by proxy, and sat in the office in his big wooden chair, neatly cushioned with a bit of rag carpet, or else out on the piazza, while his wife managed things. Poor Mrs. Bill Trumbull! Even the reputation of being a "capable woman," which was cheerfully accorded her by even the most hard-working and critical farmers' wives in Broughton, was hardly a fit compensation for her life of toil, though it was all the visible compensation she had.

"Wal, I guess Mis' Trumbull'll see to you," was her husband's invariable answer to those who came with produce to sell, or to those who wanted rooms or dinners; then he would shift his legs a little, and fixing his blue eyes upon the questioner, he would say, "Nice morning," or, "Quite a spell of rainy weather," in the softest, most winning voice, with such good-fellowship in it that most persons dropped at once into a chair and began to talk, responding thus to an unmistakable appeal. In short, Bill Trumbull was lazy,—incorrigibly, hopelessly, shamelessly lazy,—as only that man can be who grows up among thriving, pushing New Englanders, and instead of catching some of their ambitious spirit, is driven to the opposite extreme. Yet everybody liked him: he would leave his chair and walk to the farthest end of the village to prescribe for a sick cow — he was prouder of his skill as a cow-doctor than of anything else except "Mis' Trumbull"; his blonde, handsome face with its long yellow beard was the first one that the village babies used to learn; he was an almost infallible prophet in politics and had twice been sent to the Legislature. No one ever came to "Trumbull's" without feeling at home as soon as he arrived, and being sorry when the time came to go.

It was a great shock to the community — as the county paper expressed it — when Mrs. Bill Trumbull sickened and died. The cause of her illness remained something of a mystery. Some thought it was nothing but "malary," others that it was "a kind o' run of low fever"; there were a few who were sure she must have had a cancer; all agreed that she had "looked sickly" for some weeks, that she had grown thin; a few of the more observing ones had noticed that her voice had become querulous and sharp, and that she had complained as never once before of being "driven." But gradually the interest in her malady became absorbed in the more engrossing question, whether the sad occurrence would make Bill Trumbull "step 'round." Upon this point opinion was divided even among those who knew him best, if indeed it could be said of such a public character that there were any who knew him best. The problem, however, did not long remain unsolved; human nature vindicated its impugned consistency; Bill Trumbull did not "step 'round." He seemed dazed for a while. When matters were referred to him for decision, he began more than once his old reply, " guess Mis' Trumbull'll see to that "; then recollected himself, while a vague, hurt look came into his blue eyes, and answered by some indefinite conjecture. The hotel had long been mortgaged, and all Mrs. Trumbull's efforts had not been successful in clearing it of the encumbrance. The crisis came rapidly now. In the autumn " Trumbull's " was sold at auction, and was bought in by a man from the Center.

The new owner's experience in keeping a hotel was not large, but he had been the proprietor of the railroad restaurant at the Center, and brought with him an air of enterprise and a familiarity with the ways of the great world that made an impression upon Broughton. He was a small, black-eyed, restless Welshman, who professed great faith in the future of Broughton as a summer resort, and began at once to talk "improvements" to the regular hangers-on at the office. All that winter he was busy with his schemes, and before the roads were fairly settled in April, teams from the Center began to haul lumber for "repairing" the hotel. The building, though fifty years old, was in perfect preservation; a solid two-story structure, with a basement in the rear, which was made necessary by the rapid falling off of the land from the street level, and which was used as a kitchen in summer. On the right, as one entered, was the big square office; the parlor and hall filled the remainder of the front, while behind was the long dining-room and a diminutive winter kitchen.

The Welshman's first wish was to secure a more imposing exterior. He thereupon erected a two-story extension upon the front, tearing down the west wall of the parlor and dining-room to connect them with the addition. On the ground floor, beyond the parlor, he put in a reading-room or smoking-room, with a hardwood floor and stained pine mouldings. Behind the reading-room, in the rear of the new part, he built a couple of bath-rooms. The remainder of the extension, above and below, was devoted to bedrooms, separated by the thinnest of partitions, and reached by a long hall down the middle of each story, lighted only by a window at the end. A broad piazza was erected along the whole front, including the old part, and around the flat roof of the piazza there was some talk of having a railing, so that the rooms on the second floor might have a piazza of their own, but this was finally deferred until another season. The whole hotel was now painted a bright yellow, with muddy brown trimming. "Trumbull's," like most of the other houses in the village, had been white, with green blinds. But the Welshman preferred yellow, as being more modern; at the hardware store where he had bought his prepared paint they told him that they sold three pounds of yellow to one of white, nowadays.

Then came the question of naming the hotel. The proprietor's first instinct was to name it after himself, "The Evans House." He hesitated, however, and got some one to sound Bill Trumbull as to the advisability of the name.

Trumbull had taken up his abode with a married daughter, across the street, but spent most of his waking hours at the hotel, where his chair still stood in the office as of old. "The Evans House?" he repeated, when his opinion was privately asked. "Wal, I dunno: it might be good. 'Trumbull's,' now; why, everybody round here knows who I am. But s'pose a man was to come along here and ask who Evans was. You'd have to say, 'he's a feller from the Center who used to keep a restaurant down there'; and I s'pose," he added reflectively, "that most folks'd say he kep a darn poor one." This sentiment having been duly reported to Evans, he changed his mind about the name. Then he thought of calling it "The Mansion House," but that was on the whole too common. "The Broughton Arms" suggested itself to him as being euphonious and as having a sort of flavor of the old country about it which might attract summer boarders. But here again he was not positive enough in his conviction to decide without consultation, and the ignorance that prevailed in the village about the appropriateness of the "Arms" part of his idea was discouraging. Finally he hit upon "The Broughton House." If it was not particularly original, it was at least unobjectionable.

The farmers looked curiously at the staring sign in gilt letters upon a black ground, the name of the printer, a Center man, in quite readable letters in the corner. It was in the form of an arch, one end springing from the office extremity of the piazza, and the other supported by a black post sunk in the newly gravelled space in front of the hotel.

"Trumbull's" had never had any sign, nor needed one, except the rusty square of copper dangling on the office corner, which had creaked there in the wind ever since Andrew Jackson's time, when the house was known simply as "The Tavern." But the farmers were cautious about expressing any opinion, and had a certain respect for any man who had money to spend.

It was June before the repairs were completed. Evans had planned to renovate the office, but his ready money was nearly exhausted. He was deterred from it, too, by Mr. Collins, who came up in May, as usual, for a week's fishing, and who threatened never to come again if the old office were touched. Evans disliked to lose an influential patron at the outset; and when Collins explained to him that the huge beams that supported the ceiling, dark with fifty years' exposure to the air, but sound to the core, were actually fashionable, and were being put into many modern hotels, he gave up his proposed improvements. The office remained intact. On one side was the yellow-painted counter from behind which, in the old days, glasses of flip had been served to guests and to the village worthies. On the walls, which were covered with a closely figured paper, variegated by vertical stripes of blue, hung a map of the county roads, a map of the United States in 1840, and a portrait of Daniel Webster, *lithographié par Julien*, representing the statesman clad in his blue coat with velvet collar and black stock. Every one in the village knew that face, with the drooping mouth, sunken cheeks, domelike forehead, and steady, wistful eyes under the shadow of the gloomy brows. Tacked near it was a fly-specked woodcut of James G. Blaine. The fireplace was a noble one, with a wide hearthstone of marble, tipped more or less into uneven levels, but uncracked by the huge fires of half a century. The sides were adorned with marble facings, and it was surmounted by an oak mantel-piece. On one side of the latter, at distances ranging from eleven to sixteen inches from the end, were numerous notches, recording the length of captured trout, the longest being the memorial of a famous four-pounder caught in the Johnson brook away back in the sixties.

Along the brown, rough-hewn beams that traversed the ceiling were hooks, which before the days of jointed rods had been used for hanging fish-poles.

There, too, hung a musket which Bill Trumbull's grandfather had brought back from the campaign along the Hudson in 1777, and a rusty cavalry sabre which Trumbull's younger brother swung in his right hand when he rode to his death in a nameless village of Virginia. No one had had the heart to take them down. High in one corner was nailed a crotch of a tree, on which were a stuffed wild cat and a Cooper's hawk, both of them rather the worse for time and moths. Everything in the office, it will be seen, had an air of the past — a conservative, tranquillizing quality. The very chairs around the fireplace were hospitable; solid, iron-clamped ones as they were, strong enough to tip back in, — the comfort of two generations of tired fishermen, chilled travellers, and genial country loafers. What stories they had heard!

Notwithstanding its new management and fresh paint, the first season of the Broughton House was not particularly successful. June and July were unusually cold and wet, and few people left the cities. August was a better month, but none of Evans's guests stayed so long as he had hoped for, and some of them openly deserted him on finding that some of the farmers were willing to take boarders. He could not understand this. There was Calvin Johnson's, for instance, a big old-fashioned farmhouse, where the folks were respectable enough — even the village school-teacher "hayed it" there through the summer for his board; but there were no modern conveniences there, not even a chance to hire teams. Why should any one prefer Johnson's to the Broughton House?

In vain did Evans arrange, upon his long piazza, lines of cane-bottomed rocking-chairs, painted an attractive red. In vain did he furnish the reading-room with files of the county papers, together with the *Springfield Republican, Harper's Weekly,* and the *Semi-Weekly Tribune.* In vain did he induce the stage-driver to attach to his dashboard a big placard, "To the Broughton House," as he drove through the Center. The harvest of boarders did not ripen. A few people who had formerly spent a while in August at "Trumbull's," came as usual; but even these spoke disrespectfully of his cherished improvements, and one told him that his plumbing was a crime. The men preferred the office to the reading-room; the ladies kept asking after the old waitresses in the dining-room, — neat farmers' daughters from the neighborhood, whom Evans had replaced, for the most part, with Irish help from the Center; and both men and women seemed to pay more attention to Bill Trumbull than they did to Evans himself.

When the season closed, the Welshman was dismayed. He had not made two per cent upon his investment. All the autumn he fumed. He began to suspect that Broughton people distrusted him as a newcomer. Perhaps the temperance folk objected to the reputation which his restaurant at the

Center had enjoyed. He resolved therefore to identify himself more thoroughly than ever with the town, as his fortune depended upon the popularity of the hotel. He became a regular church-goer, much to the private delectation of his cook and stable-boy. There was a new minister in Broughton that winter, a clear-voiced, straightforward, likable young man, — Arthur Ellerton. The sermons were not long, and Evans found himself concurring with the prevailing opinion that the minister was a "smart one." He felt, too, that he was weekly growing more respectable, in his own eyes and in the eyes of Broughton. He was unmarried; otherwise he would have undoubtedly taken a pew. When the time came for the town-meeting in March, Evans was active in distributing "no license" votes, and was fluent in his announcement of his purpose to keep a strictly temperance house. So far, so good; but he was frightened at the idea of having another summer like the previous one.

In May, Collins arrived; but the spring came late, just as it had done the year before, and there was too much snow-water in the brooks for successful sport. Collins waited day after day, smoking tranquilly in the office with Bill Trumbull; but the brooks were still high. The woollen business was dull, he said; the mills were doing almost nothing, and he might as well be in one place as another. Then came some business letters, a couple of telegrams sent up from the Center by telephone, and the manufacturer went off hastily, to return three days later with a case of new rods and a trunk. He explained to Evans and Trumbull, laconically, that there had been a cut-down at the mills, then an ensuing strike; that, as some repairs of machinery were necessary and the market was flat, the mills would not be started again until fall.

"So I may stay here all summer," he added; "and if I do, Bill, I won't go back without that big fellow down in the Hollow. I saw him twice last year, and he's a three-pounder if he's an ounce."

Evans slid out of the office, stroking his black, pointed beard in nervous delight, his keen eyes snapping at the prospect of having the manufacturer as a guest for two or three months. If he could only get a few others for permanent boarders, he could trust to a hot summer and his improvements of the year before — even if some of the old patrons did not seem to like them — to attract "transients" enough to carry him through. His mind reverted, as it had done often before, to the school-teacher. As a permanent boarder, John Sonderby would add character to the house.

The Welshman learned, by some inquiry, that Sonderby did not expect to work at Johnson's, as he had done the previous summer, Johnson having now hired his men by the year; further, that Sonderby was undecided about spending the vacation in Broughton, but that as he had no home of his own, it was very possible that he might do so, especially as there was a chance of his remaining in the village through another winter. Evans lost no time in offering him room and board at such a low figure that the school-teacher packed up his few effects, left his uncomfortable room near the academy, and found himself by the middle of June quartered at the Broughton House. The proprietor had offered him any room he liked, and was evidently disappointed at Sonderby's taste when the latter chose one of the old rooms over the office, adjoining the one occupied by Mr. Collins, instead of going into the extension, and taking a room newly fitted and papered. But Evans did not feel sufficiently familiar with the academy teacher to remonstrate, and after all, it only left one more of the new rooms for somebody else.

Collins and Sonderby had sat beside each other at table for a week or two, and in the feeling of permanency which arises from seeing more transient guests come and go, were beginning to get well acquainted. Neither was much of a talker, but they made some progress. Collins was ten years the elder, and liked the younger man's ways. One morning at breakfast as Evans was passing through the dining-room and stopped for a moment at the head of the table where they sat, to chat with them, — Evans being strongly impressed with a hotel-keeper's duty to cultivate acquaintance with his patrons.— Collins gave him a brilliant idea.

"If you like to have two 'regulars,' the manufacturer was saying in his deep voice, now slightly quizzical in its inflections, "why don't you get some more of them? There is Bill Trumbull; he would make a good one. Why do you let him go across the street to eat and sleep? Or what's the matter with the Floyds? Why can't you get them to board here?"

Evans looked sharply at him. "Perhaps so, Mr. Collins," he laughed. He was somewhat afraid of Collins, and never knew just how to take him.

"Of course you can," Collins went on, his handsome dark face breaking into an ironical smile. "They have been here three days, and Floyd is tired of housekeeping already"— and he turned his attention to his steak again. Evans passed on, meditatively.

At dinner-time the Floyds were there. Sonderby came a few minutes late, having spent the morning over the physical apparatus in the deserted, dusty rooms of the academy.

He found Collins listening to a stoop-shouldered fellow of twenty-six or seven, who sat opposite him; a carelessly dressed man, with his flannel shirt unbuttoned at the throat, though held in place by a soiled pink tie. Sonderby scarcely glanced at him, but the impression was somehow unpleasing. Opposite the school-teacher was the artist's wife, a slender woman, in a close-fitting black jersey, her face singularly destitute of color, her dark hair drawn back from her forehead and knotted behind. She looked up as Sonderby seated himself and bowed timidly. She had big, shy eyes. Sonderby remembered that he had been introduced to her the year before. As he murmured something about having met her, her husband checked himself in his remarks to Collins and eyed the newcomer.

"I beg your pardon," exclaimed Collins; "I thought you knew each other. Mr. Floyd, Mr. Sonderby."

The men bowed.

"You are the school-teacher, I believe?" said Floyd. The tone was just a trifle patronizing.

"Yes," replied Sonderby. His manner was not communicative.

"You are staying here in Broughton this summer?" the artist continued.

"Yes."

Floyd looked at him curiously an instant, then took up the dropped thread of his talk to Collins.

"You see," he went on, gesticulating with a long forefinger slightly dirtied with Roman ochre, "my theory of landscape is just this: —"

Sonderby did not feel particularly interested, and gave his attention to the soup. He exchanged some commonplaces after a little with Mrs. Floyd, and when she happened to say that she was a native of Broughton, — he had already noticed that she used Broughton locutions in her conversation, — and had attended the academy in her girlhood, he remembered what he had heard about her. It was she whose aunts had lived in the low, unpainted cottage next to the hotel, and the removal of one of them and the death of the other in the preceding autumn had brought her into possession of the property. She and her husband had been in Broughton the summer before, and had stayed with one of the aunts, but this season, as Collins had said at the breakfast table, the Floyds had expected to keep house in the cottage themselves.

"I don't much care," she said to Sonderby, speaking of the sudden change in their plans. "I'm not very fond of housekeeping. But my husband thought we should like it better here."

Evans had, in fact, proposed to board them at such a ridiculously low rate, that they had not hesitated a moment in coming.

"I hope you will not be disappointed," Sonderby said politely. "How do you fancy the changes in the hotel? It must seem strange to you if you were brought up next door and have always known it as it used to be."

She was about to reply, when she noticed the Welshman standing in the kitchen door near by, watching his four "regulars" with intense satisfaction.

"Hush," she exclaimed, with a warning smile, so bright and confidential that Sonderby found himself instantly attracted to her. They changed the subject.

After that Sonderby got on very well with her. She had a soft voice, lower in pitch than the voices of most New England women, and at times almost indistinct. She spoke with a shy swiftness, when she spoke at all, and the teacher had difficulty in catching all she said.

During the whole dinner hour Mr. Floyd talked incessantly, in a self-conscious, preternaturally weighty fashion, which Collins, who seemed to know him pretty well, did not take with entire seriousness. Indeed, it seemed to Sonderby that Collins was slyly bantering the artist and drawing him out, without the latter's suspecting it. Floyd had an easily remembered face, and Sonderby recollected that he had taken a dislike to it a year before. It was not that Floyd was ugly, — though, indeed, with his high cheek-bones, flat cheeks, a nose broken out of line by some accident in boyhood, thin light hair, growing far back on his square forehead, weak-looking eyes, and a bad mouth, he could scarcely be called handsome. Sonderby never noticed such things in detail, at least in a man. Yet he felt there was a kind of pretence in the artist's expression, a lack of real dignity or worth in the man's bearing. But this, after all, was only the impression of the moment.

When the four came out of the dining-room together, they stood for a moment in the parlor, aimlessly. The Floyds seemed to have no idea of returning to the cottage.

"We might sit on the piazza for a while," suggested Collins, resigning mentally his customary after-dinner smoke with Trumbull in the office. "It would rejoice the heart of Evans, anyway," he added; "his chairs haven't been very popular."

"All right," said Floyd; they strolled out upon the broad piazza, and Collins drew some of the big red chairs together into a group in front of the reading-room. Floyd pulled out his cigarette-case, and offered it to Sonderby.

"Thank you; I don't smoke," said Sonderby, regretting, after all, that he had to refuse the first friendly overture the artist made him.

"Do you object to my pipe?" asked Collins, turning to Mrs. Floyd.

"Oh, Phenie don't care," interrupted Floyd. "She's used to it. Aren't you, Phenie?"

"I should think I ought to be," was the answer.

Sonderby wondered why her husband called her "Phenie," and tried to guess from it what must be her name.

A light June breeze was blowing down the piazza, and Collins moved his chair so that the smoke from his briarwood might not be carried into Mrs. Floyd's face. She thanked him as if somewhat surprised at his thoughtfulness. Sonderby's chair was nearest hers, after this change of position on Collins's part. Floyd rocked vigorously a few moments, then got up and balanced himself along the flat railing of the piazza, resting his head against the post and crossing his feet upon the rail, while he blew idle rings of smoke and watched them drift and break.

The four were still in their relative position a half-hour later. Evans regarded them silently from the office door, in triumph. He had waited so long to see those chairs filled, and the new piazza appreciated. He only hoped that in the growing familiarity of his guests, the fact would not leak out that he was charging them three different prices for board. But in the glow of that exultant moment he could have explained anything satisfactorily. As he turned away and passed through the office on the way to the kitchen, he allowed himself, for the first time since he had taken the hotel, to address a disrespectful remark to Bill Trumbull.

It never rains but it pours. That afternoon the stage deposited a whole family at the hotel. As Evans received them, and gave sharp directions to the driver and the stable-boy about the disposition of the trunks, he was a happy man. If there was any cloud in his sky, it was that his regular boarders were no longer sitting upon the piazza, when the stage rattled up to it. That would have given such an air of life to the hotel. But it mattered little: and the mail brought four or five inquiries about rooms for July and August. At last! How often Evans had imagined himself receiving those letters!

By the end of June the Broughton House was half full. Evans firmly believed that the luck had been brought him by the quartette of "regulars." Their mutual acquaintance seemed to progress steadily: every day, after dinner, they sat together either on the piazza or under the trees in front of the cottage next door; in the morning they often spent hours watching Floyd sketch, though the artist sometimes left his work altogether for a fishing-jaunt with Collins. The second Sunday after the Floyds came, Collins, in some freak, persuaded them to go to the Congregational church, making Sonderby join the party; and the four had listened, decorously enough, to Arthur Ellerton's sermon, and had been scrutinized gravely by Arthur Ellerton's wife. But they were to be seen together most regularly in the evening, after supper, when they took the curious old mahogany card-table from the parlor, and placing it upon the piazza outside, sat down to play whist. When it became dark, they had the big reflector lighted over their heads; and if it grew cool, as it was likely to do, even in these July evenings up among the hills, they retreated to the stuffy little parlor, and played on, till long after the other guests had retired.

The Saturday evening when Sonderby was invited to take tea at the parsonage was the first time in three weeks that the whist had been broken in upon. Collins and the Floyds had sat a long time upon the piazza that night, waiting for him, when Mrs. Floyd thought she caught a glimpse of the school-teacher among the elm-tree shadows on the other side of the street, and it was Collins's mellow "Hullo" that called him from the darkness and silence of the deserted street, across to the light and the murmur of voices on the Broughton House piazza.

III.

Two or three days after that Saturday evening, Floyd was pacing up and down in the sitting-room of the cottage. One hand was thrust deep into his trousers pocket; the other held a crumpled letter. In a low rocking-chair by one of the windows sat his wife, leaning back so that her head rested upon the calico cushion, and her throat showed white. From moment to moment she pushed her foot against the iron framework of a dust-covered sewing-machine in front of her, to rock her chair. Her hands were lying in her lap, the fingers clasped, and palms turned from her in a way that brought into relief every line of her slender arms.

Her dark eyes were fixed now on the ceiling, and now on the restless form of her husband. Altogether it was a graceful, piquant figure, with manifest nervous power; but just now she was cool, provokingly cool.

"Well?" she said, in her light voice, with the slightest upward inflection.

He shrugged his shoulders, making with the hand that held the letter a curiously vague, impotent gesture.

"Well, Billy?" she repeated.

He took another turn before replying. "What's the use?" he muttered. "You don't understand me; you don't even try."

"Don't be too sure, Billy."

"No — you, nor none of you," he cried, stopping in his walk. "You don't know what an artist is; you can't appreciate the artistic temperament."

"I have had nearly three years of it," was her answer. "I should think I ought to know something about it by this time." She smiled faintly, showing a glimpse of her fine teeth, but the smile was hard.

"Why can't you make allowances, then?" He hesitated, seeing that she had spoken ironically.

"Allowances?" she repeated, in an indifferent tone.

"Yes," he cried. "You seem to think that it makes no difference where I am or what I see. Can't you understand that a man has got to have inspiration from something? What is there in this dusty little country town? How can a man paint here? Who appreciates him? Who cares anything about art? How do you expect me to do my best work up in this God-forsaken place? I ought to be over on the other side again. I ought not to have come back to America before I was half ready. Just think of being over there to-day, — over in Munich again, — and then think of being — here."

As Floyd uttered the last word he swept his eye

over the low room. Its uneven floor was covered with a rag carpet; the hair-cloth furniture was rickety and old-fashioned; on the walls, which were papered with an ugly flowered design, there hung in black oval frames, suspended by green picture-cord, daguerreotypes of Mrs. Floyd's maiden aunts, Tryphena and Tryphosa. A carefully framed photograph of Mrs. Floyd herself, at the age of ten, hung under the picture of Aunt Tryphena. There was not much else in the room. Both windows were wide open, but the hot sun of the July morning failed to penetrate the thick-leaved lilac bushes planted close under the eaves of the cottage. In one of the lilacs a chipping sparrow, frightened by the sound of Floyd's voice from off her second set of eggs, was fluttering anxiously. Otherwise there was perfect stillness, save possibly the intermittent creak of Mrs. Floyd's rocking-chair.

The contrast between Munich and Broughton was evident enough.

The artist began to pace the floor again, moodily.

"I'm sorry you don't like it here, Billy," said his wife. "You seemed quite fond of staying last summer. Aunt Tryphena would feel real bad about it; she set a good deal of store by you, and if she had only known you wouldn't have liked the house, she might have sold it and left us the money instead. But it was all she had. And it's too late now, anyway. I was brought up here. It's different for me." She spoke slowly, and the irony had all gone out of her voice, leaving there nothing but helplessness.

But Floyd was stung by the reference to their circumstances. He had scarcely enough money to pay their board through the summer, and the cottage had been left to his wife, by her aunt's will. The little that they had was hers.

"You are always throwing my poverty in my face," he exclaimed. "Is it my fault? Is it my fault that Mr. Watson—" He hesitated, glancing at the letter in his hand.

Mrs. Floyd's colorless face flushed a little. What he had said was grossly untrue.

"You're not very fair, Billy," she said.

"Perhaps not; it's hard to be fair when everything's against a man."

She tapped her foot against the sewing-machine, but made no reply. What was the use?

"I've stood it long enough," he went on, in a petulant, high voice. "I have no chance here. There is no sympathy for me; nothing but curiosity. It kills enthusiasm, that does. Over there it is all different. An artist is given his place, the place that belongs to him, the first place. Yes, I say! Phenie, why can't you stop looking at me that way? You sit there with those thick black eyes of yours, as if you were blaming me for something. Haven't I done everything that man can do? The fact is, I'm out of my place here. I have genius— they said so over there, though not in so many words — they never do that. I know I've got something great in me. You can't appreciate me — none of you can. It takes an artist to sympathize with an artist. I'm tired of it all, and I'm throwing away my chances too. It can't last forever — it is too hard."

He closed melodramatically, with the same impotent gesture as before. His wife watched him with inscrutable eyes. She had heard this tirade so often that she knew it by heart, and could have prompted him when he stopped for rhetorical pauses. But to the captious, vain babble to which she was accustomed, there was added this morning an excitement of manner and a personal resentment against herself which were unusual, and which she conjectured at once were caused by the letter.

"What does Mr. Watson say?" she asked, her voice trembling in spite of herself. "Better have it out, Billy: I know he isn't fond of me."

Mr. Watson was a Chicago broker, an elderly relative of Floyd, and his patron, so far as that personage can exist nowadays. He was the only one who believed in Floyd's talent; he had sent him to Munich, he had discouraged his return to America and his marriage.

"Come, Billy," she persisted.

Brutal in his selfishness as Floyd had shown himself, he was ashamed to tell her what she asked. But he had gone so far that it would be useless to try to hide from her how matters stood, or at least, it would be useless soon.

He smoothed out the wrinkled sheet of paper and ran his eye over it again until he reached the last paragraph. Then he folded the letter once more so that the closing sentences would be all she could read, and handed it to her. She could scarcely make out the scrawled business hand, but the meaning of the words was clear.

"*Of course you understand that if this scheme works, it must be as before. The money you had was enough for you. It will be enough for* YOU *this time. You know my ideas about that subject, already. Shall be able to let you know definitely by another month.*"

Mrs. Floyd read it twice, a faint color coming into her cheeks, then fading out again. She looked at her husband suddenly, but his eyes did not meet hers. Then she tore the letter in two and tossed the pieces upon the middle of the floor, at his feet.

"That's a very nice letter, Billy, and the man who wrote it seems to be a very nice sort of man." She lay back in her rocking-chair as before, her fingers clasped again, her slipper touching the sewing-machine.

He stooped sheepishly to pick up the pieces; then put them carefully into the pocket of his sack coat. Habitually moody, he yet failed to understand the moods of his wife, and he mistook the bitter irony of her tone for that cool, light sarcasm which in New England passes for humor, and with which Mrs. Floyd often savored her talk.

"You don't seem to object to his scheme, Phenie," he laughed, with a nervous and pitiable attempt at jocoseness himself.

"Why should I?"

The terrible directness of her reply brought him to his senses. He stood looking hard at her, but no words reached his lips. Why should she, indeed, object to his leaving the country and going away from her? Was he so essential to her? This question smote upon his selfishness, rebukingly, but from that selfishness there came the swift and dangerous response: was his wife, after all, essential to him?

He had played with the idea before; it had tempted him, teased him; and now in a moment it rose before him, and beat down his guard. Still no words came to him.

Man and wife were gazing in each other's eyes. It was the supreme moment in their married life. All around them was absolute stillness, save the flutter and chirp of the sparrow outside the window.

"Billy," Mrs. Floyd said slowly, "perhaps it was all a mistake. Perhaps we never ought to have been married. I've tried hard to do what was right." The words were growing slower still. "I've never wanted to stand in your way, and I don't want to now. But that's our business, Billy;

it isn't any of Watson's." She hesitated so long that Floyd thought she had quite stopped, and then in a dry, strange voice added, "and I don't know what Aunt Tryphena would say."

There was a painful silence.

"There is another month," he ejaculated, weakly. He could not have told why he said this, except that the thought of the month's interval before another letter would come was floating at the top of his chaotic ideas.

"Yes," she replied, mechanically, but with a trace of the former irony, as if she perceived his indecision and his cowardice.

He turned irresolutely away, and going to the sofa picked up his brushes and colors, his sketching-stool, and a broad-brimmed straw hat. He was a good while doing it, hoping that she would speak, though he had no more idea what she would say than what he could himself have said. At last he walked toward the door, eyeing sideways her motionless figure. He put on his hat and glanced toward her; she was not even looking at him. Muttering something, — what, he hardly knew himself, — he opened the creaking door and went out.

Outside, a brilliant July sunlight was over everything. The yellow-painted Broughton House fairly glared under it.

The artist paused by habit, on the sidewalk in front of the cottage, and glanced toward the hotel.

No one was upon the piazza, except a child or two. He remembered that Collins, in spite of the strong light, had gone fishing, and that Sonderby had said something at breakfast about some experiments in electricity at the academy. All the better, Floyd thought; he preferred this morning, contrary to his custom, to be by himself. He turned to the east, and walked up the street leisurely. Scarcely had he left the cottage behind him when he was conscious that his spirits were rising. He drew a long breath. The sitting-room had seemed so close, and the scene with his wife had been so intensely disagreeable! But to be out of doors, that was a different matter. The vagabond instincts of the fellow came to the front, and he threw back his head, stretching his throat away from the collar of his flannel shirt, absorbing great chestfuls of the sweet air. Overhead in the elm boughs the Baltimore orioles were flashing like glints of yellow flame, and whistling their wild gurgling call. Floyd caught every vibration of that strange cry; both ear and eye had never been so intensely alive to the outer world; he noticed the shadows on the deep-fissured bark of the elm-tree boles, and stopped an instant to study the texture of the bark, and its exact shade of chocolate-brown; he saw for the first time the perfect line which an old well-sweep made, outlined against a decaying woodshed; his eye rested with keener delight than ever before on the long vista of elm-arches through which he was passing, while to right and left were gardens and orchards in sharp-cut masses of light and shade in the clear morning light, and hayfields showing already subtle tints of brown and yellow.

Main Street was almost empty, as befitted ten o'clock in the morning in the haying season. Only before Parkinson's store were a couple of unloaded wagons, waiting to be weighed upon the public scales. The farmers who drove them, bearded old fellows in shirt-sleeves and cowhide boots, stopped their random interchange of questions and queries, to stare at the artist as he sauntered by.

"The artist fellow; married Trypheny Morton," he overheard one of them explain to the other.

Floyd was irritated by the comment. "Married Trypheny Morton." It was three or four happy, irresponsible minutes since he had thought of the woman whom he had left back there in the sitting-room. But he had some capacity for shaking off disagreeable sensations, and shrugged his shoulders therefore, and strolled on. As he passed the parsonage, Mrs. Ellerton, arrayed in a freshly starched calico dress, was kneeling by a flower-bed in the front yard, surrounded by pots of geraniums, which she was transplanting. Her weight was thrown forward upon her left hand, almost sunk in the freshly upturned earth, while her right hand held a trowel, upon the point of which she steadied herself as she turned to smile at her husband, who stood in his study-gown, and with pen in hand, above her upon the piazza, joking about something. It was a charming pose,— that of Mrs. Ellerton,— and the artist drew an involuntary quick breath of pleasure as he caught sight of her. Then he remembered that Sonderby had told him that the minister's wife was interested in his pictures, and his sudden self-consciousness gave a new erectness to his figure as he walked by. He had not met either of the Ellertons, and so looked straight before him, with assumed nonchalance.

Just beyond the parsonage he turned to the left, down the North Broughton road, which joined the village street here, in front of the white, bare-looking Orthodox church. The road to North Broughton was not much travelled; indeed, it was hardly more than a couple of wheel-tracks, and the encroaching grass did its utmost to efface even these. Down hill it went, through pastures that were getting overrun along the fences with second-growth birch and maple, and then through a bit of real woodland. Soon appeared an opening again, toward the west, and the artist left the road, pushing his way through the tangle of blackberry vines and milkweed that fringed the rickety stone wall. Scrambling over the latter, he came out into a meadow, overlooking a brook and the ruins of a mill-dam. Part of the mill itself was still standing. With the brook escaping from the woods upon one side, and upon the other the white houses of the village, seen from the rear here, and half hidden by the orchards and the elms, the spot had previously suggested itself to Floyd as one affording opportunity for a landscape subject. He had thought of calling the contemplated picture "The Old Mill," and certainly Hobbema himself could never have set an old mill in a more charming background.

Floyd had planned to make a preliminary sketch for the picture upon this particular morning. He set up his portable easel, and having stretched his canvas, began to sketch in the outlines of the tumble-down building in charcoal. The first strokes pleased him; his hand seemed steadier and freer than usual. He whistled and hummed away to himself; it was such a fine morning, and here in the edge of the meadow, under the shadow of the last tree of the forest, there was so little to trouble him. Then, growing careless, he drew an unlucky line; in trying to better it he made it worse. The whistling ceased, and he began to work more slowly and carefully, but he did not regain the confidence of those first few strokes. Possibly, he thought, he might be a trifle nervous. He stepped back from the easel once or twice to study the proportion of his work; it was not so bad—no—but after all, as he finished the outlines and scanned it critically, he could not disguise from himself that it was out of drawing. He gave an impatient exclamation. Confound it! he had never half learned to draw!

Floyd was easily put out of temper with himself, and finding that after some rubbing and measuring and redrawing the sketch did not entirely suit him, he was too disgusted to begin again from the first, and therefore opened his color-box and began squeezing and mixing greens, and yellows and browns upon his palette, resolved to make memoranda of the colors at least, under this favorable light.

His eye was really good, and as he began to paint, and was conscious of reproducing cleverly the tones of the brilliant coloring before him, his spirits came back, and he felt again something of that peculiar exaltation which he had experienced as he walked down the street three-quarters of an hour before. Before another hour had passed he had accomplished a good deal. He had transferred to canvas the shadowy masses of woodland, the bright green of the meadow, through which the brook gleamed and whitened, the breadth of meadow, turning now to yellowish brown and showing here and there a strip of purest gold where the grainfields were ripening early, and in the far background the low line of blue hills, stretching on and on, shadowed now and then by the white clouds which they seemed at last to touch.

The artist had wished to make sure of these transient effects first, fearing that they might escape him; and it was not till he had nearly finished that he turned his attention to the village, in the left background. There was nothing difficult about that, and he filled in rapidly the line of foliage, and began to blotch it with white where the houses stood. He smiled as he put on a daub of ugly yellow, to represent the Broughton House. Then, as he held his broad hat in the air to shade his eyes better and give him a steady view of the hotel, a look of irritation came over his mobile face, for against the yellow there was a low brown building. He recognized the cottage, and for the first time since he had begun to paint, there crept upon his mind the thought of his wife.

His wife! Mechanically he put in the yellow. Then he wiped his brush, forgetting that he had meant to paint the rest of the white houses that peeped through the elm-trees on lower Main Street, beyond the hotel. His wife! She was not to be left out of the landscape, after all.

He folded his sketching-stool, and, throwing himself down at full length before the easel, lay there just within the line of the shade, gazing moodily toward the village.

She was there, somewhere, probably in the very room where he had left her. Perhaps she was in that chair by the window, where she sat so motionless and unregardful of him when he had come away. Confound the woman! why should she persist in being so strange? Who could be expected

to understand her! Well, what was the use of
trying? He called himself an artist: why not give
himself to the life of art? His eye fell upon the
completed sketch. The sunlight rested full upon
it now, and it seemed too crude and brilliant. It
needed toning down. This could easily be done;
but was that all? How about the drawing?
Floyd's eye was too accurate, naturally, to let him
be ignorant of the fact that there was a radical
deficiency in his work.

Well, he thought fiercely, suppose there was?
Whose fault was it? What had tempted him to
stay in America when he had come home for that
visit, three years previously, before he had half
learned what Munich could teach him?

His eye wandered toward the cottage again. It
had been Tryphena Morton.

Floyd had a dislike, common to men of his temperament, of thinking things through. It was
easier and pleasanter for him, generally, to be
guided by the impressions and sensations of the
moment. But just now his ideas had a certain
tenacious continuity, and his mind travelled again
over the whole road of his past experience. There
was his boyhood, passed in a Long Island town,
where his earliest memories were of the wharves,
and of escapades along the beach at low tide. His
first passion had been to build a boat, and his second to draw one. He drew them for years,— on his
slate in school, on brown paper in his father's gro-

cery store, on smooth boards at the lumber piles upon the wharf. Then some attention was paid to him; he was given a box of cheap paints. At sixteen he took a prize at the county fair, for a water-color. He had been very proud; yet, as he recognized clearly when he looked back at it on this July morning, it was the worst thing that could have happened to him, artistically. It made him vain, and it did not bring him a teacher. He began to try oils after that, and by the time he was twenty he could almost support himself by painting portraits. Long Island folks were not very critical. Finally he gave that up, went to Brooklyn, and got work in a lithographer's establishment. Here he began to find out his defects, to meet other young fellows, ambitious like himself; he joined an evening class, and saved his money to pay for models. Then he lost his job; and when he was almost discouraged, how like a dream it seemed when old Watson took an interest in him and said he should have "as good a chance as any of them," and sent him to Munich!

Ah, Munich! As Floyd thought of that year and a half, he turned flat over on his back, and pulling his hat down upon his face, gave himself up to alluring memories.

What days and nights he had spent in the Bavarian capital! What long mornings of work in the atelier, elbowed by young painters from every nationality in Europe, except the French! There was gaiety there and good-fellowship, the jostle of ideas, the pulse of ambition, the breath of rivalry. How just and kindly had been the criticisms of his masters! How serious had been their headshaking as they recognized his knack of handling color, unaccompanied by a mastery of the one fundamental thing in his work; how roundly had they condemned the American fashion of hurrying a pupil along to dabble with oils before he was ready for it; how rigidly had they tried to put him on the right track again, by going back to the starting-point! Floyd blushed now to think that he had been so irresponsive, so unreasonable; that he had persisted in working in color so much of the time, in spite of the laconic dictatorial warnings he received. To be sure, he had scarcely understood them at first, the language and the ideas were so new to him; still he might have gotten hold of more, though he felt, as he clinched his fingers into the meadow grass, that he had at any rate gotten hold of something. If he had only stayed longer! What afternoons those had been, when the autumn and winter light failed early, and he and his knot of friends lounged through the gay streets or loitered in the dusky Frauenkirche, to hear the vesper music; those evenings, all too swiftly passed, when they had gathered in the Hofbraüerei, the Augustiner, the Franziscaner, or in some out-of-the-way restaurant given up to the patronage of art-students, or even in one of their own attic "studios," and talked art, and drunk the health of every conceivable person or thing in foaming Münchener, and, reviling German tobacco all the while, had smoked it till they were sitting in a blue fog, — the right atmosphere, after all, for art and air-castles. Over it all was the charm of comradeship, of mutual enthusiasms and purposes. Floyd was not analyst enough to know how much of the fascination that Munich had for him lay in the selfishness of his life there, the lack of any ideals except artistic ones — and these mainly technical — the easy morality, the freedom from responsibility. He was simply conscious of having had an immensely good time, and of having learned something.

The sun had now worked its way out from behind the trees and shone so hot upon the artist that it destroyed his reverie. He pulled himself into the shadow again, and opening his eyes, gazed gloomily through the grass-blades, out over the intervening meadows, at the trim New England village before him. That was what he had come back to. Why had he been such a fool? Yonder heap of brown against the yellow of the Broughton House contained the answer — it was Tryphena Morton Floyd.

He had come home from Munich one spring, summoned by some family affairs, and was about to secure passage for his return when he met this girl. She was singularly graceful. Her shyness attracted him. The only women he had known in his absence were waitresses and models, and the quiet, delicate ways of this New England girl seemed doubly grateful to him. He fell in love. She refused him. He postponed his return to Germany, and waited, and would not give her up. She let him see something of her still, and finally her mind seemed to change and she opened her heart to him. He was lucky enough to sell some pictures; the outlook for the future seemed hopeful; he abandoned the idea of returning to his studies, and they were married.

In vain did old Watson, who disliked the girl, growl about the marriage. When he persisted in objecting, Floyd quarrelled with him. Love was enough.

And afterward? Ah, that "afterward." It came so soon, like the gray veils of cloud that drift in from nobody knows where, unaccountably and quietly, to dim the sun, on a spring morning. As swiftly as those, but less inexplicably, came to the Floyds disappointment, disillusion, distrust. He felt them sooner than she, though the wife had greater cause. His selfishness did more to make their union an unfit one, than did her failure to understand him, which was all, after everything was said, that he could bring against her. He even had times of thinking that she did understand him thoroughly, that she saw straight through him, but that she had no sympathy for his peculiarities, for his artist's moods. Whenever he felt this, his irritation against her was strongest.

Indeed, he was more than half right. When she married him she was as utterly ignorant as a New England country girl can be of all that was to him most interesting. The art-jargon that he talked was meaningless to her, however diligently she tried to learn. She had tried hard, hard as a loving woman can who feels that her husband's life ought not to be separated from her own. But the more she penetrated beneath the surface of his mind and life, the more she found of chaos, of egotism, of superficial aims, shifting desires.

She grew secretly afraid; there was so little in him that she could take hold of, depend upon. He seemed to be slipping away from her, and her love, strong as it had been, rebelled against its own impotence.

For his part, though he had perhaps loved her at first as much as he would have been likely to love anybody, and was still very fond of her, in a way, he had never been able entirely to make her out. When he first met her, this had added to her charm; but once married, he wanted to know definitely what he could expect from her. Upon this point he was never quite sure. She seldom reproached him for anything, but behind the slightly sarcastic sentences which were frequent in her talk, and which had delighted him originally, he often suspected that there was hidden a deeper and more bitter irony than appeared upon the surface. There was a power of feeling in her which his weaker nature surmised and dreaded. Floyd was a man who wanted to domineer, to be master and to make a parade of it, and the very obedience and subordination which his wife had always exhibited taunted him sometimes, as if back of that self-abnegation there was something more powerful than himself, which penetrated his shallowness, and only seemed to yield, and in reality baffled him.

Nearly three years had crept away since their marriage: years of scrimping, of cheap boarding-houses, of quarrels with picture-dealers; years, too, of health and hope and experiment. But Floyd had experienced an artistic disillusion, as well as a personal one. His pictures were called clever, but too sketchy. There were too many faults in composition. His dealer had spoken plainly to him of the criticisms he had heard; old Watson, whose fine private collection was gradually training its owner's taste, and who stubbornly insisted on writing to Floyd occasionally, was forever harping on the same subject, and Floyd had at last learned his artistic lesson, though it was a hard one for him. He must put himself again under a master; that was the decision. Vain as he was,— too vain to seek instruction in New York,— he had made up his mind at last to go back to composition-classes once more, if the way were only open. Then, later, he would take America by storm.

If the way were only open! He thrust his hand into his side-pocket and drew out the fragments of Watson's letter. Pulling up handfuls of daisies and timothy till he had cleared a few inches of turf, he laid out the pieces and slowly arranged them in their places. The fact that he had to piece his letter together in this fashion, after Mrs. Floyd had torn it in two, seemed to make it easier for him to read between the lines, perhaps to read something of his own into them.

The meaning, after all, was clear enough. Tryphena had caught it at a glance. Watson wanted him to go back to Munich, but he wanted him to go alone. Still, the cynical old broker was cautious and had given him a month, perhaps to let him arrange matters with Tryphena. Floyd had tried many a time to fancy his wife "over there" with him, but his imagination could find no place for her in the circle of his Munich life. He did not wish her there; he might as well own it to himself. He could not support her in America during his absence. After his absence was over? Would he come back to her?

Again there came to him, as in that crisis of the earlier morning with his wife, the sense of perfect stillness, as if all things held their breath and waited for his decision. No — not all things. Down across the meadow crawled a mowing-machine on its ceaseless jarring round, monotonously, mechanically. The light and shadow had

all gone from the meadow now, leaving nothing
but the hot glare of a vertical sun; yet the machine
kept on, heedless of anything but its work. The
fine, steady whirr of the toothed wheels kept biting away on the artist's ear, irritatingly. The
machine was a type of humdrum, horizonless toil,
of life without impulse, without sensation, of the
life Floyd saw around him in New England. It
was the only life Tryphena knew; it was the life
they seemed destined to live together.

The artist sprang to his feet, and leaving the
letter there in the trampled grass, paced up and
down indecisively in the shadow of the woods.
Would he come back to her?

Something far down within him said, "No," and
he found a satisfaction in listening to it, in seeming to accept it, and imagining that he had settled
the question. It was an ugly question, certainly,
and he hated any unpleasantness; but if it must
come, — he shrugged his shoulders in a fashion he
had acquired abroad.

Well, and Tryphena? Characteristically, Floyd
had considered himself first. Would she object to
the "scheme"? He remembered that he had used
this euphemistic expression to her that morning,
and he scowled as he recalled her answer, so
simple that it staggered him. "Why should I?"

In the two or three hours or more that had
elapsed since the scene in the sitting-room, he had
kept it pretty thoroughly out of his mind, thanks

to his habit of getting rid of disagreeable impressions, especially when there was fine weather to help him. But that power failed him now, and he found himself saying over again almost every word that had passed between himself and his wife. It was the first time they had ever discussed their marriage, in set words, and Floyd, after some nervous pacing to and fro, had a kind of conviction that it would be the last. He was enraged, more than at anything else in his remembrance of their discussion, at the way he had closed it. He had stood there like a schoolboy, and had stammered out, "There is another month," as if he were afraid to settle the matter; and she had answered nothing but "yes," in that curious dry tone of hers, which he was never able to fathom. There could scarcely have been a more inglorious, undramatic ending.

He paused in his walk, and pulled out his watch. It was dinner-time, and he was hungry. Men must dine, crisis or none. To go back to the Broughton House and sit by Tryphena's side through three courses and dessert, and perhaps to play whist afterwards, with Sonderby and Mrs. Floyd against Collins and himself — all that, after what had happened that forenoon, was rather commonplace and unheroic, but it was very much the way of the world.

"There is another month." Perhaps he had ended well enough, in spite of his momentary disgust at himself; and the artist felt all of a sudden that he had been analyzing as long as he could stand it. He had thought everything straight through, for once, and had finished very much where he began, in a determination to let matters take their natural course. There was no immediate crisis, after all; everything would go along just as before. Some subtle cord had perhaps been snapped, but no one would know the difference — for another month. He picked up the letter, folded his easel and stool, packed away his brushes, and holding the finished sketch carefully in one hand, took a short cut across the meadows to the hotel.

Mrs. Floyd, left in the low rocking-chair by the window, when her artist husband closed the squeaking door behind him, sat there a long while. Little by little the disturbed sparrow ceased its tremulous fluttering in the lilac bush, and settling down upon its nest again, was quite still. What was there in the fresh morning, up among the Broughton hills, that could bring a certain stale odor to the nostrils of that pale-faced, dark-haired young woman of twenty-two? Yet Mrs. Floyd became conscious of breathing an air that she remembered well. Perhaps it was only something from the Broughton House kitchen, acting on her by the subtle associations which odors convey, but Tryphena Floyd was for the moment carried far away from Broughton. She was again in the basement dining-room of a Brooklyn boarding-house, in the close, gas-heated, grease-scented air. The room was noisy with the clatter of dishes, the hurrying of slatternly servants, the well-worn jokes of the boarders. At the head of the table sat Aunt Tryphosa, dear, fat, Aunt Tryphosa, who had married an old bachelor when both their best days were long past, and who had gone to live in Brooklyn, and had been absurdly happy. Near her was a dark, shy girl from the country, her guest, and opposite the country girl, watching her with greedy eyes, was a young artist, just returned from Munich, whom the girl addressed timidly from time to time, as " Mr. Floyd."

Bah! Mrs. Floyd rose wearily, and shut the west sitting-room window. She thought it was the cooking at the hotel. In the last ten minutes she had grown old. Was it only three years since Aunt Tryphosa had invited her to Brooklyn? It was a lifetime — an eternity.

Tying the strings of an apron around her waist, she made ready for her scanty morning duties in the cottage. A tall, gilt-framed mirror hung in front of her, and, scarcely knowing what she did, she stood staring into it, still thinking of her visit to Aunt Tryphosa. Only three years? She had surveyed herself in that mirror the morning she started — a fresh-faced, ignorant maiden of scarcely twenty, with romantic notions. And now? Less color in her cheeks, more depth in her eyes, and less innocence in her heart; a womanlier figure and a woman's insight: all this had come to her in three years. How much that silent glass and gilt had seen, she thought. Her mother, whom she scarcely remembered, had dressed for her wedding by it, forty years before; so had good, queer Aunt Tryphosa; and so had she herself, Tryphena Morton, on that rainy autumn afternoon, when she had been so happy. She turned away quickly.

She passed into the bedroom, soon after that, to put it in order, moving automatically. It had been Aunt Tryphena's room once; Aunt Tryphena, the only mother the girl had ever known. Her childish memories gathered about this room; it was a sort of sacred place to her. And now it was theirs: hers and her husband's. Mrs. Floyd stopped helplessly in the middle of her work. She went out into the sitting-room, crossed it quite steadily to the wall where Aunt Tryphena's picture hung, and catching the black oval frame in both hands, burst into tears, and covered the daguerreotype with piteous kisses. Then she dropped upon the haircloth sofa, and lay there, sobbing.

An hour later Mrs. Floyd, who was a woman of narrow resources, and not, like her more gifted husband, a person to whom the consolations of nature and of art were always potent, bathed her eyes, as women do, and, finding the loneliness of the cottage intolerable, went over to the parlor of the Broughton House. When her husband came in to dinner he found her there, with the last *Harper's Weekly* uncut in her lap, talking to John Sonderby.

IV.

TOWARDS the end of the week that followed upon the Saturday evening when Sonderby had been entertained at the parsonage, the minister and his wife started out to call upon the Floyds. Mrs. Ellerton had been debating for some days her social duty in this matter, even before the school-teacher had told her something of his associates at the hotel. As the wife of the minister, Mrs. Ellerton felt that she had peculiar responsibilities, as far as calling was concerned, and some oversights on her part, at the commencement of their life in Broughton, had taught her how sensitive, even punctilious, the people in the village were, at least in their demands upon herself.

Mrs. Floyd was a newcomer in one sense, and, thus far, the obligation of the minister's wife was clear: she should make the first call. But from another standpoint it was Mrs. Ellerton who was the newcomer, and the artist's wife, as a native of Broughton, ought certainly to have called at the parsonage. She had not done so. Moreover, she had hitherto absented herself from church except on the Sunday when the quartette were there together, though Mrs. Ellerton discovered by consulting the church manual that Tryphena Morton had joined the Congregationalists in her early girlhood.

Mrs. Ellerton had a sort of intuition, too, that the artist's wife did not care particularly to be called upon; and that was certainly the opinion which Broughton people had of Tryphena's wishes in the matter, as a deacon's wife gratuitously informed Mrs. Ellerton. But, on the whole, the latter considered that it was her duty to make the call; and the performance of her obligation was considerably lightened by two facts: she was anxious to see Floyd's work; and in the second place she had taken a strong liking for the school-teacher, and she wanted to see for herself the kind of people with whom he was at present thrown. She suspected, though she could not have told why, that they were not his equals, that this long summer vacation was a time of deterioration for him; and she felt hurt by it and wondered if there were any way to help it.

Broughton women were not very scrupulous as to the time when they received calls, — provided only they were not in the kitchen, and it was neither washing-day nor ironing-day nor baking-day, — and Ruth Ellerton had acquired the habit of starting soon after dinner in order to make as many as possible within the limits of the afternoon.

Upon this particular Tuesday, however, it was nearly four o'clock before she was attired in her soft gray Henrietta, and called her husband from his study to accompany her. Arthur Ellerton was not unwilling to come. His next Sunday's sermon was in a satisfactory state of progress — indeed, it was a peculiarity of Ellerton that he was generally optimistic about his sermon, in whatever period of evolution it chanced to be. He was fond, too, of making parish calls, partly because he had not yet done enough of it to weary him, but mainly because he was fitted by nature to do it well. Ellerton met people easily; he could talk upon any subject or upon no subject; there was something in his boyish laugh and the heartiness of his manner that drew men instinctively to him, and made his calls one of his most favorable opportunities for influence upon his parish. Slightly monotonous as might have appeared to him, at times, the conversation of his deacons' wives, or of his young lady organist, there was nothing in the prospect of a call upon the Floyds to give him anything but pleasure. They had interests outside of Broughton, at any rate, and the artist ought to have something to talk about. If Ellerton scarcely possessed the conscious, strenuous desire to reach people, to influence them for good, which was a passion with his more finely organized wife, there was an unconscious, healthy benevolence about him that made him like to meet people, and caused him to effect, almost without knowing it, that impression upon others which his wife gained by means of secret trembling, and ever-renewed aspirations, and many prayers.

As they reached the post-office, on their way down the street, the mail was just distributed, and Ruth Ellerton strolled on slowly, while her husband stepped inside to get the county paper, due that day. Before he rejoined his wife, Floyd sauntered past her, his white helmet hat far back on his head, his hands in the pockets of his loose coat. The artist had been waiting for the mail: why, he scarcely knew, as he had no reason to expect anything, yet it was rarely that he failed, nowadays, to be at the office in the afternoon.

The callers turned in at the cottage gate just as Floyd reached the door. He did not notice them at first; for Mrs. Floyd met him in the doorway, bringing out in her slender arms an oddly carved cherry table. He took it from her, though not very promptly, and set it in the shade of the lilacs, in front of a bench that always stood there. Mrs. Floyd turned into the cottage again, as if to fetch something else, and at the moment when the artist had settled the table solidly upon the gravelled walk, he looked up to find Mr. and Mrs. Ellerton close to him.

Floyd bowed, with a low sweep of the helmet hat, and gave himself the privilege of a full, long look at Ruth Ellerton's face.

"Is Mrs. Floyd in?" she began — "we are glad"

— then hesitated and glanced at her card-case. The artist's stare had slightly disconcerted her.

Arthur Ellerton's frank voice followed quickly upon her pause. "I don't know that we need any introduction," he said, in his cheery, incontrovertible fashion of uttering a commonplace; "but, Mrs. Ellerton, this is Mr. Floyd." Then stretching out his quick hand, before the artist could murmur the conventional reply, the minister added, "I am very glad to make your acquaintance."

Floyd bowed slightly, and his eyes wandered to Mrs. Ellerton again.

"Shall we stay here?" asked Floyd, "or will you come inside?"

"Oh, it is so pleasant here," smiled Mrs. Ellerton, and she glanced toward the bench.

"My wife is just bringing out some chairs," explained Floyd. "We were going to play whist," he added, then bit his lip as he thought of the infelicity of his remark — the more so as Mrs. Ellerton said instantly, "Oh, you mustn't let us interrupt a whist-party!"

At that instant Mrs. Floyd appeared in the doorway, holding in front of her the cushioned rocking-chair that usually stood by the sewing-machine. It seemed heavy for her, and both gentlemen started to take it, but Ellerton was the quicker.

"Mr. and Mrs. Ellerton are here," said Floyd.

Mrs. Floyd bowed, and a little color came into her pale cheeks.

"Won't you be pleased to sit down?" she asked.

It was the beginning of a phrase that Aunt Tryphena had taught her in her girlhood as the polite formula of hospitality. The remainder of the expression — "and make yourself to home" — Mrs. Floyd had gradually dropped in recent years, as she became conscious that most persons in Brooklyn did not use it.

"Thank you. How pleasant it is here under the lilacs!" exclaimed Mrs. Ellerton, as she seated herself at one end of the oak bench.

"It is pretty in the summer time," answered Mrs. Floyd, taking timid possession of the rocking-chair near by. "Aunt Tryphena used to set a great deal of store by them — the lilacs, I mean. They used to be the handsomest in town."

"Yes?"

Mrs. Ellerton's eyes grew soft as she looked at Mrs. Floyd's black dress, and remembered that the first funeral Mr. Ellerton had attended after they came to Broughton had been that of Aunt Tryphena.

"I am very sorry," she added, gently, "that we could not have known your aunt."

Mrs. Floyd lifted her dark eyes an instant, for reply, and they looked into Ruth Ellerton's with a sort of appeal, pathetically brief. Then they fell to the ground again, and left Mrs. Ellerton with a helpless desire to say something intimate and tender to her. But she knew the time had not yet come for that.

"You have very pretty roses here, Mrs. Floyd," broke in Ellerton.

Floyd had gone into the cottage for another chair, and the minister, without noticing particularly the opening words of the conversation between his wife and Mrs. Floyd, felt that the tone of the talk was not as breezy as it should be.

"Yes, sir," replied Mrs. Floyd. "They were Aunt Tryphena's." This time she did not raise her eyes at all.

Ellerton went on persistently, in his way, oblivious of her reticence. "What do you call these white ones, with the pink-tipped petals?" he demanded. "I don't remember that I ever saw anything like them before. Have you, my dear? Just look at them."

They turned to the straggling rosebush, whose burden of late roses was shaded by the clump of lilacs. The minister picked a bud, and showed to his wife the exquisite line of deep pink that ran across the edge of each petal.

"Lovely!" she cried. "How very lovely!"

"Isn't there any name for them, Mrs. Floyd?" he repeated.

"Well, Aunt Tryphena used to call them the Smith roses," she answered, slowly. "He was a missionary to foreign parts, and planted this bush before he went away."

"Indeed," exclaimed Mrs. Ellerton, rather vaguely.

"I wonder what Smith that could be," remarked the minister, reflectively. "There was a Richard J. Smith who went from somewhere in New England. He was the one who accomplished such a great work in Ceylon, you remember."

Neither of the ladies looked as if they did remember.

"Yes, it was wonderful what that man went through. If it was Richard J. Smith, and he planted the bush here before he sailed, it is very — historic."

He hesitated a trifle before the last word, and seemed to have a suspicion that his ending was somewhat ineffective.

Tryphena Floyd said nothing. Mrs. Ellerton felt that in spite of Arthur's conversational gifts, their acquaintance with Mrs. Floyd was not progressing rapidly. By this time the artist had brought out a couple more chairs, and Ellerton turned toward him.

"Didn't you say something about playing whist?"

"Inadvertently," replied Floyd. "But the others are not yet here."

"Ah? Well even a pastoral call ought not to break up a whist-party, I suppose," laughed Ellerton.

Floyd was surprised to hear such tolerant language from the parson.

"Do you play?" he asked at a venture.

"No, not since my college days," responded Ellerton. "It takes too much time. The most I have done in that direction is to play a half-dozen games of cribbage with my wife. And I don't know that even that would be regarded in Broughton as being very ministerial," he added, with the freedom that came with talking to people who did not really belong in town.

"My dear," interrupted Mrs. Ellerton, "you must be careful of what crimes you accuse yourself." Arthur was so careless sometimes!

The artist was watching stealthily the gay smile into which her grave features lightened. She turned toward him suddenly, before he could look away.

"Mr. Sonderby told me that he played whist with you a good deal," she said.

"Yes, he plays with Phenie — with Mrs. Floyd, I should say — against Collins and myself. Do you know Collins?"

"No, I do not," replied Mrs. Ellerton.

"He's coming over pretty soon," the artist went on, glancing toward the Broughton House. "He doesn't have much to do, either, in this lively town. Don't you find it lively, Mrs. Ellerton?"

She did not like the tone of jocular familiarity upon which he had just ventured, but answered, smilingly:

"There is at least more to see and hear now than there is in March and April. It certainly is not very lively then. But I should think the quiet of the place, and the beauty of it, would be just what you would most like, — for your painting, Mr. Floyd."

She spoke the last rather timidly; for she had rarely met a veritable artist before, and did not know whether she ought to refer, before people, to that which she had grown up to consider a great and divine gift.

" Why, of course," Floyd began — and then hesitated, happening to discover that his wife was watching him with that impenetrable look of hers. She was grateful to the minister's wife for those appreciative words about Broughton — " the quiet of the place, and the beauty of it "— and wondered if Floyd would say the same things to this delicately bred woman that he was in the habit of saying to herself.

" Of course," Floyd continued, " Broughton is a very good sketching-place. I have made a great many studies here. And it is the home of my wife." He did not look at his wife as he uttered this gallant sentiment, or he might have detected upon her thin upper lip a line he well knew.

" But you see, Mrs. Ellerton, I am the only man who comes here to paint, and there are no persons here who care at all about art — unless the present company are excepted," he added, awkwardly. " There must be a sort of atmosphere before a man can do his best work : a sort of — " and he stopped for a suitable word.

Mrs. Floyd leaned back in her rocking-chair. It was the old story on which he was started, after all. For once in her life she interrupted him in it.

" Perhaps, Billy, she would like to see some of the things you have been doing. And Mr. Ellerton."

" Oh, if you would be so good, Mr. Floyd," cried Mrs. Ellerton. It was more than she had dared to hope for. " Would it be very much trouble ?"

Floyd was already on his feet. " It would give me the greatest of pleasure, Mrs. Ellerton," he answered, bowing to her so markedly that she found herself disconcerted again, and almost disliking him. She did indeed dislike his bony, irregular face, his small, watery eyes, and the way he stared with them; but he seemed, except for that, gentlemanly enough, and she supposed that allowances must be made for artistic eccentricities.

He came back presently, bringing an armful of canvases, and setting up his easel in front of the door, he put one sketch after another upon it, while Mrs. Ellerton watched them hungrily, hardly daring to make any comments lest she should say the wrong thing. She leaned forward from her seat on the bench, holding across her lap in both hands her best lace parasol; her husband stood behind her, resting one hand on the back of the bench, and making gay remarks about the pictures he liked best. Mrs. Floyd had moved her rocking-chair to give the visitors a better light, and did not seem to follow very closely the succession of the studies as her husband explained them. There were many clever things, undoubtedly, in the collection, and they showed pretty well what Floyd's artistic experience had been.

Most of them had been done either in Munich or since his return, and Mrs. Ellerton recognized — or thought she did — some of the qualities which her reading had taught her to look for in the modern Munich school. Mrs. Ellerton knew the names of one or two of Floyd's teachers; she even had at the parsonage a photograph of Defregger's Madonna, and when she had summoned up her courage she began to ask questions, some of them childishly simple, others — relating to the purposes of modern art study, and the ideals of the Munich school — so puzzling that he could not answer, nor indeed really understand her.

But not all his subjects were Munich ones, and she was glad when he replaced the *genre* sketches, with their monotonous repetitions of earthen and pewter beer-mugs, bread and cheese and radishes, and the charcoal studies in composition, by some memorials of an Easter trip to Venice. There were bits of landscape here that were really admirable for their atmospheric quality, especially some water-colors done at the Lido and out at Torcello. The scenes in Venice itself were not so good, —

the architecture being noticeably weak, — but the water and the sky and the boats were almost always capital.

When Mrs. Ellerton praised these things particularly, Floyd brought out two or three finished pictures, painted on the Long Island shore since his return, and finally he produced a portfolio containing some of his Broughton sketches. Many of these were of familiar objects along Main Street, and were quickly recognized, to Floyd's secret pleasure. There was one of the Broughton House piazza, the perspective all askew, but with a felicitous representation of Bill Trumbull asleep in his chair in the foreground. There were two or three of the whist quartette, in the act of playing; but these were barely more than caricatures.

"Why, who is that?" suddenly cried Mrs. Ellerton. Floyd was trying to get the best light for a tiny canvas on which a man's head had been painted in oils.

"Can't you guess?" said Mrs. Floyd. "I tell Billy that it is the best thing he has done this summer."

It was a square, bearded face, with unmistakable power in the heavy jaw and firm-set mouth.

"Why it must be — it is — Mr. Sonderby, isn't it?" asked Mrs. Ellerton, slowly.

Floyd smiled triumphantly.

Mrs. Ellerton reached out her hand, took the head and scrutinized it. There was a massiveness and dignity in the portrait which surprised her, so out of keeping was it with most of Floyd's work.

"How long did it take you to do this?" she asked. She felt that she ought to say something, and yet she did not wish to tell Floyd what was in her mind.

"Oh, three or four hours, one Sunday morning," he answered, carelessly; then remembered he was talking to the parson's wife, and felt rather abashed.

She did not seem to notice the latter part of his remark, but contented herself with saying:

"I think it is remarkably good, Mr. Floyd; I have never seen just that look in Mr. Sonderby's face, — I know him so little — but, — " and her voice fell a little, — "I suppose an artist sees the best that is in a face — the strongest and noblest features — and tries to make these permanent. I was reading the other day what Walt Whitman says about Lincoln: that there was in his eyes a deep, latent sadness beneath his smile, that none of the artists caught the whole expression of his face, and that one of the great portrait-painters of two or three centuries ago was needed."

Floyd watched her attentively, though he really was noting the exquisite color in her cheeks and the gray of her eyes more than what she was saying. He had never heard of Whitman, and hardly knowing what answer to make, caught at her closing words.

"The old masters," he said, somewhat flippantly.

"Yes: Holbein, for instance."

She mentioned two pictures by Holbein, in the Munich Gallery, which she knew well enough through prints. To her bewilderment, Floyd seemed not to be acquainted with them.

"We don't care much for those old fellows," he explained. "Of course it's all very well if you've got time enough; but there is so much to learn in the modern schools nowadays. There's the Salon, for instance; if you want to know how to paint, there's the place to see how it's done, instead of bothering your head over those old cracked and dirty pictures — the Lord only knows who painted them — in the Pinacothek."

Against this she rebelled.

"But surely if Holbein were alive now and were to send a portrait to the Salon, every one would see the difference."

"Oh, a difference, of course," he admitted, with a patronizing smile. "But that isn't saying that it would be any better, is it?"

Obviously, Holbein's name meant nothing to him. But before she could answer, there was a rustle in the lilac bushes behind her, and she turned to see a solidly built man of thirty-five, bareheaded, with a dark, oval, handsome face, step into the group, having crossed by a short cut from the hotel. He threw away his cigar as he recognized the strangers. Mrs. Floyd introduced him to the Ellertons as Mr. Collins.

"Having another exhibition, Floyd?" asked the newcomer, seating himself upon the artist's sketching-stool, which stood near Ellerton's chair.

"Yes."

"Sorry to have missed it," replied Collins, with a tranquillity of tone which implied that his regrets were not to be taken too seriously.

"Did you go down to the Hollow?" inquired Mrs. Floyd.

"Yes, I've been there again. He rose twice to-day, but wouldn't touch anything."

"Mr. Collins is a great fisherman," explained Mrs. Floyd.

"There's a big trout down in the Hollow," Collins went on, turning politely to Mrs. Ellerton, without noticing Mrs. Floyd's interpolation, "and I have a try at him almost every day now. He's a queer fellow, and he never rises at anything except in the most unlikely time of the day. I used to go down there before breakfast and after supper, but now I'm trying him after dinner, and on the shiniest, hottest days I can find. He's a contrary one, I can tell you."

Mrs. Ellerton smiled appreciatively. She liked his deep, resonant voice, and the deliberate, self-contained way he had of talking.

"My husband will be interested in your efforts," she said. "He is fond of fishing, too."

Collins turned his dark eyes scrutinizingly upon the minister, as if to see whether he were worthy of being admitted into the guild of sportsmen.

"I think we met down near Calvin Johnson's a while ago," Ellerton remarked; then added, with a frank laugh, "I suppose you were sorry to see me; I certainly was to see you."

Collins twinkled; the parson did not seem to be such a bad fellow.

"The Johnson brook has been poor this year," he replied. "There was too much high water until that day we were there. I took three or four pounds out of the meadow, though; but you had the start of me in the woods."

"Yes; I got about forty there, most of them little ones. By the way," — and Ellerton lowered his voice a little, as befitted the discussion of the secrets of their craft, — "I noticed that you were using a white fly that day. Did you try that in the woods at all?"

Collins hitched his stool a trifle nearer to Ellerton.

"Well, I don't remember about that. I use a worm in the woods a good deal. I've just got a new book of flies this afternoon," reaching for his inside pocket; "don't you want to take a look at them?"

"If Mrs. Floyd will allow us," assented Ellerton. It was exactly what he had wished for.

"That's all right," Mrs. Floyd answered, indifferently. "Billy, haven't you anything else to show Mrs. Ellerton?"

"Oh, you have been so good, Mr. Floyd," exclaimed Mrs. Ellerton, "you mustn't give yourself any more trouble. But it has been such a treat to me."

"I haven't much else here — except this," the artist answered, as he placed upon the easel the picture of the old mill, done a couple of mornings before. Opening his penknife he scraped off carefully a few grass-seeds that had blown against the fresh paint and had dried on.

"Do you remember it?" he asked.

Mrs. Ellerton took a long look at the canvas through her gloved hand, as if it were a glass.

"Why, the landscape seems perfectly familiar — it is the view from the North Broughton road, behind the parsonage, isn't it?"

"Correct."

"But the details — the mill — I don't think I have ever seen that — have I?"

"Perhaps not; it is a little off the road. I was down there the other morning, and saw you setting out some plants as I went by."

"Oh, yes — it was Tuesday? Or Wednesday?"

"Thursday," said Mrs. Floyd, quietly.

Floyd did not reply, but Mrs. Ellerton detected a scowl on his face, as he suddenly picked up the pictures. She feared she had not shown enough attention to the last one.

"Please may I see that one moment more?" she asked, taking it in her hands. "Oh, here are the houses along Main Street, and the parsonage, too!" she cried, delightedly. "Isn't your cottage here? You must like so much to put that in if you can. It must be charming to paint your own home. No, there is nothing but the Broughton House," she decided, in disappointment.

"You must admit that the Broughton House is much the more prominent object in the landscape, Mrs. Ellerton," replied Floyd, fluently.

"Yes; but don't you think it is ugly? The cottage is such a beautiful old place that I should think you would like to paint it for its own sake. And you have left it quite out."

"Perhaps he thought that the two didn't go well together," suggested Mrs. Floyd, doubtfully. "One thing sort o' kills another, sometimes."

Floyd was busy strapping up his sketches, with his back turned to his wife, and made no reply.

"My dear," called out Arthur Ellerton, suddenly, "Mr. Collins is going to show me some of his tips, over at the hotel; we shall be back in a couple of minutes. Will you excuse us, Mrs. Floyd?"

The latter nodded, and the gentlemen slipped away. Mrs. Ellerton was just a trifle annoyed. Arthur was so forgetful of conventionalities sometimes! There he was making a first call, and excusing himself because he wanted to see some bamboo fishing-rods. Yet she was glad to have him enjoy himself, and find a congenial spirit in Mr. Collins: it was not every day that Arthur could talk about out-of-door sports without being misunderstood, the dear hard-working boy!

While Floyd was carrying his pictures and easel into the cottage, the women were left alone. Ruth Ellerton started one subject of conversation after another, but with slight success. The hostess seemed shy; and though she replied to Mrs. Ellerton's questions straightforwardly enough, there was a peculiar terseness, almost curtness, in her brief answers, that made her seem non-communicative. She made it easy for one to infer, too, that prevailing standards meant little to her, and yet she gave this impression more through her tone than through her words, for what she actually said was commonplace enough.

Floyd did not reappear for a while; Ellerton's couple of minutes had lengthened to ten or fifteen; and Mrs. Ellerton felt as if her call had already grown into what the Broughton people would call a visit, and that even the latter was extending itself to unfit proportions. She was heartily glad when she saw John Sonderby enter at the front gate. If her husband would only come, the quartette could be left to their whist; in the meantime the school-teacher's appearance would bring a new feature into the conversation.

Sonderby came down the walk deliberately,

planting his feet solidly at every step, as was his custom. He pulled off his straw hat as he caught sight of Mrs. Ellerton, and shook hands with her somewhat formally, nodding to Mrs. Floyd as he did so.

"You're very late, Mr. Sonderby," said Tryphena Floyd.

"I know it," was the reply; "I've been trying to work out something at the academy."

"Did you get it?" asked Mrs. Ellerton, eagerly, not having the remotest idea what "it" was, except that Sonderby was interested in physics and spent some of his time over the apparatus at the academy.

"Yes," he replied, looking straight at her.

"I knew you would," she cried; then blushed to think that she had betrayed what was in her mind. Unconsciously it had flashed over her as he spoke, that a man with John Sonderby's square-set face would get whatever he set out to get.

The school-teacher made no answer, though a puzzled smile crept into the corners of his eyes and mouth, as he saw Mrs. Ellerton's heightened color. A quicker man would have said something graceful, but John Sonderby had never had much practice in saying graceful things to women. He sat down upon the bench, and leaning forward, began to fan himself with his hat.

"Where is Collins?" he asked of Mrs. Floyd.

"Over at the hotel."

"Didn't he come?"

She nodded. "He's gone over to show his rods to Mr. Ellerton."

"Oh."

There was a pause. Then Sonderby changed his hat into his other hand, and turned to Mrs. Ellerton, who was seated at the opposite end of the bench.

"Have you seen the pictures?" he asked.

"Indeed I have," was the enthusiastic answer. "Mr. Floyd was so kind! I can't tell you how much I enjoyed it."

The last sentence was addressed as much to Mrs. Floyd as to the school-teacher, and it was the former who answered:

"Billy likes to show them."

"I should think he might," said Mrs. Ellerton, appreciatively. Then she remembered that during that evening at the parsonage, Sonderby had spoken of Floyd's fondness for talking about his work, and she was struck by the similarity of the tone in which both these persons had commented upon the fact. She did not quite like Mrs. Floyd's way of speaking: there was too little reverence in it for the husband's art.

"It must be a wonderful pleasure to you, Mrs. Floyd," she said, "to see these beautiful things growing under your eyes, and to feel that you have a part in them."

"Yes?" There was an appreciable rising inflection in Tryphena's voice, enough to puzzle Mrs. Ellerton.

"Were you abroad with your husband?"

"No." She did not even look up.

"That would have been so delightful,— to be there together,— would it not? Don't you think so, Mr. Sonderby?"

"Oh, yes," exclaimed Sonderby, hastily.

"Perhaps he will feel like going again some time. Mr. Ellerton and I want to go so much."

Mrs. Floyd made no response, except to twist tighter about her slender fingers the cheap blackbordered handkerchief that was in her lap. Sonderby fanned himself persistently.

Mrs. Ellerton discovered that she was almost provoked. Of all hard people to talk to, these two were certainly the hardest. If Arthur were only there!

She could not know that underneath Sonderby's stolid manner there was hidden almost a nervous desire that she and Mrs. Floyd might get on well together. He was anxious that these two women should not misunderstand each other, so different as they were. Ever since his evening at the parsonage he had been wishing that they might meet, that they might be friends. There they were at his side; and though he felt that he understood each one of them, somewhat, he instinctively saw that they were making no progress toward mutual acquaintance, and that he was not helping them.

Mrs. Floyd was in one of her silent moods, which seemed to Sonderby to have increased within the past few days, and which appeared beyond reach of any conversational artifices that the school-teacher possessed. Mrs. Ellerton was glancing furtively toward the hotel, hoping that her husband might be coming. Sonderby racked his brain for something to talk about, then remembered that she had asked him a question about etching, the previous Saturday, which he could not then answer.

"Oh," he exclaimed, "I have looked up that matter about the preparation of the plates for drypoints, and I think we were both right, in part." And he proceeded, to Mrs. Ellerton's great relief, to give a detailed and careful explanation of the process in question. But part of the time she was only pretending to listen; she was really thinking of Floyd's portrait of Sonderby, and whether it was stronger than his face actually was, and what was his place in this Broughton House quartette, whose acquaintance she was making.

She had been suspecting all along that he was of finer grain than the others, and that they were not doing him any good. Yet she had found Collins exceedingly agreeable; and though she hardly liked Floyd, she was sure that his artist qualities must be the result of some high and noble strain in him, which she had not sufficiently taken into account, else how could he have such appreciation of the lovely things in the world? She could even almost forgive his ignorance of Holbein. As for Mrs. Floyd, the minister's wife felt a tenderness for her in her evident bereavement, and a pity for her shyness; but she was irritated that Mrs. Floyd's talk should be so unsympathetic, and she wondered why John Sonderby seemed to know the artist's wife so well, and what sort of an influence the latter was likely to have over him. Ruth Ellerton was a woman, as well as a minister's wife.

Just as Sonderby was finishing his explanation, Floyd joined the group, and a few moments after Ellerton and Collins came strolling over from the hotel, the latter with a fresh cigar in his fingers. They had had a glorious fishing talk, ranging from the trout-brooks of Ellerton's boyhood, in Western Pennsylvania, up to the great salmon of the Restigouche and the St. John, where Collins had fished repeatedly.

Mrs. Ellerton rose at once, and her husband pulled out his watch, and then laughed.

"Excuse me, my dear," he cried. "A whole half-hour! Well, I declare! Mrs. Floyd, will you pardon me for running away?"

Mrs. Floyd, who had risen too, smiled at him. She could understand the voluble, cheery young fellow so much better than she could his wife, who seemed, in some way, off up above her. The ladies shook hands. Then Ellerton stepped forward in his turn, and while Mrs. Floyd put out her hand to him — much less timidly than she had extended it a moment before to take the daintily gloved hand of his wife — he seemed to remember his pastoral function, and said something about the church, turning to Floyd likewise as he spoke, but not changing his key at all, and referring to a church service as simply as he had to a fishing-rod. That was a part of the charm of Arthur Ellerton.

Sonderby happened to be standing by Mrs. Ellerton, and in the moment of waiting she turned to him.

"Have you decided about next winter?" she asked.

"No," he answered, bluntly. "The truth is," and his small blue eyes looked squarely into her great gray ones, "I can't decide. I don't know but I'm letting the summer decide for me. And — do you think it makes much difference, anyway, where a man is?"

"Oh, it does make a difference!" she exclaimed, with a troubled voice. "You mustn't think that it doesn't!"

"Come, my dear," interrupted Ellerton, gaily. "We have effectually broken up the whist-party, I fear. Next Monday then, we will say, Mr. Collins, at five sharp. Good afternoon, all."

The others bowed.

"Pardon me, madam," cried Collins, as he took a quick step forward and snapped a big rose-bug deftly from Mrs. Ellerton's collar; "but you were carrying away something from the premises."

She thanked him, and under cover of a general laugh, the Ellertons withdrew.

Floyd stood looking at Mrs. Ellerton's tall figure as she disappeared. He had seen the crawling rose-bug sooner than Collins, and might have had the smiling thanks himself, if he had not hesitated. Confound it, but she was a superb woman for a parson's wife, and how she had praised his pictures! Women like that could appreciate him.

"Well," said Collins, "how about that whist?"

"There's time for half a dozen hands," replied Sonderby, looking at his watch. Mrs. Floyd had already placed her rocking-chair at the table, on the opposite side from the bench. Sonderby pulled off his coat, and spreading it over the bench for a cushion sat down to play as her partner, looking very comfortable in his gray flannel shirt.

"It's your deal, Floyd," Collins remarked; "remember we have the lead now," and he produced the well-used markers.

But Floyd seemed to be out of temper, for some reason or other, and made a misdeal.

V.

Five o'clock of the next Monday morning, however, did not see Collins and Ellerton starting upon their fishing excursion. It witnessed, instead, a downpour of rain so persistent and heavy that it put even trout-fishing out of the question. The rain had indeed begun upon Saturday afternoon, shortly after the stage had brought an unusually full quota of strangers to the Broughton House. A few drops fell before the mail was distributed.
Bill Trumbull, standing at the southeast corner of the hotel piazza, and slowly surveying the different points of the compass, was surrounded by a group of the newcomers, anxious to learn the probabilities. It is curious how soon strangers in a New England town will detect the most weather-wise natives, and how respectfully they will accept whatever decisions the experienced weather prophets condescend to give them. Bill Trumbull had watched New England weather too long, and was too old a hotel man, to be over-positive in his declarations as to the weather in store for Sunday; but beneath his cabalistic remarks about "a wet moon," and the "wind backin' 'round," there was certainly revealed a conviction that they were "in for a wet spell."

"You see," he remarked, benevolently, pointing with his pipe toward the gray folds of cloud that were steadily wrapping themselves around the southern and eastern hills, "the wind is settin' right from the west, just as it has ben all day. But those 'ere clouds to the east'ard keep a comin' up all the same, 'n when you git the wind comin' up one way, and the rain comin' up the opposite, — at least 'round here, — yes ma'am, I'm a-pointin' toward the east — why, then the rain never stops till the Lord stops it."

Sure enough, by supper-time there was a spiteful shower, which whipped tiny branches from the elms all along the street, laid the thick July dust, and freshened the grass wonderfully. But after the shower had passed, there were no signs of clearer weather, and a fine rain kept falling as it grew dark. Evans glided around the piazza, among his guests, and promised them better things for the morrow, in spite of the opinion expressed by Bill Trumbull, between whom and Evans no love was lost as time went by. Trumbull watched Evans now with some amazement, and confided to Collins his sarcastic opinion of the Welshman's knowledge of Broughton weather.

Notwithstanding the dampness, the whist quartette played for a while upon the middle of the piazza, in the light of the reflector. It grew chilly finally, and when Mrs. Floyd had coughed once or twice, Sonderby proposed that they should go into the office, where there was a big blaze in the fireplace. Trumbull was in his accustomed seat, telling fish stories to a gentleman who had come up that afternoon. A lady with eyeglasses was inspecting the adornments of the office, more particularly the portrait of Daniel Webster, and the map of the county roads.

Mrs. Floyd seated herself in one of the hospitable wooden chairs by the fire, and extended her feet as near as she dared to the burning maple logs. The school-teacher sat next her, while Floyd and Collins filled their pipes and listened — the latter for the twentieth time — to the account Bill was giving of the way he and his younger brother had once taken twenty-five pounds of trout in one day out of the Johnson brook. It was before the war that this famous fishing occurred, and with each year Bill's narration of it grew more thrilling and richer in detail. The stranger absorbed it eagerly, and once or twice when the tale reached a situation so remarkable as almost to appear unveracious, Bill Trumbull turned gravely to Collins for confirmation, which Collins's own experiences seemed perfectly adapted to supply. The "Broughton House" stopped with the piazza and the new part, after all; here in the office the atmosphere was still that of "Trumbull's." A sort of miraculous air it was, in which every listener breathed in a predisposition to faith, and where the veriest sceptic might be convinced by simply pointing out the indubitable length of certain trout cut as an imperishable sign upon the oak mantel-piece.

But suppose one does not care for any of these things? Suppose the person sitting in "Trumbull's" is a woman, looking back upon an isolated childhood, an ignorant girlhood, an unsatisfying marriage; a woman with strong yet variable impulses, with yearning affections, and an empty heart; a woman looking forward to the great crisis of her life? Or suppose the person is a man, likewise with a lonely youth behind him, a man powerfully moulded in mind as well as body, but never brought under the dominion of an inspiring purpose; a man whose best years had been selfish, solitary ones, who is touched at last by a profound solicitude for a woman whose deepest grief he can only guess at, and toward whom he can ill define his own feeling, save that he wonders if the feeling, whatever it may be, is stronger than his will?

For persons like these, "Trumbull's" can do nothing. They may sit there side by side, and gaze steadily into the glowing mass of maple embers, while the flame plays on their faces; they may well see strange shapes and forms of things deep down in the glowing innermost heart of the burning coals, and the fire may whisper to them and answer their mute questionings, perhaps; but they will not hear any of Bill Trumbull's fishing-stories.

"Phenie," Floyd had to cry at last, "Collins is speaking to you."

Mrs. Floyd started and looked around at her husband. The stranger and the lady with eye-glasses had gone. Collins was rapping the ashes out of his pipe.

"Want to sing?" he asked.

"Oh, yes, if Mr. Evans won't put us out; it's too cold over at the cottage, and I'd rather stay here. But I'm not sure that the people who have just come will appreciate our singing, Mr. Collins."

She spoke more than she commonly did, as if to make up for her inattention at the beginning.

"Well, they'll have to get used to it," drawled Collins, rising. "And Evans won't put us out. Will he, Bill?"

Trumbull chuckled. "I guess not."

"Come on, Sonderby," said Collins, as the trio crossed the hall to enter the little old parlor, where stood a battered, yellow-keyed melodeon.

"No," replied Sonderby, without taking his eyes off the fire, "I think I'll stay here."

Trumbull refilled his pipe, silently. He never went into the parlor of the hotel nowadays.

Collins seated himself at the melodeon, with Mr. and Mrs. Floyd standing on either side, and began to turn over the leaves of a song-book. He knew enough about music to play his own accompaniments fairly well, and he could sing a magnificent bass, of sensuous richness and remarkable compass, though he was not always strictly on the key.

He was passionately fond of singing, and had persuaded the others to keep him company, though they did not add much to the musical value of the performance. Mrs. Floyd could carry the air pretty well, after she had learned it, and Floyd was trying to persuade himself, after having disastrously failed to persuade the others, that he could sing tenor. Sonderby sometimes stood up with them, not caring to shut himself out of the circle, and chased the air a little, an octave below, but he had no illusion as to the nature of his success.

But to-night Sonderby kept staring at the fire, while the trio sang one song after another. Collins was in high spirits, and persisted in alternating selections from Moody and Sankey's hymn-book with the more worldly melodies, singing all with equal fervor. The mixture pleased Floyd, whose reverential sentiments had never been much developed, and did not seem to shock Mrs. Floyd, who sang straight through whatever she happened to know, and hummed the rest, without seeming to care much what it was all about.

Out in the office Bill Trumbull smoked and listened, and called once, greatly to Collins's delight, for a repetition of a well-known revival hymn, though he did not tell them that the reason he wanted to hear it again was that it had once been a favorite with "Mis' Trumbull." The rain kept surging against the office windows at intervals, and now and then the wind would find its way down the huge winding chimney and brighten the maple logs with its sudden breath.

The "rainy spell" had set in, in earnest.

After a while Floyd come back and stretched himself out in a chair by Trumbull, muttering something about a duet and not being wanted. There was some preliminary turning of leaves and trying of keys, and then Collins's superb voice broke in with the words of a song he had picked up in a chamber concert at New York, the preceding winter.

> Kiss me to-day,
> Wait not the morrow;
> Waiting is sorrow,
> Love me to-day!

Then Mrs. Floyd's faint, but clear soprano made answer, —

> Love me to-morrow,
> Like me to-day;
> Kisses betray,
> Kiss me to-morrow!

and the bass began again, —

> Kiss me to-day,

only to meet the soprano's, —

> Kiss me to-morrow,

and the contest recommenced, until the parts, through inextricable weavings of phrase, and change and interchange and repetition of entreaty and denial, blended at last in a soft minor chord, and one could not say which had triumphed.

"To-day" and "to-morrow"—"love me"—"like me"—there is the true stuff for a song there, however the phrases be written or however they may be sung.

Perhaps John Sonderby thought so, as he sat there moodily, and watched with his irresolute blue eyes the leaping of the irresolute blue flames. "To-day"—"to-morrow"—"love me"—"like me"? His heart was in a tumult. It had been closed too long upon the rest of human kind, and neither man nor woman had ever come into his life to stir it very deeply. But a change had come. A great master of tender speech prayed once for those who are initiated by sorrow into the brotherhood of the great human family; yet sorrow is not the only initiator: her sister, pity, has an equal share in the divine and beneficent task. Pity had opened his heart wide.

In vain did he lean forward, and with unsteady hand push the pieces of the breaking log together to make a hotter flame, and try to close his ears against those haunting catches of music. "Love me?—Like me?" He had to take his turn with the rest of the world.

When Collins and Mrs. Floyd had finished, they found Sonderby standing with his back to the fire.

"Good night," he said, as they came toward the fireplace. "I'm going to bed."

As he disappeared up the staircase, Collins remarked:

"He seems a little blue to-night."

"The rain," put in Mrs. Floyd, "is enough to make any one blue."

"Oh, it isn't the rain that ails Sonderby," rejoined Collins. "The truth is, he ought to get out of Broughton. He needs to be waked up. I put him on the track of a job in Boston, two or three weeks ago, that would just suit him, with an electric company. Sonderby is a good fellow, but he is a little slow; and the longer he stays in Broughton, the slower he'll get. Isn't that your experience, Bill?"

He turned to Trumbull, facetiously. Trumbull had listened with interest to Collins's attempt at analysis, but did not altogether agree.

"Wal," he said, deliberately, "those winters when I was down to Boston, in the Legislature, I naturally took some account of the folks down there, 'n I didn't find any that was smarter — that is, the smart ones — than smart folks right here in Broughton. That ain't it. Some folks are born smart — pushers, drivers, — you know. There was Mis' Trumbull," — and he hesitated, while the vacant look came into his eyes.

"You mean," said Mrs. Floyd, gently, thinking to help him out, "that it doesn't make any difference where one lives."

Floyd made an impatient exclamation.

She went on without heeding him — "that if you're born to be smart, you will be smart; and that if you ain't —"

"You won't," assisted Collins.

"Exactly." concluded Bill Trumbull, looking admiringly at Tryphena Floyd, whom he had always liked, ever since she was a child. "Wal, I 'spose I must be gittin' across the street. Nigh on to ten o'clock, ain't it? Sho! Pesky rain, ain't it? Good night — good night," and he shuffled off.

"We must go too," said Mrs. Floyd.

"Haven't you any umbrella?" asked Collins. "Here, mine is in the corner. You ought to have some rubbers too."

"She won't need them," said Floyd.

Collins looked doubtful. "See here, Johnny," he cried to the stable-boy, who had just come into the office. "Take a lantern and show them to the cottage. Find a dry place to get across, now."

Mrs. Floyd looked up at the manufacturer, gratefully. "Thank you," she said.

When the stable-boy came back, and set down his dripping lantern by the fireplace, Collins had gone, and the office was empty. The boy blew out the lamps, and pulling Bill Trumbull's cushioned chair close up to the dying fire, dried his fingers and his heavy shoes, and amused himself by trying to find horses' heads in the coals. He fell asleep after a while, and when he awoke, the office was so dark and dismal, and the rain tapped at the windows in such a ghostly fashion, that he locked the front door of the silent hotel, and climbed up to the attic to bed.

All night long the rain fell, and from time to time the thunder rumbled over the hills, yet so distant was it that one could hardly have told whether it were thunder, or only the roar of a freight train climbing a long grade down at the Center, whence a favorable wind sometimes carried the toilsome sound even as far as Broughton.

Sonderby, wakened for a moment, thought that it was the midnight freight, and falling to sleep again, dreamed that a train was carrying him away from Broughton, and that his heart was strangely light; yet that he did not wish to go, and tried to leap from the platform, but failed, for his feet were so heavy that he could not stir them. Then the dream changed, and he was bow oar in his college boat again, pulling desperately; but instead of his college mates the boat was manned by the minister and his wife, Collins, and Mr. and Mrs. Floyd. Mrs. Floyd was pulling stroke, her slim white arms bare and rigid, and she quickened the pace till the felon on his hand hurt so cruelly that he woke.

It was almost morning, and he did not go to sleep again.

When he came down to breakfast, Collins was already there, his high spirits of the preceding evening fortified by a good night's rest, and undeterred by the prospect of a rainy Sunday. He talked to Sonderby a good deal about the electric company in Boston, and seemed pleased when the school-teacher said that he had been thinking the matter over seriously, and was rather inclined to go.

"That's right," approved Collins. "You ought to get out of this place, Sonderby, and make some money. You are just the man they want, I know. You'd better write in the morning that you'll take the offer."

"Well," hesitated Sonderby, "there is no especial hurry. I understood that their busy season did not begin for three weeks or so, and that any time before that —"

"But that's not business," Collins interrupted. "If you're going at all, there's no time to spare. You want to get acquainted with the ways of things down there before the busy season begins. Why don't you go right off?"

"I — can't," replied Sonderby.

The manufacturer eyed him, sidewise, narrowly.

"You can't, eh? Why the dickens can't you? Not that I want to get rid of you, my boy," he added, in a more kindly fashion. "It would knock our quartette higher than a kite. But because I am loafing up here half the summer, waiting for those devilish strikers to get ready to go to work, that's no reason why a young fellow like you, with this big chance all ready for you, should sit around in this little country town, and get hayseed in your hair."

Sonderby laughed.

"It's no laughing matter," persisted Collins, seriously. "I tell you the quicker you get out of Broughton and into the A. S. & F. Works, the better off you'll be. And now I've said all I'm going to. It's none of my business, anyway."

"I am very grateful to you, Collins," said Sonderby, earnestly.

"That's all right. Now if you'll only pack up, I'll believe you. You hang along as if there were some woman in the case: as if—"

"Hush up!"

Collins stopped, lifting his black eyebrows a trifle. He had only been joking in that last sentence, and Sonderby had spoken angrily. Ah! And Collins closed his eyes as he took a long, meditative draught from his coffee-cup.

Tryphena Floyd had just come in, and was taking her seat opposite Sonderby. Her husband followed her, a moment later, and the conversation turned, naturally enough, to the subject of the weather.

A Sunday morning in a New England country town! Most of the people who had come up from the Center in the Broughton stage the day before had a definite vision of the morrow that awaited them. It should be a bright morning, just warm enough to make one realize how hot it would have been in the city, and there should be enough breeze to bend the meadow grasses, and rustle in the elm-tops, and waft the white clouds slowly on their way. It should be a quiet morning, with hardly any sound except from the bobolinks, until the church-bells began to ring, and the farm wagons to rattle by on their way to church; and in the white meeting-house itself the windows should be wide open, and if one did not like the minister, he could help himself to a big old-fashioned palm-leaf fan, and look outdoors. across the stone walls and country roads and raspberry bushes to the meadows. and dream his childish dreams over again, and gently fan himself to sleep.

But alas! this particular Sunday morning in Broughton was destined to be a disappointment to the visionaries.

The elm-tops swayed in the wind, indeed, but they shook showers of drops from their dripping leaves; the road along Main Street was three inches thick with mud. the grass in the meadows was lodged with the violence of the storm, and a cold rain fell incessantly. The wind had blown the rain in upon the piazza of the hotel, and the chairs were so wet that no one could sit out there. Evans ordered a fire built in the sheet-iron stove in the parlor, and another in the fireplace in the office; and the guests tried, dispiritedly, to make themselves as comfortable as they could.

The quartette of "regulars" had some difficulty in arranging their programme for the morning. Floyd, who was in no humor for work, even had the weather permitted, proposed whist; but Mrs. Floyd would not play, and Sonderby did not seem enthusiastic. Collins said he had some letters to write; but when Floyd challenged him to a game of euchre, he seemed willing to defer them.

"Evans," he remarked, calling the proprietor into a corner of the office, "Mr. Floyd and I are going to have a little game of euchre up in my room. And — Evans — the morning is likely to be cold."

"Yes, sir," replied Evans, intelligently. "With lemons?"

"If you please."

Though Evans affirmed in the March town-meeting, and everywhere else, that he kept a "strictly temperance house," it was evident that he was not without experience in the art of running a hotel. The Broughton farmers who voted "no license" religiously every spring, after having consumed hard cider all the winter, would have been shocked enough if they had known of the Welshman's sub-cellar.

When Collins and Floyd went upstairs, the school-teacher and Mrs. Floyd were left in the parlor, standing with three or four other people around the sheet-iron stove. Mrs. Floyd seemed ill at ease there, and after replying once or twice to Sonderby's attempts at starting a conversation, she whispered to him. "Come, let's go over to the cottage."

He followed her into the hall.

"Why not?" she asked, seeing his inquiring look. "We can build a fire in the sitting-room. I don't know why I didn't think of it before."

Sonderby took his hat and umbrella without a word.

"Wait till I get on my rubbers," she said, eagerly.

Then holding his umbrella over her, he piloted her across the stable road, now a rivulet, and under the drenched lilac bushes, to the front door of the cottage.

It happened that Collins, who had just stepped to the window of his room to open the shutters, caught sight of the pair under the umbrella. He looked at them reflectively until they disappeared, but for some reason or other he made no comments to Floyd.

Tryphena, pulling off her waterproof and rubbers in the tiny hall, opened the door of the sitting-room.

"Will you walk into my parlor?" she cried.

Sonderby watched her silently as she ran across the room and closed the bedroom door. Then she took off the top of the square, soapstone stove, and surveyed the inside.

"What do you think?" she demanded. "Don't

you believe it will heat up? It's most worn out, though."

Sonderby took the heavy top from her hand, and looked down into the huge, sooty interior. His only answer was a smile, and that a rather vacant one; for the sight of her hand, tense in its hold upon the soapstone lid, had made him think of his dream of the night before. Was she the stroke oar, and was she setting a pace too quick for him, in spite of all he could do?

He gathered himself together. "Oh, I guess we can manage it," he said. "Where did your aunt keep her kindling-wood?"

She led the way to the woodshed, in the rear of the cottage, and gave him a basket which he filled with chips and bits of old apple-tree wood, she helping all the time, in the highest spirits.

"Give me the basket," directed Mrs. Floyd, "and bring an armful of wood. You must make yourself useful, if you expect me to take care of you."

He picked up three or four sticks.

"Now bring one of those big chunks," she ordered. "Aunt Tryphena used to have them left big on purpose. Oh, I don't mean at the same time with the others!"

He had stooped and lifted a huge knot of maple, in addition to what he held before.

"How strong you are!" she said, admiringly, then blushed a little and started for the sitting-room, Sonderby following. He put down his armful in front of the stove, breathing hard, but not altogether because of the weight he had carried.

"We must have some paper now," Tryphena exclaimed, and going to the paper-rack that hung against the wall by the window, she pulled out two or three dusty copies of the *The New York Observer*.

"Don't you think these will burn?" she asked.

"You mean that they are dry enough?"

"Well, Mr. Quickness! Yes."

He was beginning to catch her infectious spirits. Tearing the papers and crumpling them into loose balls, he filled the bottom of the stove, and covered them, as artistically as he could, with the least mouldy chips, and a few splinters of wood. Then Tryphena struck a match, turned the rusty damper in the pipe, and touched off the papers. They smoked prodigiously, but no flame appeared, and she dropped on her knees and blew at the lower draught, laughing meanwhile.

"Help," she bubbled. "You don't help at all."

Sonderby knelt too, and taking a big breath, blew steadily upon the smoking paper, while Tryphena, her cheeks full of color with the unusual effort she had made, watched him eagerly. A thin flame spurted, then another.

"All right," said Sonderby, getting up and brushing involuntarily the knees of his trousers.

"You're not very complimentary to my floor,"

she commented; "but never mind. Now let's sit down and be comfortable."

Sonderby had never seen her so gay. She brought her own low rocker for herself, and pushed toward him a high-backed, deep-cushioned chair, that had been the peculiar property of Aunt Tryphena. As they seated themselves on opposite sides of the stove, it came over Sonderby that he had been a fool; that she was nothing but a girl — a girl of twenty-two, like three or four who had been under him at the academy — that she was girlishly happy at heart, after all, and that his fears for her, and his nervous dream about himself, were the purest nonsense. He breathed freer. How light her talk was, too, as she rattled on, about Collins and Bill Trumbull and the lady with eye-glasses, and the last game of whist, while the fire crackled merrily in the old stove, and the wet lilac bushes dripped against the windows!

There was such an odd flavor of sarcasm in all she said, such a quaint way of putting things. Sonderby had hardly more to do than to express his assent or dissent. Moment by moment a weight was rising from his heart. He had been a sort of well-intentioned idiot, he kept thinking to himself; he ought to have known that he knew nothing about women.

He, John Sonderby, boating-man, school-teacher, posing as the discoverer of a woman's secret, the sentimental meddler, the suspecter of his own motives, the dreamer of unhealthy dreams? It was really too absurd.

He put the knot of maple into the stove, and gave himself up to the happiness of frank, cosey companionship with a woman he liked. An hour passed, — the happiest hour he had ever known.

They fell to comparing notes about their childhood, and it appeared that their circumstances had not been unlike. Sonderby's parents were no longer living, and for years he had had to shift for himself. He told Mrs. Floyd about his college life, about the way he happened to come to Broughton to take the school, and how he had stayed along for three years. She listened amusedly to some of his teaching experiences, understanding thoroughly, on the one hand, the strong hold he had upon his pupils, which had made the academy more prosperous under his management than it had been for many a year, and appreciating, on the other hand, the prevailing Broughton dubiousness as to the status of an academy teacher who seldom went to church, who omitted the extempore prayer from the devotional exercises with which the school session opened, and who talked to his scholars so earnestly about common morality as to give rise to the suspicion that he was a Unitarian.

She made him laugh, in turn, by telling him some of her own adventures in the academy as a schoolgirl, and little by little he found that he was constructing for himself the whole of her life up till the time of her marriage. He felt as if he knew her better than ever before; and though she did not once mention her marriage nor her husband, honest John Sonderby had a conviction that that was sacred ground upon which she would not enter with him, however strong their feeling of comradeship might be. He wanted to ask her advice about himself, about the position with the A. S. & F. Company. So strong was his revulsion of feeling against the mood he had been in the night before, that he was conscious of a longing to consult her about leaving Broughton, feeling that that very act would be a kind of expiation of the fact that on the preceding evening leaving Broughton meant chiefly to him an abandonment of her.

"I should like," he said, "to ask you about something that concerns me pretty closely."

"Yes?" she answered.

If he had not been intent on what he was saying, he might have noticed that a sort of lassitude had gradually taken possession of her. The sparkle had begun to go out of her eyes, and the brilliant, transient mood seemed to have left her weary.

"I have had a good position offered me in Boston," he went on, "with the A. S. & F. Company."

"You are going away," she cried, drearily. "I heard you say so to Mrs. Ellerton; Mr. Collins told us so last night. You are going away."

"I don't know," he stammered. "The salary — It is a very good position."

"Oh, yes," she said. "The money. Of course. We must have something to live for — money — or art."

The sudden bitterness of Tryphena's voice frightened him. It swept away the security in which he had been sheltering himself all the morning, and the old fear and uncertainty rushed back upon him.

"I may not go," he stammered again. "I don't know."

"You are going," she murmured, and he thought he saw a terror steal into her eyes.

"No," he cried, blundering straight to the heart of the matter, "I won't go if I can stay and help you."

There was a long instant of silence. Then she rose and stretched out her slim white hand; and Sonderby thought, even in that intense moment, of his dream.

"John Sonderby," she said, quite simply and quietly, taking his right hand, "you are a good man. But you can't help me. No one can help me."

Then she relinquished her grasp, and sinking into her chair, covered her cheeks with her hands, but not enough to hide the swift-coming blushes. Sonderby stood looking at her, crushing down a fierce desire to take her in his arms.

"I'm tired now; I guess I'm too tired."

He understood her, and turning without a word, opened the door, and strode out into the rain.

At the door of the Broughton House Collins met him. "Floyd beat me at euchre," he remarked, peculiarly, "and he felt so well over it, that he got Johnny to drive him down to the Center. Shouldn't wonder if he didn't get back till to-morrow."

"Is that so?" replied Sonderby, dryly, hardly knowing what he said, or what Collins really meant, though the slight odor of whiskey punch that clung to the manufacturer might have enlightened him. As the school-teacher passed the door of the parlor, he saw the lady with eye-glasses seated at the melodeon, turning over Collins's music, which still remained on the rack from the previous evening. While he was mechanically mounting the stairs to his room, she began upon the soprano of the duet:

> Love me to-morrow,
> Like me to-day;
> Kisses betray,
> Kiss me to-morrow!

and poor Sonderby, gripping the balustrade with one hand, stopped to listen and thought of the night before, and saw again the crouching figure he had left in the cottage, and felt a passionate wrath rising in his heart against Floyd, against Collins, and against the whole vulgar, brutal world.

VI.

Mrs. Floyd did not appear at dinner. Collins was in a jovial frame of mind, and, failing to get much talk out of Sonderby, tried with some success to cultivate the acquaintance of the table-waitress, a recent arrival from the Center. The school-teacher ate silently, except when his left-hand neighbor, the gentleman upon whom Bill Trumbull had exercised his story-telling gift, questioned him about the drives and the scenery near Broughton. Sonderby replied as courteously as he could, and, though his mind was not really on what he was saying, he surprised himself by an unusual fluency and readiness.

When the dessert was served, Collins tried him again.

"What are you going to do this afternoon, Sonderby?"

"I have something to do at the academy."

"What, Sunday?"

"Yes, some reading." As a matter of fact, he had not thought of the afternoon until Collins spoke.

"I didn't know but you'd be over at the cottage again," said Collins, encouragingly, balancing a piece of berry pie upon his fork.

Sonderby made no answer, and Collins dropped the subject.

"By the way," the manufacturer inquired, as Sonderby was folding his napkin, "have you written that letter yet?"

"Not yet," was the stiff reply. Sonderby felt the blood rising to his face. Collins smiled imperturbably; and Sonderby, the impotent wrath coming into his throat again, left the table.

"Who is he?" said the waitress, familiarly, as she stood by Collins's chair.

"He's the school-teacher, Kittie," replied Collins, holding out his glass for some ice-water, "and a first-rate fellow. He's a little off color to-day, though."

While Collins was smoking his after-dinner cigar in front of the fireplace, he noticed that Sonderby walked through the hall, hat and umbrella in hand, without glancing into the office. The manufacturer strolled over to the window, curious to see whether he would keep his word about going to the academy.

Sure enough, Sonderby turned to the right, and trudged off toward the academy, his feet sinking almost to the ankle at every step, in the water-soaked gravel of Evans's newly made road. Collins watched him with a smile, and, sauntering again to the fireplace, stood with his back to it, contemplatively, while he finished his cigar. If the manufacturer had any new ideas on that rainy Sunday, he kept them to himself. After a few minutes he went up to his room to write his letters.

John Sonderby, meanwhile, unlocked the front door of the Doric-pillared academy, and entered the dusty room where the working hours of three years of his life had been spent.

He leaned his dripping umbrella against the desk whence he had ruled his little world, and the desk and the room seemed to him smaller than ever before. He went into the "laboratory," as he was fond of calling the tiny recitation-room that contained the scientific apparatus of the academy, and flung himself into a chair before the acid-stained table. Upon the rear of the table were ranged a row of books upon physics, the one subject in which he had hitherto felt a strong and permanent interest. He had economized strictly, in order to buy these books, and to purchase much of the electrical apparatus that was scattered about the room. The hard-handed school committee of Broughton had indeed been willing that the pupils of the academy should learn something about the telephone, after the wire had been put up between the village and the Center; but their appropriation of money for purposes of experiment was so ridiculously small that the teacher had to pay most of it out of his own pocket. It was in making some experiments with a telephone-switch, one day, that Sonderby hit upon an expedient for simplifying the number of wires then in use.

He communicated this idea, which, it is to be said, he was not able thoroughly to work out, to an expert connected with the A. S. & F. Works, and it was to the correspondence which ensued that Sonderby was really indebted for the offer of a place with the company, though Collins, who had had business relations with them, had indeed spoken a good word for the school-teacher.

Sonderby sat in his chair, gazing across the table stupidly at the row of text-books. If he cared more about physics than about anything else in the world, it was singular that he did not open one of those books and satisfy himself. He had not read much for three weeks past. He had spent hours upon hours every day with his friends at the Broughton House. He had grown to be quite well acquainted with them, as he thought. Yet as he sat there it came over him that he really knew nothing about Floyd, nor about Floyd's wife. Why was it that he could not help her, that no one could help her? He had suspected for some time that she was unhappy, that her husband did not care for her. For two hours he had been sure of it. Yet what had that to do with him, the almost-discoverer of a patent telephone-switch?

Pity, the initiator, had done her task for him in those weeks of summer, and he was no longer what he once had been. He had a confused consciousness of a resolve to shield that woman, if he could, when the time came to serve her, though meanwhile the sight of her white hands stirred him as if in a dream, and his breath grew quick and his head whirled. . . .

John Sonderby, school-teacher, roused himself at length, and seizing Clerk Maxwell's *Electricity and Magnetism*, opened it at the chapter on "Conduction in Three Dimensions," and resting his elbows on the table, and his head upon his hands, he read fiercely hour after hour, till the dusk closed in upon the sombre laboratory, and he could see no longer. Then he locked up the academy and went home, chilled by the dampness and his long sitting in one position, but feeling steadier and walking more erectly than when he came.

The dining-room of the hotel was already emptied. The waitress, Kittie, looked at him curiously, while she brought him some cold roast beef, with tea and huckleberries. Collins's remark about Sonderby's being off color had interested her, but she failed to make much out of him. He noticed, with some relief, that Mrs. Floyd had been at supper. He took pains to walk through the parlor and reading-room, as he went out, and satisfied himself she was not there. Looking in at the office door, he saw several of the guests grouped about the fireplace, but Collins and Bill Trumbull, who were in the centre, were the only ones he knew. Clearly, Mrs. Floyd had returned to the cottage.

He stood for a while in the front door of the hotel, his hands in his pockets, looking out into the gloomy rain, and wondering how he could spend the evening. He was in no mood for the society of the group in the office; he had been alone all the afternoon, and fond of solitude as he had commonly been, an evening spent in his own room seemed rather lonely to him. He saw that there was a light in the sitting-room of the cottage; but something told him that Mrs. Floyd would not wish to see him, had he even for his own sake dared to go.

The bell of the Congregational church began to toll, sounding heavily down through the swaying elms. Sonderby took out his old silver watch: it was half-past seven. Why not go to church, for once? This had been a strange Sunday; indeed, not a Sunday at all. He liked Ellerton since he had come to know something of him; the minister was a straightforward fellow, who said what he thought, and would always say it in thirty minutes. On the whole, why not go to hear him preach? The service would last an hour or so, and by that time, Sonderby reflected, he might possibly be tired enough to go to bed, and to sleep without dreaming.

He slipped quietly out of the door, and taking up again his soaked umbrella, started for the meeting-house. He could not help glancing at the cottage as he passed, but the curtains were drawn.

There were in the muddy street few church-goers, and most of these were young. He overtook one of his pupils, a stooping, overgrown girl of sixteen, and walked along with her, evidently much to her surprise and pleasure. As they mounted the knoll on which the meeting-house stood, he saw that the front doors were unopened and the audience-room unlighted.

"Why," he said, "isn't Mr. Ellerton going to preach?"

"Oh, no," she replied. "Don't you remember? It is the second Sunday of the month, and the Young People's Society meeting takes the place of the preaching." She spoke with some pride. Sonderby would have retreated, but that he was ashamed to do so. Besides, they were nearly at the lecture-room entrance, and it was too late. He entered with his pupil, but left her at the door and sat down in one of the rear seats. When he looked up, as the bell finished tolling, the room was half full of people, and in the leader's chair, placed in front of the pulpit, sat Ruth Ellerton. She gave out the opening hymn, and the stooping girl in whose company Sonderby had come started the tune vociferously. While it was singing, Sonderby picked up one of the cards that were strewn plentifully about the seats, and ran his eye over the list of topics and leaders for the devotional meetings of the Young People's Society of Christian Endeavor. He had heard a good deal during the preceding winter, in a casual way, about the Y. P. S. C. E., which had been started soon after Ellerton's settlement in Broughton, but the school-teacher had never taken any particular interest in the organization. He recognized now, in the neatly printed schedule, the names of many of his pupils, and wondered that they had courage enough to take such a prominent part in the meetings.

Opposite the date of that Sunday, July 15, was the name of the leader, Mrs. Arthur Ellerton, with the topic, "Be not weary in well-doing," and a reference to a Scripture passage. His scrutiny was interrupted by a little fellow, who got up noisily from his seat to offer the school-teacher a hymn-book, which Sonderby, seeing that several persons were looking at him, accepted with the best grace he could muster, and sang the last two stanzas with tolerable correctness. Then Mrs. Ellerton, in a low voice and with an evident embarrassment, said, "Let us pray," and, closing her eyes, rested her head upon her hand and began the opening prayer. Sonderby had never heard a woman pray, and was profoundly touched by it. The grave, sweet voice, the absolute simplicity, the reverence, the desire, — these things moved him as no petition had ever done before. He did not dare look at her till she had raised her face, and then he noticed the red spot on her forehead where her hand had pressed, and the moisture in her gray eyes. After a moment's pause, she read the chapter in the Epistle, repeating, for emphasis, the verse selected for the special topic of the evening. Her voice grew clearer as she went on, and by the time the second hymn was sung, and she began to talk, it seemed to Sonderby that she was as self-possessed as she had been at her own tea-table.

"Be not weary in well-doing, for in due season ye shall reap if ye faint not." There is the accent of conviction in those words which carries its own weight without the necessity of comment. Ruth Ellerton tried to do no more than to point out how the personal character of the writer gave significance to his exhortations and his testimony, and then to show the application of the words to the members of the Broughton Young People's Society of Christian Endeavor.

For everybody in Broughton worked, she said with a smile (apparently forgetting Bill Trumbull), and the main thing was to learn to do one's work without weariness; that is, without weariness of spirit, for to be tired in body did no one any harm. Purposeless work was what made us weary. One must work with an inspiring motive, feeling that God has given him that special work to do, because he was fit to do it; and the work that God gives people is very likely to be work for others.

That was really all she said, though she explained and illustrated it in a good many ways, with rare tact and adaptation to the particular persons before her. She forgot all about Sonderby, after the first sentence or two, and gave herself up to making the half-grown boys and girls, and the few older persons present, feel the force of what she was saying. Only once or twice did she seem to be talking more to herself than to her audience, and then she quoted Longfellow's *Dante*, and used some words that Broughton folks were not in the habit of hearing. Her tone grew more intense and rapid as she went on, and once or twice, without knowing it, she gesticulated slightly with the hymn-book that she held in her hand. The room was very still as she finished. The Young People's Society of Christian Endeavor was unboundedly loyal, almost reverential, toward its founder.

"And now the meeting is open," she concluded, taking out her watch and laying it on the table with a business-like air that seemed a trifle incongruous. "We mustn't have any time wasted. Let us first, however, sing another hymn."

Sonderby opened his book and sang the hymn through with the rest. Then the stoop-shouldered girl repeated a verse which had indeed no particular reference to the subject of the meeting, but which was sufficient to discharge the weekly obligation she had assumed in becoming an active member of the Y. P. S. C. E.

A young farmer from out on the North Broughton road rose and made some "remarks" so thoroughly in the New England vernacular that many of the village young people laughed, but so completely in sympathy with the leader's ideas that she smiled at him, assistingly, in a manner that would have turned the head of a more imaginative youth. Then came another hymn, some more texts of Scripture, and two or three bits of religious poetry quoted by the village girls.

A small boy, the son of Parkinson, the storekeeper, offered prayer. So the meeting ran its course, until every active member of the society had taken some kind of part, and Mrs. Ellerton rose punctually upon the minute, and gave out the closing hymn.

John Sonderby, to tell the truth, did not follow the progress of the meeting very closely, though in some of the things that were said he felt a curious interest. He sat a good deal of the time looking at the leader, with all the rest of the audience blurred out of sight for him. He was comparing Ruth Ellerton, as she sat there in her black silk, her masses of brown hair glistening in the light of the lamp on the pulpit, her face partly in shadow, the strongest lines of it thrown out into unusual relief, — he was comparing this radiant, helpful woman with another black-dressed figure, which had stood opposite him that morning in the sitting-room of the cottage, a slender, mournful figure, with rigid hands and appealing eyes. But something else than this, strongly as the involuntary contrast had moved him, was in Sonderby's mind. He was thinking of himself. In the simple words of the minister's wife — nothing more in themselves than what the Christian Church has been reiterating for a great many hundred years — there had come to him a rebuke for his own way of life.

"Purposeless work;" would not that describe much of his existence? So powerfully had the events of the last twenty-four hours impressed his emotional life, that he now perceived certain things with a strange vividness, albeit they were seen in an atmosphere as unreal as dreamland.

As the meeting broke up, he came to himself with a start, and would have slipped out of the door before the others, had not one of his pupils stepped up to him and asked about something connected with the academy. He answered as well as he could, but made clumsy work of it and lost time, so that when the pupil left him and he stooped down at last for his hat, it was only to find Ruth Ellerton standing by him as he straightened himself up. She already had on her waterproof, and was going home.

"Good evening, Mr. Sonderby," she said, holding out her hand. "It was very good of you to come on such a rainy night."

He murmured something or other.

"Didn't you think the young people turned out well?" she exclaimed. "Some of them came from way over on the road to North Broughton."

"Very well," he assented, and they walked down to the door together. She hesitated a moment on the steps, over which was playing a thin line of precipitous drops from the eaves above. She wanted to hold up her best black silk under her waterproof, but she had in her hands a Bible, hymn-book, and package of Y. P. S. C. E. cards, besides the parsonage umbrella. Sonderby, by an intuition remarkable for him, guessed at her dilemma, and without a word took her books with one hand, and held his own umbrella over her head with the other.

"Oh, thank you," she cried, and they started down the hill toward the parsonage. "Mr. Ellerton is preaching down in the Center to-night," she explained; "and so you see I have to carry my own impedimenta. He always makes fun of me for having so much." The reaction from the responsibility of leading the meeting made her very light-hearted.

"Won't you come in?" she asked, as they reached the parsonage gate.

"Just to the piazza," he answered. He was thinking that he had lived three years in Broughton and had never taken a woman under his umbrella in all that time, and to-day he had had two there — Tryphena Floyd and Ruth Ellerton.

"I hope you have had a pleasant Sunday," said Mrs. Ellerton, as they stopped at her steps. "It has been so very dismal outside."

"Well," he answered, handing the books to her, "I have been doing some hard work."

"Have you?" she replied, gravely. "What was it?" She wanted to have him come in, but did not dare ask him again.

"On 'Conduction in Three Dimensions,'" said Sonderby.

"Oh!" She was waiting for him to say something more, and had too much tact to refer to that which came naturally into her mind; namely, his working on Sunday.

"Yes, but it's what you would call 'purposeless work,' I suppose." And he added bluntly, "You hit me pretty hard to-night."

She did not know what to say. "But —" she began.

"I don't know what I work for," he went on, bent upon expressing himself. "I never have known."

"Why," she said slowly, after a long pause, "I must stand by what I tried to say to the young people, Mr. Sonderby. If 'Conduction in Three Dimensions' is what you are best fitted for, then" — and her voice trembled a little — "isn't that what God has given you to do? Only, one must do it unselfishly — for others — because God has given it to us. Oughtn't that to give a purpose to any kind of work?"

The words had come slower and slower at the last.

He hesitated for an answer. The muffled rattle of a wagon could be heard out on the North Broughton road, and the rain kept dripping from the Virginia creeper.

"I don't know," confessed Sonderby, finally. "Perhaps so. Good night!"

"Good night!" she said, and put out her hand again, but it was so dark that he did not see it.

VII.

NEXT to a rainy Sunday, a wet Monday is perhaps the most disheartening punishment that the goddess of New England weather can impose upon those who have failed to propitiate her. It is curious, indeed, that Monday should be so unpopular the world over. However widely people may differ in their theories about Sunday, they agree, with a singular unanimity, that Monday, even under the most favorable conditions, is something of a trial to the spirit.

For those who make Sunday a day of pleasure-seeking, as well as for those who strive to make it a day of grace, Monday is "the day after." If it happens to be rainy, so much the more unfortunate. City streets never look so cheerless as on such a morning, when laborers, demoralized by their holiday, go straggling to their work; and when even those people who on Sunday have made high resolves and received new inspirations, find their enthusiasm chilled by the sweep of the wind and rain around the street corners, and soiled by the very sight of the sticky, slippery pavements. It seems discouragingly hard to take hold, to begin again, unless it chances that one is lucky enough to be so busy that he cannot give a single instant to the analysis of his feelings.

In the country, too, a wet Monday morning is universally resented. Even in those dry seasons when the farmers, gathering round the steps of the meeting-house before the Sunday sermon commences, have agreed that it is about time for the minister to begin to pray for rain, they have a suspicion that a showery Monday is too prompt a response to their wishes to be genuinely providential. But Broughton farmers, in this particular July, had no need for any rain. The haying was late, as it was, and the satisfaction that they had experienced upon Saturday afternoon, in the reflection that if it had to rain at all, Sunday was a good time for it and it would be over by Monday, gave way, by breakfast-time on Monday morning, to a philosophic ugliness of temper.

Over the wide stretches of upland that made up the township of Broughton the clouds hung low and heavy, and the rain still fell upon the soaked meadows just as it had been falling for forty hours. The cattle in the pastures, who had stood out in the full downpouring of the cool showers of Saturday evening, had by this time got heartily enough of it, and stood huddling their steaming hides together under the oaks and elms and maples, that stood singly or in groups of two or three in every bit of pasture-land.

There was more wind in the tree-tops, though,

than had blown before since Saturday, and it came in veering gusts, that to the knowing observers indicated that the end of the storm was not many hours away. Nevertheless, any haying for that day was out of the question.

Tons of hungarian and timothy, all over the township, had been so long soaked, standing in the meadows in half-cured cocks, and so much oats and corn had been lodged by the great wind of Saturday night, that the farming folk of Broughton might have been pardoned for feeling out of sorts.

Yet a genuine New England farmer, no matter how deep may be his disgust at rain which comes at a wrong time, will rarely have any open words of discontent at the weather itself. He keeps those, under such circumstances, for his wife.

The proprietor of the Broughton House, however, had no wife upon whom to vent his wrath, nor did he have any scruples, not being a native of New England, about cursing its climate. Poor Evans had made many rash predictions on Saturday evening, and when Sunday proved them false, he had only plunged in deeper by vouching that the Monday skies would be as blue as Broughton winds could fan them. Here was Monday morning come, and the driver of the Center stage was stamping with his rubber boots upon the piazza, holding the dripping lines in his left hand, while the horses stood with drooping ears and sunken tails, as if it were night instead of morning, and the closely drawn curtains of the stage were already splashed with mud, just in coming from the post-office to the hotel.

"All aboard!" cried the lanky driver again, and the lady with eyeglasses, enveloped in her waterproof, climbed in, followed by the gentleman interested in Broughton fishing.

He had been protesting in the office against the amount of his bill, demurring more particularly to the extra charge for the fire which had been built on Sunday morning in the stove in the parlor. He paid it; but Evans did not feel inclined to accompany him to the piazza, as was the Welshman's custom with departing guests. The driver buttoned the curtains over the door, stepped across the wheel into the front seat, and pulling the boot well up around his waist, clucked to his horses and started off, but with none of the usual morning brilliancy of style.

After the stage had gone, the hotel seemed rather deserted. The remaining guests kept to their rooms. As for the "regulars," Collins and Sonderby had had breakfast together without much conversation, at the ordinary time. The teacher had slept like one of his own schoolboys, and he went down to the academy shortly after breakfast, for a dogged morning's work. Mrs. Floyd had come over for breakfast very early, had eaten a little, and slipped out before any one else entered the dining-room. Her husband did not come at all.

The reason for Floyd's absence from Broughton at that hour was perhaps more readily appreciated by Arthur Ellerton than by any other person. When the minister rose at a quarter of five to see whether the weather permitted his fishing engagement with Collins to be kept, the noise of the shutters, as he turned them to look out into the gray fog through which the rain was sifting, woke Mrs. Ellerton. Her husband finished his brief survey of the weather, and fond as he was of fishing, was not sorry at the prospect of a couple of hours more sleep, being tired after his hard Sunday.

"Did it go off well, down at the Center, Arthur?" asked Mrs. Ellerton, drowsily.

"First-rate," was the response, as Ellerton closed the shutters again, and drew down the curtain.

"Oh, by the way, I saw our friend Floyd at the Center hotel, just before the evening service."

"Did you?" said Mrs. Ellerton, more sleepily than before.

"He was very glad to see me. In fact, he wanted to insist on my taking a drink with him."

"Arthur!" exclaimed Mrs. Ellerton.

"Fact. I believe the clerk got him to go to bed, after a while, though. I'm sorry enough." And the minister, as if in recognition of the fact that nothing could be done about Floyd then and there, proceeded to go to sleep in his sensible fashion. But Ruth Ellerton lay awake, shocked and troubled, until Mary Jane jingled the rising-bell at the foot of the front stairs.

In the course of the forenoon a buggy from the Center deposited Floyd at the cottage door. He had slept off the effects of his Sunday indulgence, and had nothing to remind him of it except a headache and a misty remembrance of having made a fool of himself — somehow, somewhere — in connection with Arthur Ellerton. Whatever may have been the welcome his wife gave him at the cottage, the artist did not remain there long after his return. He strolled over to the Broughton House, turning up his coat-collar against the rain, not seeming to care that he was spoiling the shine which his shoes had received at the Center hotel.

Collins was in the office, wrapping a split tip with silk, and hardly took his eyes off his delicate work as Floyd came in.

"Look out!" he cried, as the artist was about to take the chair by his side; "don't sit on my glue-pot, man."

True enough, the chair held a tiny glue-pot made of brass, and a collection of silk threads and colored feathers, from which Collins had been amusing himself by making some flies.

The artist took another seat and stretched out his feet to the fire. Bill Trumbull made some remark about the weather, with a covert reference to the state of the roads between Broughton and the

Center, which Floyd appeared not to understand. When Collins finished winding the silk, and fastened it with a skilful half-hitch, he turned to Floyd and regarded him a moment with a kind of grin, which might have been construed as a silent reflection upon the consequence of Floyd's victory at euchre. But he said nothing, and the three sat there, with Evans as a morose onlooker at Collins's deft handiwork, until dinner-time.

The quartette sat down together that noon, for the first time since Sunday morning. John Sonderby had not seen Tryphena since he left her in the cottage, and his hand trembled as he unfolded his napkin and looked across the table at her. He expected to detect some change in her, or at least that there would be some constraint in her manner toward himself. But Mrs. Floyd returned his gaze as tranquilly as she had done at any time in the few weeks during which he had known her. She even seemed more cheerful than usual, and certainly looked prettier, for she had put some white ruching in the wrists and neck of her black jersey, for the first time since her aunt had died. Was it merely a whim of the moment, like the gaiety of Sunday forenoon, or was it the beginning of a deliberate detachment of herself from her past life? At any rate, she was in good spirits all through dinner. Floyd kept his peevish temper in the background, and Sonderby tried to blot the preceding day out of his mind and to imagine that all was going as well with the Floyds as it seemed to.

Collins had had rather a confined morning, and was the least talkative of the four, but his eyes went keenly from Floyd to Tryphena more than once as the dinner progressed.

While dessert was serving, Mrs. Floyd declared that from her seat, which commanded a glimpse of the hills toward the southwest, she could see a bit of blue sky. As the rain was still blowing against the dining-room windows every few minutes, the others doubted her assertion; but she claimed that the drops on the windows were shaken from the elms and then carried by the wind, as if it were real rain. By and by she admitted, just as they were rising from the table, that her blue sky had in some way disappeared; but when the quartette went out to the front piazza and watched the west wind send patches of gray cloud scudding over the elm-tops, so low as almost to touch them, while in the northeast a blue-black heap of thunder heads kept piling itself higher, Tryphena persisted that it was nothing but "the clearing shower."

She appealed to Bill Trumbull, who was picking his way across the street to the hotel, after his dinner in his daughter's house, to know if she was not right.

"Wal, I guess you be," decided Bill, half because he really thought so, and half because he didn't like to disappoint Tryphena. However his decision was reached, it settled the matter, and all agreed that the wet spell was drawing to an end.

"Now let's celebrate by some whist," cried Mrs. Floyd.

Collins assented.

"Phenie's ahead now, and is more anxious to play than she was last week," remarked Floyd.

"Oh, Floyd, stop your growling, and go and get the markers," ordered Collins; and the artist shrugged his shoulders and obeyed. The schoolteacher was the only one who seemed not to wish to play.

"I had something to do at the academy," he explained, rather feebly.

"Since when?" said Collins, ironically.

"Since the middle of June," was on Sonderby's lips, when he caught Tryphena's eyes. She was looking at him with that shy, friendly glance, which had attracted him to her the first day they met.

"Please," she whispered.

She had never said that to him before, and John Sonderby forgot all about certain resolutions he had taken that morning, and the problems of Conduction in Three Dimensions.

For an hour and a half the quartette sat in the hotel parlor, around the old mahogany card-table, and John Sonderby and Tryphena Floyd held everything.

At last Floyd threw up his hand in disgust.

"It's no use to-day, Collins," he cried. "Let's have a smoke."

They all rose, and Tryphena put the table back into its place.

"Well, I don't know," said Collins, taking out his watch. "It's getting rather late. Suppose we take another look at the weather."

Mrs. Floyd's "clearing shower" had not yet passed, but the rain was light now. All overhead there were thin places in the clouds, and in the west more than one strip of blue. The pile of thunder clouds in the northeast had altogether sunk away.

"Sure enough," Collins remarked, "that last prediction of Bill Trumbull's did the business. No, Floyd," he added: "we'll take that smoke another day. I'm going up to call on the parson."

"On the parson?" repeated Tryphena, in such surprise that the others laughed at Collins's expense.

"Exactly," replied Collins, imperturbably; "the parson and I were going fishing this morning if it hadn't rained."

The manufacturer turned away, smiling, and went up to his room.

The remaining three stood on the piazza a few moments longer. Sonderby thought of going down to the academy, to take up the work he had planned for the afternoon; but by this time he was in no mood for it, and could not bring himself to go.

"Sonderby," said Floyd, yawning, "what do you want to do?"

"Billy, wouldn't it be a good idea for you to get shaved?" suggested Mrs. Floyd.

Floyd passed his fingers over his lank, unshaven jaw.

"Very likely," he answered, although somewhat irritated by his wife's advice.

"I don't know but I'll go over to the barber's shop with you, and sit around during the operation," volunteered Sonderby.

Neither of these men altogether liked the other, but circumstances had thrown them so together that upon this afternoon each of them preferred the other's company to being left alone.

"All right," Floyd replied, and lit a cigarette. Then the two men got their hats, and leaving Mrs. Floyd to turn over the papers in the reading-room, started up the street toward Parkinson's store. The first glints of sunshine were upon the elm leaves and the grass, but the clayey soil of the sidewalk was still slippery, and the road, where they crossed it in front of Parkinson's, was ankle-deep with mud.

The "general store" of Mr. Parkinson had been familiar to Broughton people for a generation. Built in the solid, ample style of architecture that characterized the original Broughton tavern, the store had been more fortunate than the hotel, in preserving its original form and something of its original color. A dingy white was still its prevailing tone, though the front, around the doors and window-casings, was ornamented with bands of blue and yellow, the result of a transient enthusiasm of Mr. Parkinson for prepared mineral paints. A broad piazza ran along the front, reached from the sidewalk by three steps, the lower one of which was splintered all along its edge by the grinding of innumerable wagon-wheels against it. Standing on the piazza, between the windows and the door, were a long box of scythe-blades, a bundle of wooden rakes, a patent three-tined pitchfork, and a pile of empty cheese-boxes that had been returned from the Center. There was a bench there too, and a couple of chairs. Within, two dark-painted counters, running the whole length of the store on either side, were laden with the most desirable or newly arrived goods in stock. The right side of the store was mainly occupied with dry goods: piles of flannel and calico, packed away on fly-specked shelves; blue pasteboard boxes marked "Buttons," "Thread," "Hose," protected by a sliding glass door; and a few rolls of black silks and cashmeres. On the left were the groceries, boots and shoes, and the hardware. Overhead, on plentiful hooks, were displayed tin and wooden pails, oil-cans, rubber boots, lanterns, and a few choice hams. In the "L part," at the rear, which was accessible by a side entrance to which teams could drive up, was stored a full line of flour and feed, kerosene oil, and molasses, together with an assortment of single harnesses, marked down, and warranted for a year.

But it was by virtue of its proprietor, rather than through any distinctive excellence or abundance of the goods offered for sale, that Parkinson's store had gradually driven every rival establishment out of Broughton, and built up a reputation among the surrounding towns. Mr. Parkinson was a little fat man, with a sleek laugh, who never spoke disrespectfully of any one, and asked no one's advice in regard to himself.

He had come to Broughton as a clerk in this very store, thirty years previously, and after a while had become partner and then owner. His talent for collecting bills, and his blameless manner of life, had given him for years the office of treasurer of the parish, and his name was often mentioned for deacon in the church, though it was the opinion of the older and most influential members of the Congregational body that Samuel Parkinson, in spite of the gray in his neat beard, and his fifty years, was still too young to serve in so responsible and dignified a capacity.

If Parkinson had any disappointed ambitions, however, no one ever knew it. He watched the markets, was hospitable to all travelling salesmen, listened to the talk of the farmers around his big rusty-bottomed stove, and went down to Boston three or four times a year to look around for himself. He bought very cheap, and in the majority of cases sold very dear — though there was a minority of magnificent "bargains at Parkinson's" that kept the housewives of Broughton in a continual flutter.

Mr. Parkinson always averred his regret that his successive rivals in Broughton abandoned the effort to compete with him. "Competition is the life of trade," he used to repeat, smilingly, from behind his counter; but though it may have been the life of trade, it was generally the death, commercially speaking, of Parkinson's competitor. It was in accordance with his amiable theory of political economy that he built, closely adjoining his own store, a tiny one-story structure, which he rented successively to a boot-and-shoe man, to a ninety-nine-cent venture, — a branch of the Center establishment, — and to a widow, who, attracted by the growing reputation of Broughton as a summer resort, hoped to sell ice-cream, cake, and confectionery during the summer months.

From each of these tenants Mr. Parkinson had blandly required six months' rent in advance, and then had amused himself by conjecturing how long the experiment would last, how many customers would be attracted to the neighborhood of his own store in the meantime, and how cheaply he could buy in the bankrupt goods at the close. Broughton could support exactly one store, and Mr. Parkinson knew it.

His latest tenant, however, was less of a rival than any of the preceding ones, being none other than a barber.

A barber-shop was something entirely new in Broughton, and the townspeople looked upon its striped pole with an excusable pride. From the day when the township was settled, under the stockades of a fort against the Indians, down to the time when Otto Meyer, a native of Bavaria and a recently naturalized citizen of the Center, concluded his arrangements with Samuel Parkinson, the good people of Broughton had shaved themselves and cut their own — or rather one another's — hair.

Of late, to be sure, the village butcher, in his leisure moments, had acquired a good deal of skill in giving boys what he called a "fighting cut," for the sum of ten cents each. To the more aspiring among the farmers' sons, especially in the winter season, about the time the annual singing-school commenced its sessions, the butcher administered his so-called "fancy cut," which left the hair long on top and short up to the ears, and which, when treated plentifully with oil, looked very smooth and was well worth the fifteen cents it cost. But the butcher, even in his most ambitious moods and in spite of his proficiency with keen-edged tools, never dared to shave anybody, and indeed it would have been a gallant man who would have risked the operation.

The male population of Broughton, therefore, were favorably disposed toward Otto Meyer and his scantily furnished shop. The smart pole took away something of the rusticity of Main Street. Some of the younger men in the village fell into the habit of getting shaved at Meyer's regularly, and he had also more or less custom from the guests of the Broughton House. Floyd had been one of his most faithful patrons, during the artist's stay in town. Meyer had left Bavaria to escape military service; and Floyd, finding that the barber had been in Munich, never tired of exchanging with him impressions of that city. The conversations were carried on mostly in German: for Floyd found that he could make himself understood, and it rather tickled his fancy to lie back in a barber's chair, up among the hills of Broughton, and talk familiarly about the Hofbraüerei, and the gilded state chariots of the mad King Ludwig. Meyer's knowledge of Munich, to tell the truth, was limited to these two subjects; but they possessed a perennial interest, and the more Meyer talked with Floyd about them, the more fluent did the latter's vocabulary become. By dint of unlearning all he had acquired previous to his emigration to America, Meyer had become a very decent barber; but he was vastly conceited about his skill, and dogmatic in regard to everything that concerned his profession. He did not conceal his contempt for the average inhabitant of Broughton, and declared that nothing but the over-supply of barbers at the Center had driven him up to this hill town, ten miles from a railroad. Toward "Mr. Floyt," however, he had a great respect, as was due to a man who had seen the world and could therefore tell when a razor was well handled.

When Sonderby and Floyd tried the door of the barber-shop, they found it locked.

"Where is Meyer?" Floyd called out to Parkinson, who was standing in the doorway of his store, his hands behind his back, his rotund form comfortably arrayed in white linen trousers and an alpaca coat.

"Meyer, Mr. Floyd, is, I presume, asleep," was the bland answer.

"Asleep?" growled Sonderby.

"Without doubt," continued the storekeeper. "On Mondays, gentlemen," and Mr. Parkinson brought his hands to the front and smoothed out with them a wrinkle in his coat, over the pit of his stomach, "Meyer is generally inclined to sleep — to slumber, I may say. But I will try to rouse him if you wish it." Mr. Parkinson, with a charitable smile at the weakness of his fellow-men, opened the side door of the shop, and went up the back stairs to the room where Meyer slept. The German usually felt so lonely on Sunday that he went down to drink a glass of beer with his comrades at the Center; but once there, he could scarcely confine himself to the single glass which he usually mentioned to himself as his excuse for going.

"Oh, I see," remarked Sonderby, who had never interested himself in Meyer enough to become acquainted with the German's peculiarities. He was about to say something more, but checked himself, remembering that Floyd, too, had spent his Sunday at the Center.

"Well," said Floyd, flushing somewhat, "it's none of Parkinson's business." He did not look at the school-teacher as he spoke, but wondered whether Collins had said anything about that game of euchre. Sonderby slapped vigorously at a mosquito that had just alighted on his coat-sleeve, but made no reply.

Mr. Parkinson descended the back stairs of the shop and announced that Meyer would be ready for business directly.

"Let's sit down over here," suggested Sonderby, moving toward the bench on the store piazza; "we might as well be comfortable." There had grown up some rivalry among the trio of men at the Broughton House about finding the most easy seats and making a parade of their idleness.

"I should hope so," replied Floyd. They dropped heavily upon the bench, and leaning forward, rested their elbows on their knees.

Collins went by upon the other of the street, on his way toward the parsonage. He was carefully dressed, and carried his gloves and a silver-headed umbrella in his hand. He glanced at the store, in passing, and waved his umbrella in recognition of his acquaintances.

"Now there goes a man," remarked Floyd, confidentially, "who can drink like a fish, if he wants to, and never show it. Oh, Collins is a deep one! He's a mighty moral fellow, he is, to go calling on the minister!" The artist chuckled in satisfaction at his superior knowledge of character.

Sonderby resented that smirching laugh. "I don't know anything against Collins," he said, deliberately.

"Oh, neither do I," was the mocking response. "Collins is quite a saint up here in Broughton. But in New York —" He shrugged his shoulders.

"Well?" demanded Sonderby.

"Oh, I don't know anything about him, any more than you do."

"Why don't you shut up, then?"

It was Floyd's turn to take offence. "What's the matter with you?" he cried, hotly.

At that instant Meyer unlocked the front door of the shop, and sticking out his frowzled head, glanced around with his sleepy eyes, and called "Next!" as automatically as if he had been working all day. Both men laughed and forgot their incipient quarrel.

"Go ahead, Floyd," said Sonderby. "I'll wait. If he gets sufficiently waked up on you, I'll take a turn later."

Floyd disappeared within the barber-shop, leaving to the school-teacher the possession of the bench. Mr. Parkinson came to the doorway again, but failed to engage Sonderby in conversation, though through no fault of his own. Sonderby was somewhat out of temper. He had planned at breakfast to work steadily this week, morning and afternoon, whatever happened; and here was already another afternoon spent like so many previous ones. He wondered whether he had will-power enough to carry out anything, good or bad.

He was disgusted with Floyd; partly on account of the artist's Sunday indulgence, and partly on account of his just-uttered insinuations against Collins. There was a deeper reason, too, for his distrust of Floyd; but this he could not as yet formulate exactly; he only knew that since Sunday morning he had been justified in it. Yet what was the use of puzzling and troubling himself any longer about other people's problems? Why not cut himself loose from it all, write an acceptance to the A. S. & F. Company, and leave at once for Boston? Why not? It was for the same reason that he did not go to the academy that afternoon, when Tryphena Floyd asked him to stay and play whist, and had said "Please": he could not go; that was all. But whether it was right or wrong for him to stay, he could not have told for the world. Whichever it was, he was in an uncomfortable state of moral irritation.

He was not left long, however, to a solitary occupancy of the store piazza. It was getting nearly mail time; the period of the day when, if at all, the village awoke to a semblance of life. The sun had come out at length to stay, and was as hot as if it realized the huge task of drying which was awaiting it. Farm wagons began to rattle into Main Street, their owners having found some excuse for hitching up, toward the close of an idle day, and driving into the village, even if it were only to call at the post-office, and to inquire the price of granulated sugar at Parkinson's.

Sonderby was watching one of these wagons, which he thought was from Calvin Johnson's, when a young fellow of nineteen stepped jauntily from the store, and after a moment's examination of the school-teacher, tapped him on the shoulder.

"How do you do, Mr. Sonderby."

"Why! Hullo, Harry," exclaimed Sonderby, in some surprise. "I didn't know you were here."

"Yes. Been up on a vacation; but I'm getting sick of it," responded the newcomer, who had been a pupil of Sonderby during the latter's first winter at the academy.

"Yes?" asked Sonderby, looking with curiosity at the boy, as he helped himself to a seat on the bench, and took out his cigarette-case.

"Oh, Lord, yes! it's too slow. Have a cigarette?" and young Duffield, albeit a trifle bashfully, extended his case to his old school-teacher.

Sonderby declined. "How do you like Boston?" he asked.

"Tip-top," said Harry, buoyantly, giving a slight hitch to his ready-made trousers, to keep them from bagging at the knees as he sat. Sonderby noticed that his patent leather shoes were badly worn off at the heels, and while the boy was lighting a cigarette and sucking it into a state of animation, the school-teacher studied his very high collar, very red tie, the brown Derby hat, a trifle stained, that he wore well back on his head, and the heavy ring that adorned his little finger. Two years had evidently done a good deal for the farmer boy.

"How are you feeling?" inquired Sonderby, who found it hard to get much variety into his questions.

"Keen as a brier," was the prompt response.

"You're with the same firm?"

"Yes, sir. Every time. Blank & Blank's" — and he named a huge dry goods house — "is a good place to stick to, if you once get in. They're a square firm. Of course" — apologetically — "you can't strike for big pay right off. You have to wait a while. Now I've had an advance in my salary once already, and I'm going to tackle the old man for a raise the first of September. That's the only way. Keep right at 'em. Make 'em give it to you."

He did not find it necessary to explain that the

advance referred to consisted in the change from seven dollars a week to eight — less than day-laborers were making on his father's farm.

"You think you'll keep to dry goods, then?"

"Certain. Why, my chum has only been with the house two years longer than I have, and he's now a floor-walker. Draws his fifteen dollars every Thursday night."

Sonderby did not seem particularly impressed by this tale of affluence.

"Say, but ain't it quiet up here in Broughton?" Harry went on. "Makes a man restless, don't it?"

"Well, I don't know," answered Sonderby, doubtfully.

"Oh, it's all right if you like it," admitted the boy. "Only it's dead. Deader'n Julius Cæsar. There ain't anything going on. I tell you I was surprised to see a barber's pole here, last week."

"He's a pretty good barber," volunteered Sonderby.

"Oh, yes, I tried him Saturday. Of course he ain't what he'd have to be at Young's or the Parker House."

"He isn't, eh?" Sonderby knew these famous hostelries only by name.

"Oh, Lord, no!" From young Duffield's commiserating tone one would have hardly suspected that his acquaintance with Young's and the Parker House had been gained simply by walking by them.

There was something of a pause. Harry pulled out his silver watch, jingling the big gilded chain as he did so.

"Five-three," he remarked. "It does beat the record how slow time goes. Told father I'd stay up in the street till six, and see if there wasn't something going on. Well, say, how do you like it here, Mr. Sonderby?"

"Very well, very well."

"I suppose so, or you wouldn't have stayed here so long. Three years, ain't it?"

"Three years," repeated Sonderby. "It doesn't seem so very long."

"It don't, eh? Well, if you ever get tired of it, Mr. Sonderby, you'd better try Boston."

Sonderby rather enjoyed the youth's assurance.

"You think I'd like it, do you?"

"Certain. Couldn't help it. There's a teacher now at our boarding-house: Professor — something or other. Don't know as I know just where he teaches; but perhaps if you wanted to come down, we could work something through him. Say, you'll let me know, won't you, if I can do anything for you?"

Harry Duffield had had a great respect for Sonderby, ever since the teacher had collared him one day, during that first winter, and he would have been happy to use his present superior position for the school-teacher's good.

"Certainly," replied Sonderby. "Very glad to."

"Well," said the boy, rising and taking out his watch again. "Five-ten. Guess I'm off. They'll be looking for me down home. Glad to have met you, Mr. Sonderby."

Sonderby got up and shook hands with him. There was not so much muscle in Duffield's grip as there had been on the day of their brief and never-repeated struggle at the academy. "Good by," said Sonderby. "Good luck to you."

"Thank you. Same to you. Say, you'll let me hear from you, if you come, won't you?"

Sonderby nodded.

"Well, hold on," exclaimed Harry; "ain't that Calvin Johnson's team? What's the matter with my riding down home? It ain't the best walking in the world to-day over these backwoods roads."

Sonderby was well acquainted with the big iron-gray farm horses that were approaching, having worked through many a long day with them, the preceding summer. The driver of the team was Rufus Johnson, Calvin's oldest boy, a stalwart, sunburned fellow, somewhere in the twenties. He pulled up his horses so that the wagon, upon which rested a new hay-rick, might be weighed upon the scales, and kept his seat, awaiting Parkinson's leisure.

"Hello, Rufe," called out Duffield.

"Hello, hello!" cried Rufus, in return, and twisting the lines around the brake, he jumped clumsily to the ground.

"Glad to see ye, Harry." He mounted the steps of the store, his trousers tucked into his boots, his unstarched linen shirt open a little at his powerful throat. Pulling off his broad-brimmed straw hat, he mopped away, with the back of his hand, the sweat from his forehead, and shook hands with young Duffield. Then he caught sight of the school-teacher.

"How d'ye do, Mr. Sonderby," he said, a smile spreading over his broad face.

"How d'ye do," replied Sonderby, putting his hand into the hearty grip of the young farmer.

"I can tell ye we miss ye," exclaimed Rufus. "How's your muscle? Arms sunburned yet? I told father this morning that I guess we'd have to have Mr. Sonderby to mow that swamp for us. Ain't forgot it, have ye?"

"No," replied Sonderby, with a laugh, "not yet."

The year before he and Rufus had started to mow with scythes a swampy piece of meadow not accessible to the mowing-machine, and, proud as each was of his strength, neither one of them wanted to try over again which was the stouter mower. Each had tried to tire the other out that day, and both had succeeded.

"Why don't ye come down to see us?" demanded Rufus, hospitably. "Mother keeps saying that the maple syrup will be all gone before Mr. Sonderby gets a taste of it."

"I've been meaning to come," apologized Sonderby. It was the old story among the farmers, this reluctance of Mr. Sonderby to move among them socially. Nothing but their admiration for him as a disciplinarian, and perhaps a lurking sympathy with his stubborn fashion of suiting himself in whatever he did, kept them from taking serious offence.

"Wal, jest come right along," reiterated Rufus. "Ye don't have nothing to do, do ye? Say, you're stopping at the hotel now, ain't ye? Well, won't ye tell that feller there that does so much fishin' that we've just posted our brook? Father says we might jest as well have a few of those trout ourselves."

"All right; I'll tell him."

"Thank ye. Good day. Come down, won't ye?" Rufus turned to Duffield, who had been rather left out of the conversation.

"What were you saying to me a minute ago, Harry?"

Duffield explained his unwillingness to walk over the Broughton roads when a team was handy.

"Sure 'nough. The ground is a little bad. Hadn't really thought on't. Ef ye'll wait jest a minute, till I can git my hay-rick weighed, and some salt and turpentine, we'll go right along."

He started in search of Parkinson, followed by Duffield. Sonderby sat down again, eying the pair, as Rufus shouldered his way through a group of loafers that had gathered by this time at the store door. As the school-teacher thought of the superb physique of the fellow, with a sort of envy, too, of his calm, steady way, there came suddenly into his mind an old bit of village gossip he had once chanced to hear, which averred that Rufus Johnson had "kept company" with Tryphena Morton the winter before the latter went to Brooklyn.

Now Sonderby's imaginative nature had never become much developed, and two months before he would have no sooner found himself speculating on the probable happiness of a marriage between such persons as Tryphena Morton and Rufus Johnson, than he could have found himself envying the young farmer's calm and steady way. A temperament of this latter quality he himself possessed, he had been used to think, and what had he to do with Broughton's gossip about its young people? But just now he could not help wondering whether the gossip were true, and what Rufus used to talk about when he went home with the girl from singing-school, and why Tryphena had not liked him, if indeed she had not.

His speculations did not end when Floyd came out of the barber-shop. In response to Meyer's repeated "Next!" and after exchanging a word or two with the newly shaven Floyd, who said that he would just stroll over to the post-office, Sonderby took his seat in the barber's chair to have his beard trimmed. The random word with

Floyd seemed only to intensify the curiosity with which Sonderby's mind attacked the possibilities of the case. He turned it over and over, examining what would have been the chances of Tryphena's being happy had she never left Broughton. He recurred to it with nervous pertinacity, whenever the barber's efforts to engage him in conversation diverted him for an instant from the subject. Meyer persisted too in talking about "Mr. Floyt," and found great amusement in sly references to the Center and Mr. Floyd's Teutonic appreciation of the real uses of Sunday, until Sonderby, who finally guessed that Meyer had seen the artist on the day before, stopped him in disgust. But closing Meyer's mouth could not keep Sonderby from thinking about a certain country girl who had gone down to Brooklyn and left behind her the people who knew her best. All that had come to her since was a consequence of that.

If Sonderby did not have at this moment the peculiar moral insight that had seemed to come to his aid the evening before as he looked at the problem of his own life, he had at least such a sense of detachment from the lives immediately about him that he was conscious of assuming toward them a new critical attitude. The life of Tryphena Morton Floyd seemed to pass before him for review, and for the instant no sympathy for her deflected his judgment. There reappeared to his mental vision the figure of the young fellow with whom he had just been talking. — Harry Duffield. Harry, too, had gone down to the city: Boston or Brooklyn, it was all the same. How many thousands of these New England farmer boys there were, who drifted each year to the larger cities, cheated first by false ideals of the glories of business life behind a counter, and deliberately blinding themselves afterwards to their real situation and prospects! Retaining of their country origin only a certain physical endurance, an originality of phrase, and a ready humor which made them popular, how vain and evil and small they grew! With what ill-concealed disdain did they look back upon the serious, simple toil of their fathers! They got restless in the country now after a few days; the largeness, the slow patience, the gravity of country life, was utterly gone from them; they were flippant, shallow.

It would have done no good now for Ellerton to repeat his merry catalogue of the great Americans who have sprung from obscure country towns; Sonderby, in the mood he was in, would have matched Harry Duffield and other youths like him against all of them. By very force of contrast, Sonderby thought of Rufus Johnson, the grip of his big fist, his kindly, slow speech, and his comrade-like questions: "How's your muscle?" "Arms sunburned yet?" There was a man who was not out of his place.

Meyer had pulled the apron from Sonderby's

neck for the last time and had looked inquiringly at the school-teacher for a minute or so, before the latter realized what was going on. Then he got out of the chair, surveyed his beard in the glass, paid Meyer a quarter, — the school-teacher did not have many in his pocket, — and went over to the Broughton House for supper. But the train of thought which was started in the barber-shop continued all that evening.

When Sonderby went to bed, he looked out of the window, and felt the fresh northwest wind on his face, and saw that the sky was starry again. The rainy spell, with the confinement and overstrained emotional life of those two days, was past. Yet he was still thinking of Tryphena Morton and Rufus Johnson and Harry Duffield. As he closed the window, Rufus's questions reverted to him once more, and going to the lamp that stood on his bureau, he stretched out his forearm. The blue veins crossed and knotted themselves upon the white skin, as he clenched his fist and stiffened the muscles, but there was no color except faint blue and white. The brown, which had been burned so deeply into his arms by two months' exposure to the sun as to be visible far along into the winter, was all gone. The unused muscles were trembling already from the violence of his clench. Sonderby dropped his hand moodily, and with something of his old habits as an athlete still upon him, searched in the bureau drawer for a tape measure. Then he pushed up his shirt-sleeve to the shoulder, and doubling his arm, put the tape around his biceps. He studied the figures — once — twice; then with a muttered exclamation of disgust he threw the tape into the drawer again, as if the dimensions of his upper arm were symbolical of a great deal. It had measured fifteen inches before he trained down for his last boat-race; it was more than fourteen at the end of the summer at Calvin Johnson's; it was barely over thirteen now.

VIII.

Ruth Ellerton amused her husband exceedingly, albeit without any intention on her part, by her account of the conversation she had had with Mr. Collins, upon that Monday afternoon. It was not until more than a week after his call that she happened to explain at length the way in which she had entertained the manufacturer.

In the absence of her husband, who had driven over to Cannck Corner, in the mud, to call on a paralytic woman, Mrs. Ellerton had been sitting in his study reading an article on " Labor Troubles," in a well-known Review.

It was characteristic of Mary Jane, who answered Mr. Collins's ring, that knowing her mistress to be in the study, she opened the door and ushered Mr. Collins in there at once, without preliminary formality. Mrs. Ellerton came forward to meet the caller, Review in hand, and it was perhaps natural that they soon found themselves discussing the article she had been reading.

What Emerson said of the children of New England, as they were in the two decades of 1820 to 1840, that they " were born with knives in their brains," is as applicable to the New Englanders of the last two decades of the nineteenth century as it was to that earlier generation. It is even more applicable, perhaps; for the anatomizing of society is more keen and thorough, intellectual questionings having taken a broader range than they did then, and the development of certain social tendencies having reached such a stage that questions and answers have been forced upon the most unwilling. There is far less interest in theological controversy than there was then. In spite of the constant discussion of theological problems, and the transient hubbub of excitement around some subjects whose doorways open upon a theological hinge, people are coming more and more to a tacit understanding of each other, and to a willingness to work together religiously upon lines drawn far within what would fifty years ago have been regarded as the innermost boundary between the essentials and the non-essentials. The relation of man to God, the possibility of human knowledge in regard to all the ways of God to man, are very differently conceived, and very differently and much less talked about, than they were then. They are left to the individual conscience. The public interest has largely turned to the relations of man to man. Sociology has for the time being usurped the place of theology as a subject for popular discussion and debate.

Ruth Ellerton was a child of her generation, a generation which gives to women the same education as to men, and in so doing places them under equal obligations to face the social questions of the day. Born of a family stock whose male members had followed, for the most part, the ministry or the law, the girl had inherited a vigorous intellect, and an independent fashion of reaching her own conclusions. She had the exceedingly rare gift of taking serious things seriously. One of her earliest recollections was that of lying awake at night, and puzzling painfully over what had been told her in Sunday-school. As she grew older, and learned to interpret less literally what she read and heard, these puzzles of her childhood disappeared for the most part, though they came back now and then to haunt her with a vague trouble.

Her girlhood, passed in one of the largest New England cities, had brought to her more responsibility, and more of an insight into the social condition of the poor in town life, than falls to the share of the average young woman. At the time of her marriage to Arthur Ellerton, she was busying herself, heart and soul, in an association for work among factory girls; and was secretary and treasurer of an organization for building improved tenement houses. Indeed, Ellerton used to affirm, shaking his head solemnly, that it had been a close struggle between the tenement houses and himself, as to who should win her permanent affections; though Ruth never had any answer to this accusation, except a smile.

Her marriage, and removal to Broughton, changed entirely the method of her practical efforts in benevolence ; but it did not abate her interest in the discussion of philanthropic and social topics, as presented in papers, magazines, and books. She rarely had opportunity to talk about these things nowadays, except with her husband, and his ideas upon many of the subjects that interested her were not particularly fruitful. Arthur Ellerton had never lain awake puzzling about anything. His theological notions had been formed mainly in the seminary of his choice, an institution which kept itself popular by the judiciously non-committal balance it managed to maintain upon points of controversy.

Having once investigated a theological question, particularly if under the guidance of one of the sound but fair-minded professors he was fond of quoting, Ellerton never had any desire to recur to it again. For himself, he had " settled " it, and as he cared but little to impress upon others the particular shade of belief that was his own, and as in the multiplicity of his pastoral work he found scanty time for reading or thinking upon speculative subjects, he certainly got along under his system very well indeed.

But Mrs. Ellerton was surprised — and in another minister she would have been disappointed — at his lack of interest in certain questions in which she had always felt a vital concern. Yet her love for him was so great, and her respect for his ability and honesty so unswerving, that her surprise at her husband usually merged into a contrite feeling that perhaps she herself had not been wise in giving the matter so much importance.

She overlooked, too, much of her husband's ignorance about Young Women's Unions, and the sanitation of tenement houses. There was in their present parish but little need of such things. Scarcely a poor family was to be found in the township, except at Canuck Corner, and among the Irish people who were buying up little by little the cheaper farms in the outskirts of Broughton, along the road to the Center. Grinding poverty and the herding of people together into foul quarters, which had created the familiar conditions for Ruth Ellerton's city work, were unknown among these hills. To be sure, the problems involved in the task of stimulating this country town into a more vigorous religious life were extremely difficult; but Ellerton, with health, courage, common-sense, and abundant consecration, was grappling with them as best he could, and learning something every month. Arthur was doing so splendidly in his own parish work, Mrs. Ellerton often reminded herself, that there was really no necessity for his filling his brain with facts and theories about systems of rent, co-operative schemes, building associations, single-taxes, rights of employees, and obligations of employers. She had been proud enough of him when there was talk of forcing the resignation of the village postmistress, that spring, because of a change in the national administration, and Arthur had so far forgotten the conventional inactivity in politics expected of a minister that he had been one to call a meeting to protest against the postmistress's removal, and had introduced into his "long prayer," on the next Sunday morning, a pointed reference to the principles of civil-service reform. Yes, Arthur's heart was in the right place, she knew; but nevertheless she was likely to choose the hours when he was away for reading articles upon her favorite topics.

The entrance of Mr. Collins into the study at the point where the author of the paper on "Labor Troubles" had reached the elucidation of the familiar principle that the interests of employer and of employee, though apparently different, were fundamentally the same, seemed to Mrs. Ellerton to be singularly well-timed. She knew that Mr. Collins was a woollen manufacturer; and he had hardly seated himself and made some polite remark about her reading which he had interrupted, when she began to ply her visitor with questions about the subjects suggested by the article.

Collins was taken unawares. He had never had a woman make such inquiries of him before, and the questions themselves were not easy to answer off-hand. He had put on his good clothes and taken his gloves and best umbrella in order to make a call at the parsonage, and thus to show himself well disposed towards the minister, to whom he had taken a liking. Certainly he had not overlooked the fact that there was a Mrs. Ellerton at the parsonage, though in the few minutes that he had seen her at the Floyds' he was unable to get any more definite idea of her than that she was tall and had a fine face. But now, instead of the leisurely talk he had expected with Ellerton, about the weather and the fishing, with perhaps a few commonplace phrases thrown in to the minister's wife, whom he expected to sit dutifully by, here he was alone with Mrs. Ellerton, who looked very pretty in a close-fitting gray dress with a bunch of sweet-peas in her bosom, but who had nothing particularly dutiful or meek in her manner of address, and who was cross-examining him rapidly about his obligations as an employer of labor.

It was rather hard. What added to the peculiarity of the situation was the fact that Collins's employees were at that moment engaged in a long-continued and sullen strike; and, though Mrs. Ellerton was ignorant of this, Collins suspected that she knew it, and winced more than once under her apparently innocent interrogations. When he gradually got over his surprise, however, and saw that she had a genuine interest in what she was talking about, and that she really knew nothing of the strike, he entered into the spirit of the thing and told her much that she was curious to know.

Collins was a thorough-going business man, when he chose to be, and inherited from his father, who had established the Collins Woollen Mills, a shrewdness and executive ability that in times of ordinary prosperity had assured him a liberal income and had enabled him to extend widely the original plant. But just now the times were hard and apparently growing harder, and in the little manufacturing village where Collins, like his father before him, was a virtual autocrat, matters had taken such an unpleasant turn as not only to make him glad to stay away for a while, but also to make him willing to inquire seriously whether there were any real dangers — as many people alleged — which threatened the manufacturing industries of New England.

With the best intentions in the world, however, on the part of both Mr. Collins and Mrs. Ellerton, they could not long stand on common ground in their discussion of the labor problem. He spoke, naturally enough, from the point of view of a business man, who had grown up into the Collins Mills, and took the world as he found it. But if Mrs. Ellerton could not understand all the technical phraseology employed in the business world, which Collins used as if it were perfectly familiar to her, throwing in only occasionally a deferent "you know," she puzzled him equally, if not more, by the ideal standards which she insisted that every employer should follow. Mrs. Ellerton was perhaps as much indebted to Ruskin and Tolstoi for her political economy as she was to Labor Bureau Reports and the United States Census, and when she talked about "self-sacrifice in trade," and the "higher law binding upon capital," he did not have the remotest idea what she was driving at. They struggled on for a while, but by and by he referred irreverently to her "law of self-sacrifice in trade" as "the blessedness of getting left," and then she suspected that he recognized no higher law in trade than that of self-interest, and she was quite sure of it finally when her "New Political Economy" went dismally to wreck against his commonplace but apparently incontrovertible maxim, that "it takes two to make a bargain."

Nevertheless, with feminine persistence, she did not altogether abandon the field of discussion to which she had led the conversation. The question of the protective tariff was that summer attracting the public attention more than usually, and Ruth had been trying diligently in her spare moments to find out exactly what were the advantages of the high-tariff system under which the people of the United States were then living. The more she read, the more sceptical she grew as to these alleged advantages, possibly because the most able and attractive literature at her disposal was unanimous in attacking the existing system. The presence of Mr.

Collins now gave her the first opportunity she had had for months for talking with a business man whose interests were closely concerned in any proposed changes in tariff legislation.

She was eager to ask him about several things which her husband would hardly have been expected to know. But to her astonishment she soon found that Collins had never given the subject any thought worthy of the name. He had inherited the Collins Woollen Mills, and a theory of the paternal relation of the government to them, at the same time, and did not question either inheritance. Surprised at a woman's interest in purely economical subjects, he answered carelessly, almost humorously, until he discovered that this gray-eyed, fresh-cheeked young woman sitting there by the pastor's desk, her foot almost touching his own, was involving him in a gross contradiction. He had assented, without thinking of the consequences, to her postulate that the woollen manufacturers and the wool-growers had identical interests, but after two or three more of her innocent questions he began to stumble, and was forced to admit, before her series of interrogations ended, that it certainly looked, from the outside, as if under the present condition of things the interests of growers and manufacturers were diametrically opposed. Then, in spite of his politeness, Collins began to grow nettled at the peculiar way the minister's wife had of amusing a caller. She saw that she was treading on dangerous ground, and was almost minded to turn the conversation to the subject of the Broughton House, when a letter she had received that morning from her old home came into her mind. The letter was about tenement houses, and she could not resist asking Collins about the method of rent in use at the Mills village. He explained, a trifle impatiently, the policy of the company, and heard with some incredulity her excited exposition of the plan then on trial by the association with which she had been connected. His impatience gave way to a mild disgust when she asked him about the system of drainage in use at his company's cottages. He did not know anything about the drainage in the first place, and in the second, his vocabulary for expressing himself on such subjects had never been tested by the presence of a feminine auditor, and he found the conversation embarrassing. He feared, too, that he was not making the best impression in the world on the minister's wife, and felt that the fault lay in her intruding her interest into subjects that lay solely within the scope of the masculine comprehension. Finally he lost his temper, and in defence of the cottages under his control, asked by way of comparison if she had ever been at Lawrence or Lowell. On her replying in the negative, he used, in describing the way the operatives along the Merrimac lived, a simile so brutal that it shocked her, as he intended it should, and before she could fairly recover herself, he changed the subject so markedly that she took the hint.

The last five minutes of his call were charming. As if in recognition of the fact that she had been boring him, Mrs. Ellerton did her utmost to put him in good humor, and with a woman as pretty as the minister's wife for a hostess, Collins was not after all a caller very difficult to please. He went away with a delightful, if slightly confused impression of her, left a message for Mr. Ellerton, and promised to come again.

When Mrs. Ellerton gave her husband, one day when she was in the mood for it, a detailed description of her discussion with Collins, he went from one peal of laughter into another, and the more accurate she grew in her repetition of their mutual questions and answers, the more entertainment did Ellerton seem to find in them. He never took his wife's researches into economic subjects with quite the seriousness they deserved, and, as has been said, he did not share at all her zeal for the improvement of tenement houses.

"Well, what was that shocking thing he said about Lawrence?" he asked. "It seems that that put the finishing touch on that frivolous discussion."

"Arthur, it was perfectly horrid!" she cried, earnestly. "And he said it in such a cold-blooded way."

He waited for her to repeat Collins's remark.

"Why," and she uttered the words as if they soiled her lips, "he said that the operatives there live like — *like worms in a bait-box* — and that the factory owners don't mind it if they do."

It was Ellerton's turn to grow grave. "Rather a forcible figure of speech, my dear, I'll admit," said he.

"Well," he added, after a moment's pause, in which Mrs. Ellerton had shut her eyes as if to close something out of her vision, "I must say this: he's taken his comparison from something he's familiar with. He's a fisherman through and through. And that reminds me, if we're going trouting together before this season closes, I must go down to the hotel now, and make an engagement with him."

Ellerton crossed to his wife's chair, and bending above her, kissed her forehead.

"Good by, my dear, I'll make Collins take that back. He didn't dream of your really remembering it, I know. But if there were more people in Lawrence like you, Ruth, I don't doubt that it would be better for Lawrence — that's all."

IX.

When Mr. Ellerton reached the Broughton House in search of Collins, he found the piazza tolerably well filled with summer guests, but there was no one in the long line of red rocking-chairs whom he recognized. He entered the office and looked around for some one of whom he might inquire for Collins. The room was empty, except for a couple of little city misses in tennis-suits, who were laughing at the lithograph of Daniel Webster. The minister turned to go out again, when he met Bill Trumbull, who was coming in.

"I wonder if you can tell me where I shall find Mr. Collins," Ellerton asked at a venture.

"Wal, I guess so," replied Trumbull, benevolently, seating himself by way of preliminary in his cushioned chair. "Let's see," and he struck a match on the bottom of the chair, while with the forefinger of his left hand he pushed the tobacco tenderly into the bowl of his pipe. "Mr. Floyd, he's workin' this afternoon. Got an order for a picture yesterday, clear from Chicago. The schoolteacher, he's down to the academy. Collins — lemme see; Mrs. Floyd, she's gone red-raspberryin', all alone. Mr. Collins, — oh, now, come to think of it, I guess you'll find Mr. Collins down to the Holler, tryin' to git that 'ere trout."

The minister sat down at this point, yielding to the spell that usually came over those who stood up before the seated and conversationally inclined Trumbull. "I don't believe he'll git him," continued Bill. "Along in June, when Mr. Collins come up here, he says to me, 'Bill, I won't go back without that trout down in the Holler.' I didn't say nothin', but thinks I, you'll have to ketch 'im first."

"He's a big one, is he?" inquired the minister, who remembered that Collins had said something about this fish on the afternoon at Floyd's cottage.

"Big one?" ejaculated Bill, and he took a long pull at his pipe. "Of course he's a big one. When you have a hole under a rock like that, with water eight or ten foot deep, you don't ketch nothin' else but big ones. The little trout are afraid to go there, don't you see? Afraid they'll git gobbled up by the old ones. I never yet see this trout, though," admitted Bill, dispassionately; "Collins says he's a three-pounder."

"He is, eh?" cried Ellerton, excitedly.

"Yes, sir! But I don't think you can ketch that trout with a hook. I told Collins — says I, why don't you go down there some night with a torch 'n spear him? But Collins said he'd be —" Trumbull remembered he was talking with the minister and hesitated an instant — "darned if he'd spear that trout himself, or let any one else spear him, with a lot more about it's bein' unsportsmanlike. Now, when I was a boy, if we couldn't git 'em one way, we would the other. Anything to git 'em. There wa'n't so much talk then about 'sportsmen,' but we used to git the fish, by Johnny —"

"Ah, ha!" threw in Ellerton, to show his interest.

"Yes, sir. Did you ever see a three-pound trout? Do you know what they look like?"

"No," answered Ellerton, modestly. The largest brook-trout he had ever taken weighed a pound and a quarter, and there had been glory enough in that.

"Wal, just look at that mantel-piece." Bill waved his pipe toward the fireplace. "Do you see that narrer notch, not the end one, but the narrer one?"

"Yes," said Ellerton, who had jumped up to examine the mantel-piece.

"That trout weighed two pound ten ounces. Pretty close on to three pounds, ain't it? There was a boy caught that trout, not more'n five or six years ago. Jerked him right out of the water, with a crooked hardhack pole; 'n I guess the boy was about as scared as the fish was. Ran all the way home, anyhow, holdin' onto the trout with both hands, 'n draggin' the pole behind him along the road. Didn't dast take the hook out of his mouth, ye see, for fear he'd git away."

Ellerton laughed, with a remembrance of his own boyish rapture, when he caught his first trout, from a tiny stream in a Pennsylvania meadow. "What's this end notch?" he asked.

Bill Trumbull settled himself more comfortably in his chair and crossed his legs. "That end notch?" he repeated, as if to give the minister fair warning. "That, sir, was cut close to the end of the tail of the biggest trout that was ever ketched in the town of Broughton." He waited a moment, to give these solemnly uttered words their due impression. "That was back toward the end of the war, in the spring of 1864. Just an even four pounds. Samuel Parkinson weighed that trout, and says he, 'If that fellow had had one more fly for breakfast, he'd weigh over four pounds.'"

But just here, in the very prologue of the narrative Ellerton knew was coming, it occurred to the minister that Collins might be catching a three-pound trout at that very moment; and much as he would have enjoyed the history of the four-pounder taken in 1864, the possibility of seeing the smaller fish actually landed was more tempting.

"Well, I declare, that was a big one," he interrupted. "Look here, Mr. Trumbull, do you think Mr. Collins would mind my going down there and watching him?"

"I dunno's he would," replied Bill, slowly, dissimulating as well as he could his disappointment in not being asked to finish his story. "You know enough to keep still, don't ye, and keep out of sight?"

"Oh, yes," laughed Ellerton. "How do you get down there from here? I've never been there but once."

"Go right down the cow lane behind the stable," directed Bill. "You'll have to cross a little bit of medder, but I guess 'twas mowed yesterday. Then follow the path right through the pasture, and there you be."

"Thank you. I rather believe I'll go down."

"Wal, I guess 'twon't do no harm," said Bill, with good humor beaming from his mild, vague eyes. "I told Collins, sez I, 'that trout ain't going to be hooked.' Still, you can't never tell, in trout-fishin'. He's goin' to try a couple of banty chickens for bait to-day. Curious kind of bait, too, now, ain't it?"

"It is, indeed," replied the minister. "Good day," and he shot out of the office, brushing in the doorway against the two little girls in tennis-suits, who had been listening with great interest to the conversation, and who were trying to get up courage to ask Bill Trumbull about the stuffed wildcat in the corner. But they did not dare, and ran away after a while, with laughing whispers, leaving Bill to sit alone before the fireless hearth, and to perfect certain commendatory phrases about the parson that were forming themselves in his mind, in spite of his chagrin at Ellerton's premature departure.

Ellerton picked his way through the stable-yard, vaulted over the bars into the lane in a style that made the stable-boy envious of him, and walked rapidly down the lane toward the Hollow. It was already rather late in the afternoon, and a slight film of cloud was over the sky. Ellerton had not yet had leisure enough to get acquainted with Broughton by-paths, and he hesitated an instant at the end of the lane. On getting into the meadow, however, he found a slender path winding close to the fence, among the rank golden-rod, not yet in blossom, and the ox-eyed daisies and spirea. The grass had been cut close up to this tangled border along the fence, and lay in browning swathes just as it had fallen. Beyond the meadow, the path led over a rickety stone wall into a pasture, and here it wound up hill among quartzite bowlders, and through dark green patches of sweet-fern, brightened here and there by the purple and white blossoms of the twining morning-glory. When Ellerton gained the summit of the pasture, the Hollow opened before his feet.

A long pool lay gleaming there below. Toward it the pasture sloped steeply down, covered as on the other side of the hill with detached bowlders and clumps of fern, only that the northern slope was colder, and wet with many a tiny spring, all choked with peppermint and spearmint.

At the head of the pool, to the right, was a huge ledge with piles of broken rock, from which came the roar of falling water. All along on the north, beyond the pool and facing Ellerton as he stood, extended this high gloomy ledge, bending gradually toward the west, so that in the afternoon its shadow darkened the water. Two or three huge hemlocks were growing at the crest of the ledge, and a pair of crows were circling around them excitedly, though it was long past breeding-time. Below the hemlocks, and covering much of the precipice with their lighter green, grew birches, soft maples, and hardhacks, wherever they could gain a foothold between the crevices. A profoundly quiet place the Hollow seemed to Mr. Ellerton, in spite of the noise of water and the cawing of the crows, and it seemed a trifle lonely, too, albeit only a quarter of a mile from the village street. Suddenly he caught sight of Collins, crouching in the grass behind a long bowlder near the head of the pool, and all thought of the landscape went out of his mind in a moment. Descending carefully, though not without dislodging a few round stones which rolled down dangerously near the water, he made his way toward the fisherman, creeping the last few paces until he gained the shelter of the rock behind which Collins was squatted. The latter looked up with a nod of welcome.

"Hullo," he said, as the minister reached his side. "How d'ye do?"

"First rate," Ellerton whispered. "I hope I'm not taking too much of a liberty."

"Nonsense!" replied Collins, in his low, vibrant bass. "And you needn't whisper. The water up there makes so much noise that the fish can't hear us. I doubt if they hear much, anyway."

Ellerton swung himself over on his hip, and stretched out, regardless of the damp, clayey bottom.

"Look out for my chickens," called the fisherman, with a smile, as the minister planted his elbow almost in a Derby hat, which lay bottom upwards, propped with a couple of stones. Ellerton looked over into it, and saw two newly hatched bantams, incredibly small and noisy.

"I thought of trying some partridge chickens," Collins explained, "but they're too big by this time, even if I could find any. What do you think of the bantys?"

"Well, they're small enough," answered Ellerton. "I've heard of catching big trout with a partridge chicken, but never saw it tried."

"I've seen a Canada Indian do it," said Collins, "but that isn't doing it myself. I tried the same thing with two young field-mice the other day, but it was no use. And I had a little green frog fastened to a salmon hook and swimming all over that hole, last night, but the trout wouldn't even look at him." Collins busied himself, as he spoke, with making a gut slip-noose.

"You're sure he is there?" inquired Ellerton.

"He rose the other night at a white miller-fly," replied Collins, "but I didn't hook him. Oh, he's there sure enough. Just below that little whirlpool, in line with those brakes, is where he rose. Go on! Stick your head up and take a good look at it."

The minister peeped over the top of the rock and took a long look, uttering under his breath an enthusiastic interjection. Through the ledge, above the pool, the water had cut a straight, polished channel, down which the brook shot at tremendous speed into a round pot-hole. The rocks all around were black and slippery with the flying spray, and the pot-hole was white as milk with the churning swirl and the foam. As the brook poured out of its confined space into the broad current of the pool, a big willow stump overhung the water, on the side nearest Ellerton, and its roots seemed to catch the mighty rush of the current, and to deflect it to the other bank, toward the shelving ledge of rock. The fine purple rootlets of the tree fringed all the nearer bank, for twenty feet or more below the stump. From the willow to the opposite ledge there was a width of a dozen or fifteen feet, and a depth of ten; but the pool shoaled gradually, as it broadened, and though along the rocky side there was deep and black-looking water for fifty feet or more, the lower end of the pool was shallow, and its bottom covered with fine gravel. Here the village boys came sometimes to bathe, and once in a great while a party of little girls, watched jealously by some older woman, would dare to invade the loneliness of the Hollow, in order to dabble and wade in the shallowest places of the pool, and even to try swimming across, at a safe depth, to the ledge on the northern side.

Ellerton's rock was six or eight yards from the bank, and about the same distance from the head of the pool. The water glided past him, brimming and smooth, and he could look far down, past the purple fringe of willow roots, into the lucent amber-colored depths. He could almost see, by the presentative power of his fisherman's imagination, that the big trout was there.

"Well, I declare!" he exclaimed, sinking back on the wet grass again. Collins grinned sympathetically.

"That's about right, isn't it?" he remarked. "And now for my banty chicken."

He took one of the tiny squeaking things from his hat, gently enough, and fitted its breast into the curve of a salmon hook so that the point protruded half an inch or so above the bantam's wing. Binding the chicken in place with half a dozen turns of yellow silk thread, he knotted a strip of cork, to which were fastened some feathers, under the incipient tail of his peeping bait. Then handing the chicken to Ellerton to hold, he rapidly put his rod together, measured with his eye the distance of the cast required, and adjusted his rod. The long gut leader to which the hook was fastened was curled in tangled spirals, and Collins wet his fingers and pulled it straight. Taking the precious bait in his left hand, he lifted the upper part of his body cautiously above the rock, and while Ellerton lay flat, trembling with excitement, there was the sudden whistle of the dainty split bamboo rod, as Collins's arm straightened, and the bantam chicken soared out on the prettiest imaginable flight and landed lightly on the head water of the pool, above the stump, just where the last ripples from the pot-hole began to smooth themselves. Collins's eye twinkled; a live chick was an awkward thing to cast, but he had put it on the desired spot as deftly as if it were only an ordinary brown hackle. The chicken righted itself instantly, as its legs and wings were free, and began its fluttering and dangerous voyage down stream, hindered rather than helped by the cork, which had slipped so far back that it made the chicken's head bob ridiculously into the water, every foot or so, tipping after the manner of a young peeping sandpiper. There was breathless stillness, except for the fine click of the reel, as the bait was swept along toward the little whirlpool where the trout had last risen. It was just at the spot in a moment more, then whirled twice or thrice in the eddy, hesitated, and floated on again in its bobbing, splashing, struggling fashion; but no trout rose at it. The twinkle went out of Collins's face: he leaned far over and began to let out line, as the bait was carried down the pool, just outside of the dark shelf of rock, in the shadow of the trees. Fifteen — eighteen — twenty yards of line were out besides a six-foot leader, when Collins drew the bait across the lower end of the pool, just where the stream began to ripple again, and commenced to reel in, without a word. When the bait had crept up the nearer side of the pool to within a few yards, Collins lifted it out of the water and caught it in his hand, as it swung dangling past him.

"The cork's no help," he remarked, examining the panting, drenched atom of yellow fuzz that lay in his palm. "D'you think he'd float again without it?"

Ellerton nodded his assent, despite a certain sneaking pity for the chicken.

Collins pulled out a penknife and cut the cork loose. He stood the chicken up on his palm, and laughed at its unsteady efforts to keep its feet, and at the pertness of its black eyes. Then he tossed it into the air, and the eight-ounce rod threw it lightly up the pool again, this time placing it under the willow stump, in quieter water. There was less splashing, too, as the chicken got itself right side up, though without the cork it floated steadier than before. Again it was carried over toward the ledge, paused in the eddies, and began to glide down past the blackest water. Feebler and feebler grew the struggles and the peepings, more and more often did the tiny yellow head go out of sight. Collins shook the tip of his rod a little to make the motion of the bait more lifelike, and drew it back and forth along the lower pool, but all in vain. The three-pounder was either sulky or not hungry. When the bait floated over into the shallowest water, a dace nibbled at it, to Collins's silent wrath. He jerked it away and drew it up stream, rather limp now, and soaked out of much resemblance to a saucy bantam chick. When it was opposite the rock Collins whipped it out of the water, and with scarcely a motion of his supple wrist sent it across the pool again, below the eddy, and drew it straight in toward him rapidly, in a discontented fashion. Almost automatically, and hardly glancing at the hook, he repeated this, twice, three times, apparently making up his mind whether it would be worth while to try the other chicken. But the third time, as he pulled the bait in over the water and was just snapping it carelessly into the air toward the rock, there was an eager rush and a cleaving splash, and the huge trout, in hot pursuit, leaped half out of the water like a salmon, with wide-open mouth, and missing the yellow morsel, was driven straight toward the bank by the impetus of its spring, so that both men saw it clearly as it shot forward, then turned, with a single sullen flap of its broad tail, and darted off into deeper water again.

The men looked at each other with dilating eyes, and each caught his breath. Collins sank on his knees, twitched the wet bantam chicken, in his excitement, right into the minister's face, then grabbed it and tried to untie the silk, but, old fisherman that he was, his hand trembled so that he failed to hold the knot.

"Untie it," he whispered.

Ellerton took the chicken in his palm. It was quite dead.

"Cut it," ordered Collins. "No, it's got to be untied; I haven't any more silk. Wait a minute." He pulled out a cigar and lit it nervously.

But Ellerton had already taken the thread off, and laid the dead chicken on the rock.

"Now my hat, quick!" cried Collins. "We've got to try him with this other one: he won't come over here again."

He tied the second chicken to the hook, swiftly, puffing hard at his cigar. It took a minute, this changing of the bait, but it seemed like ten. When all was ready he crawled out to the end of the rock, cautiously, exposing nothing but his arm and head. Ellerton lay beside him, flat on his stomach in the wire-grass. The sun was down almost below the northwest bend in the ledge, and just as Collins dragged himself forward the last inch, and took a firm grasp of the butt of his rod, a shadow came quite over the water, and a hundred little ripples shivered across it.

"Now for you," muttered Collins; and once more the rod whistled and the bait flew out over the steel-gray pool.

It was a nervous cast though, and fell short. But that was no matter. The bantam shook its downy wings, drifted free of the outer circle of the eddy where it had fallen, and floated off, squeaking, just below the clump of brakes that bent down into the water. But there the big trout, not to be foiled a second time, darted up from his lurking-place, and with the waters swirling all around him as he leaped, closed his wide jaws over the trembling, frightened bit of yellow fuzz, and, with a vicious sideways shake of the head, plunged straight for the bottom. Collins struck sharply, jumping to his feet, but the rod straightened in his hand, and the empty line flew back into the air.

The three-pounder had caught the leader between his teeth and cut it as if with scissors.

Collins stood motionless for twenty seconds, staring blankly at the water. Then he took his thumb from the reel, letting it buzz until the line was wound, and then began to unjoint his rod, silently.

Ellerton, watching his smooth, olive face, clear-cut chin, and square shoulders, caught for a moment a fanciful resemblance between the manufacturer and Napoleon Bonaparte. Perhaps that was why he exclaimed:

"Well, I declare! That was a Waterloo."

Collins turned and looked at him with his luminous black eyes, not knowing whether to laugh or swear. He compromised by pulling out another cigar, and offering it to the parson. Ellerton, though the most abstemious of smokers, took it, as the most practical expression of his sympathy for the fisherman's feelings, and, borrowing Collins's cigar for a light, he blew out two or three mouthfuls of smoke before the manufacturer had said anything.

"Hang it!" finally ejaculated Collins. "I ought to have had a wire leader." He picked up his hat and put it on, and then taking the draggled, original chicken from the rock where Ellerton had laid it, and jerking it spitefully down to the dace in the shallows, he sat down on the rock himself and crossed one knee over the other. Ellerton stood in front of him, brushing ineffectually with one hand the wet clay from the knees of his ministerial trousers.

"Well," demanded Collins, his deep voice shaking yet from the excitement he had been under, "what do you think of him?"

"Think of him!" replied Ellerton; "I saw him! I didn't suppose a trout that size ever grew."

Collins smiled at the boyish sparkle of enthusiasm in the minister's eyes. "Oh, they grow," he exclaimed, knocking the ashes off his cigar; "the thing is to hook 'em."

"Let me look at the gut," said Ellerton.

Collins took it out of his pocket, and they scrutinized together the clean cut where the trout's teeth had severed it.

"Yes," remarked the minister; "I suppose wire would have been better."

It is an unusually genial fisherman who can allow any one else to join, even most indirectly, in the criticism of his own methods of procedure, and there was some asperity in Collins's tone as he replied, "But I didn't have any. Didn't bring any with me, and there isn't one within twenty miles. It wouldn't do any good now," he added; "this chicken business is played out. I shall have to wait till he has digested that salmon hook, anyway."

"Don't you think he'd rise to bait again?"

"Not right off," was the response, and Collins twinkled grimly; "not to-night or to-morrow. I propose to have him yet, though," he said, after a moment's silence, "game-law or none. There are eight days before the first of August, anyhow."

"I suppose you could spear him at night, couldn't you?" suggested Ellerton, remembering what Bill Trumbull had said at the hotel.

"Spear him?" repeated Collins, wrathfully. "Of course I could if I wanted to. So could any pot-hunter. I told Bill Trumbull that when I sank so low as to spear that trout, because I couldn't hook him, I'd never show my head in Broughton again."

The minister changed the subject, judiciously. "I suppose Bill has been something of a fisherman, in his way, hasn't he?"

"Bill?" inquired Collins, relaxing. "I shouldn't wonder. But it won't do for me to spoil any of his stories by telling them myself. I half wish he'd seen that fish in there, this afternoon," and Collins shifted his position so as to take a regretful look at the surface of the pool; "it would have been enough to keep him going for a year."

Ellerton walked over to the bank and stood with his hands in his pockets, gazing down at the waving willow roots. A frog leaped from under his feet into the water, and the sudden splash made both men start, and then look smilingly at each other.

"No," said Collins; "that trout won't jump again for us to-night. We might as well go home."

"Sure enough," replied the minister, glancing at his watch; "it's supper-time. By the way, when can we have the little fishing-trip that that rainy Monday spoiled for us?"

"Oh, any time," answered Collins, cordially; "only it must be pretty soon;" and they debated for some minutes before they could find a day and hour for which Ellerton had not some engagement.

The talk grew rather aimless after that, and by and by they started up the hill toward the village, Ellerton halting more than once to look back into the Hollow, where the pool stretched black and still. He forgot all about the conversation he had meant to have with Collins on one or two of the subjects his wife had discussed with the manufacturer. He had intended to ask Collins what he really meant about the state of things in Lawrence, and whether it was the fault of the mill-owners, the operatives, or the churches. He had had a desire to know how his new acquaintance stood on some of these social questions, not so much in the hope of getting light on the questions themselves, as was the case with his wife, but rather with the purpose of finding out what manner of man this dark-faced, gentlemanly sportsman was. He thought that the minister in the village where the Collins Mills were situated was an acquaintance of his, and by asking Collins about it he had hoped to discover what was the manufacturer's own attitude toward the church. But all these desires, sincere as they were, were for the time being obliterated by the hearty natural interest he had taken in Collins as a fisherman, and so it was about trout and salmon and related themes, and not about mills and churches, that the two men continued to talk, as they followed the winding path up the hill.

It was only a quarter of an hour before that Mrs. Floyd, returning from her solitary expedition to a neighboring pasture, had set down her heaped pail of red raspberries by the bars, at the summit of the hill, while she clambered over. She had rested there a few minutes, leaning her hands on the top bar, looking down into the darkening Hollow, ignorant of the presence of the fishermen, and thinking of the first time she had gone there to bathe in the shallow part of the pool. How the water had frightened her, as it stole up over her knees, and how dear Aunt Tryphosa, sitting on the bank, had shaken and squealed with laughter! Then Tryphena Morton Floyd looked down at her stained fingers, all scratched with the thorns of the raspberry bushes, and wondered how many times, when a child, her fingers had rested here on the bars, tinier fingers then, and browner, but just as scratched and stained. Somehow the pail seemed heavier when she took it up again, and she stumbled slightly more than once, as she followed the lonely path through the meadow to the cottage.

"Hullo!" said Collins, as the two men reached the top of the ascent, and got over the bars. "Some one has spilt some berries," and picking up and tossing into his mouth three or four big raspberries that were lying under the lowest rail, he answered one of Ellerton's queries about the Rangely Lakes, and they sauntered on towards the hotel.

X.

THE order for a picture which Floyd had received from Chicago was given by old Watson. Nearly two weeks had passed since that hot morning when Mrs. Floyd had torn Watson's first letter in two, and tossed the pieces at her husband's feet. Day after day, in this slow interval of time, Floyd had managed to be at the post-office in the afternoon when the mail was opened. He had gone with no definite expectations, for he knew that the eccentric broker would not be likely to refer again to the return to Munich until the month was past, and yet he had a restless feeling that something important might come for him at any time.

On the afternoon when the sallow postmistress handed him a second letter addressed in the cramped, familiar hand, it happened that Collins was in the company of the artist.

Floyd's first impulse was to thrust the letter into his pocket, unread; but knowing that Collins's eye was upon him, he decided to tear it open, and did so with affected carelessness. But his hand shook a little notwithstanding, and in his jerk at the end of the envelope he tore the enclosed note half across. It was an unpleasant reminder of the fate of Watson's first communication. An eager look came into his palish eyes as he read.

"Hullo!" he muttered, "I'm in luck;" and, determining to carry matters through as unconcernedly as he had begun, he passed the single blotted page to Collins.

The manufacturer ran his eye over it. "Humph!" he exclaimed. "Two hundred and seventy-five dollars for a small picture; I should think that was doing very well. It's more than I'd give you, Floyd, anyway. But can you paint it in two weeks?"

Floyd took the letter again and studied the date. Cunning old Watson had not written a word about Germany, but the price he offered for a picture "about 12 x 17" was exactly the amount of the first check he had ever sent Floyd, to pay his expenses over to Munich, and the date by which the picture was to be done was set exactly a month later than his letter of two weeks before.

"Oh, yes," replied Floyd, "I can paint it in two weeks easily." As they walked back to the hotel he talked with noteworthy gravity and conceit about his powers of rapid execution, but Collins did not seem to be profoundly impressed. However, as they reached the Broughton House, he said:

"Now, look here, Floyd. In honor of your luck we'll have a game of euchre, if you say so. You can't go to work to-night."

The artist scowled, perhaps at some inglorious recollection. "Oh, I don't mind," he assented. "Only it mustn't be for long," he added, with a deprecatory meaning that Collins understood.

"All right," smiled the latter, and entered the office to drop a discreet word into the Welshman's ear. But Collins kept the agreement, and the game of euchre was a brief one.

Next morning the artist turned over the contents of his portfolio in search of some sketch that he might use for the picture. He thought at first of the old mill, out on the North Broughton road; but he could scarcely finish that in the required time, and besides, he knew that Watson's preference would be for figure-painting rather than for landscape. He hesitated a moment, too, over the hastily executed portrait of Sonderby, and was surprised by its evident excellence into thinking that he might dress up the figure in armor and velvet — if his studio were only accessible — and call it an imaginary portrait of some mediæval character. But this was only a passing fancy. He finally hit upon a Venetian sketch — a girl leaning upon a fountain — as something which would please Watson, and which he could easily reproduce in oil. He had sketched in the fountain with considerable care, originally, and all that he wished for a background — the façade of a palace and a glimpse of a canal — his other Venetian drawings could easily supply. To be sure, he needed a model; but Tiyphena had often posed for him before, and he saw no reason why she should now refuse.

He had not spoken to her of the order he had received until breakfast-time, in the presence of Collins and Sonderby, the latter of whom showed much interest in the artist's good fortune. Tryphena listened with unusual trepidation to her husband's bombastic attempts to make light of the matter, as if it were an ordinary thing to have such conditions attached to a bargain for a picture; and when, in response to an innocent inquiry from the school-teacher, Floyd answered that the painting was going to Chicago, she felt as if something choked her. She knew then that her husband had heard from Watson again, and she did not doubt in her own mind that they had reached an understanding.

Nevertheless, so well had she learned to keep her thoughts and feelings to herself — except on those rare occasions when impulse got the better of her — that when Floyd asked her after breakfast if she would not play model for a while, he was surprised himself at her obedient, almost gentle, acquiescence.

"Of course I will, Billy," she answered. "Haven't I always?"

Those last words made him glance suspiciously at her, imagining some meaning deeper than appeared upon the surface; but her face and her tone were for him impenetrable, and the words were after all natural enough. Together the artist and his wife went into the back yard of the cottage and looked around for a suitable place for the morning's work. A fountain easily brought to mind the well-curb, and after squinting at this two or three times, Floyd decided that it would do. It was about the right height for Mrs. Floyd to lean against, and an ancient brass kettle of Aunt Tryphena's, balanced on the edge of the curb, made a tolerable substitute for the waterpot, upon which the Venetian girl in the sketch was resting her hands. The artist arranged carefully the drapery of his wife's skirts, fastening them high enough to show her ankles, for he wanted to paint the counterless slippers which the Venetian women wear on the street. As he pinned and pulled her dark flannel dress, and arranged a red shawl upon her shoulders, with momentary glances at the sketch he held in one hand, he thought with a smile of the girl who had posed for him in Venice. A stupid thing she had been, unused to posing, and unable to comprehend a word of his scanty Italian vocabulary, but patient with his pullings and twistings, and blushing withal. How prettily she had smiled when he paid her the fifty centesimi an hour! She had high cheekbones, and a broad, low forehead, with chestnut hair parting over it, like some of the old pictures in the Accademia. How she had pattered off over that little arching bridge by his *pension*, when he had done with her, her red slippers flapping and scuffling merrily along, and how coquettishly she had peeped back at him as she turned the corner by the canal! Floyd shrugged his shoulders, almost imperceptibly, as he thought of her, and then stepped back and took a critical survey of his present model. It was not bad, though, that pose of Phenie's; in fact, it was good, good enough.

"*Bellissimo!*" he exclaimed. "*Non c'è male! Sì — Sì!*"

Mrs. Floyd supposed he was talking German, and made no response, except to shift her elbow slightly where the edge of the curb began to cut it. The artist frowned; the movement destroyed a line he wanted to keep.

"No," he cried; "that won't do." Then, more considerately, he added, "Put your handkerchief under it, Phenie."

She was not so patient as the other one, he thought, setting up his easel and stool under the shadow of the grape-vine that hung over the back porch. The other one! His smile and his good-humor came back to him. What was the use of thinking of that time as of something irretrievably past for him, as he had been in the habit of doing? Past? Venice was there, never fear; and his red-slippered model, or plenty more like her. Past? The Hamburg steamer, sailing that day from New York, would make the passage, say, in nine days. He could take the train for Berlin, catch the night express southward, and be in Munich the next afternoon. There he would pick up two or three of the boys, and persuade them to make a party for Venice; and then for the morning train that he had taken before, up through the Tyrol, and over the Brenner pass, and down the long slopes to Verona; thence eastward, till in the evening the train would creep out over the marshy plains, and the salt air of the lagoons would blow in at the car-windows; then would come the long, white bridge, with the Adriatic lapping against its piers; and finally, they would hurry out of the bustling little station on to the black stairs, where the shouting gondoliers were waiting for them: they would jump in, and glide off down the Grand Canal in the darkness. Venice! It was only two weeks away from Broughton.

"Have you begun yet, Billy?" interrupted Mrs. Floyd.

"No," ejaculated Floyd, coming back suddenly to New England.

"Will you get my hat? The sun is pretty hot here. That is, if it won't make any difference for the beginning."

He brought her the hat, in momentary shame at his thoughtlessness. He had a cool seat in the shade himself. But as soon as his canvas was ready, and the picture fairly under way, he began again to plan out, in a kind of undertow of thought, the details of a trip to Europe, perhaps of the particular trip that his morning's work was making possible for him, and his wife's comfort or discomfort in her posture by the well-curb went entirely out of his mind. It seemed good to him to be at work again upon something definite, and to know now what he could count on.

The last two weeks had been, for the most part, very uncomfortable ones for the artist. Waiting, without action, is a difficult matter for the best of men under the best of circumstances; so much the more was it hard for Floyd, hesitating before a step that was to consummate his selfishness. The weather, too, had been cold and rainy, except on two or three days, and Floyd was dependent on fine weather for a good share of his happiness. Just now, of all times, to be shut up in doors with Tryphena, and to feel the mute reproach of her presence, while each of them was guessing what was covered beneath the commonplace of the other's scanty talk, was doubly trying. He had spent as much time as possible at the Broughton House, or in Meyer's shop, for ten days past, especially since that unfortunate Monday morning when he had returned from the Center with a headache, and Tryphena had said nothing to him at all; but had only looked at him, and made him feel suddenly afraid of her.

Even the whist, upon which he had relied for passing a good many hours without the necessity of saying anything, and yet with the semblance of sociability, seemed to be getting into disfavor of late, and it grew difficult to gather the quartette. Sonderby, in particular, had been growing unmanageable for a week past; had refused to play more than once, alleging that there was important work for him to do at the laboratory, and exhibiting altogether a sulky and grumpy state of temper. Collins. however, as if to make up for the moodiness of his table companion, had shown an increasing friendliness. He and Floyd had loafed a good deal together, and once Collins had insisted on taking Mrs. Floyd to drive in the best buggy that the hotel stable afforded.

"Billy," interposed Tryphena again, "this kettle is slipping out from under my arm. If you don't want to have me move, hadn't you better fix it?"

Floyd put down his brush and maul-stick, and balanced the kettle again, hardly noticing how hot it had become already in the direct glare of the sun. He stepped back to the easel and eyed Mrs. Floyd a second or two, and then went up to her and took off her hat.

"I want to get the head and shoulders — just the outline — now," he said. "No, Phenie, don't look so far to the right. Just about at those plum-trees. No, a little higher! Try looking off at the tops of those hemlocks above the Hollow: — raise your eyes a little — that's it!"

It was just the attitude he wanted for his indolent Venetian girl, waiting at the fountain.

"Can you keep it so, Phenie?" he cried.

"Oh, yes, Billy!" she answered, patiently.

He made sure of the outline with as rapid strokes as possible, but it was a matter that required careful handling, and a full half-hour had slipped by before she could put on her broad-brimmed straw hat again. She had grown faint and dizzy. Floyd, in the shadow of the grape-trellis, and well satisfied with the beginning he had made, painted on and on. He was conscious that every touch of the brush was liberating him from the bondage he was under, bringing him just so much nearer the end. He watched the slender figure leaning against the well-curb, now considering her artistically, as his model, and now practically, as Mrs. William J. Floyd. As he thought of her under these two aspects, a sardonic gleam of amusement passed slowly over his face.

Floyd was not particularly quick, mentally, but the humor of the situation grew more and more apparent. Here was his wife, quietly posing for him, in order that he might earn money enough to leave the country and abandon her! There was something grotesque about it which appealed to Floyd's fancy; a droll foreign flavor, like that of some operetta or light comedy, or like some of the atelier stories he had heard. It seemed comical that it should all happen to him, that he should be the hero of it. Then, by a singular logic, he began to persuade himself that Tryphena was playing her cards with a very fine hand, that she understood thoroughly the significance of Watson's ordering this picture, and posed for him because she wanted to hasten his going. Phenie must know as well as he that they were not made for each other; that the sooner the sorry impersonation of their rôles was over, the better for them both. Phenie could get along perfectly well without him; she owned the cottage. and she could remain in Broughton and teach school, or do something of the sort. Yes, it was clear she wanted to have him go, or she would not thus clear the path for his departure. It was no wonder she was willing to pose for him, and help the picture along! She was a deep one! Again there came over the artist the old feeling that this slight, imperturbable country girl was stronger than he, and more clear-sighted; that she could look straight through his subterfuges and excuses; could guess at his half-formed wishes, and shape her own plans accordingly; that her silent acquiescence was only a barricade behind which she mined incessantly, and against which he was ever to be baffled. But what of that? What difference did it make? A fortnight more, and it would all be over.

At no time during the two weeks now past had Floyd distinctly stated to himself that he was going away. He had never deliberately formulated the question until that bright morning out by the old mill, and then he had set it aside, unanswered. But in this interval of waiting, his will had taken to itself an unconscious strength; and now, when he came to examine the state of his own mind, he found that leaving was no longer a defiant desire, but a fixed fact, grown fixed while he had eaten and slept and idled, and now strengthened by the very weight of his moral inertia. To decide to remain in America now would have been a change of mind for him, though he was entirely unable to say when he had made up his mind to go.

And Mrs. Floyd, standing there by the worm-eaten well-curb, on the old stones which her own childish feet had helped to wear hollow, what was she thinking about?

There was time for her to think about many things, in that long forenoon. Gracefully enough she leaned there, with her skirts pinned back from her slender ankles, improvised Venetian slippers on her feet, a gaudy red shawl draped around her waist as if it had slipped down from her shoulders, her thin fingers clasped over the rim of the brass kettle, which shone in the sun till it seemed as true a gold as the wedding ring upon her hand. Her face was turned away from the painter, but by the curves of the throat, the line of the uplifted chin, and the merest glimpse of her profile, with the long eyelashes and the expectant brow, one could know that she was waiting for something.

For what? If in Venice, for a window to open in the palace opposite, for her lover to come sauntering over the bridge, for her noonday dream to dream itself out, ere she filled her water-bucket and went home. But it was not in Venice, it was only in Broughton; and Tryphena Floyd's eyes were apparently fixed on the tops of Samuel Parkinson's plum-trees, or perhaps on the black boughs of the hemlocks over the Hollow, a quarter of a mile away. The wind might brush through the plum-trees again, and shake another greengage to the ground; possibly a crow might flap reminiscently around its old nest in the hemlocks; but that was all which could happen, if one leaned there on the well-curb and watched a whole summer long. Was Mrs. Floyd really waiting for anything?

Yes. One day with fatalistic acquiescence, the next with a passion of revolt, now with dumb moods when her mind seemed not to work at all, and now with hours of fantastic gaiety, but above all with that endurance which is a part of an honest woman's heritage, Mrs. Floyd was waiting for the end of the month. A more solitary person, for one who must face the great crisis of a life, it would have been difficult to find. She had rightly said to Sonderby, in a moment when the barriers she had set between herself and others were for the moment fallen, that no one could help her. For what help was there? She had no hold upon her husband; that was the bare but the sufficient fact. She had been slowly suspecting it for a long time, and in the last few days she had felt sure of it. It was "their business" solely, as she had said, and there was help neither in him nor in herself. She had no friends to whom she could go for advice, except, perhaps, Aunt Tryphosa, and she had a conviction that Aunt Tryphosa would not understand.

Broughton folks she knew well enough outwardly, as they knew her, but the experience of the past three years seemed to set an infinite distance between her and these kindly inquisitive people with whom she had been acquainted from her childhood. She recognized the uselessness of asking counsel from any of them, even if her pride had allowed her to do so. It was her own affair. If she had made a long mistake, so much the worse for her. Her life had been aimless and empty enough, till she began to love Billy Floyd; and he, or else her love for him, had for a while filled it sufficiently. Now her husband seem to shrink, to shrivel while she watched him even, and life seemed to expand with each day, to recede from her poor pitiful experience, and leave it dwindling there; but alas! life, as it widened round her, was itself a void. Strange moods of apathy grew more frequent with her, as day after day crept by and brought no exterior change. She came to think sometimes that it made no difference whether her husband went or stayed: if he sailed for Munich when the month was up, or if he remained, and they two lived together till their hair grew white and their steps tottering, it would be the same; in either event all was over between them: their experiment was already finished.

Hotly did the sun pour down upon the back yard of the cottage, through that midsummer morning, and in spite of Mrs. Floyd's broad-brimmed hat, a faintness came over her at intervals. Posing was wearisome work, too, and for months she had had no practice in it. But exhausted as she was, it was scarcely an unwelcome way of spending her morning. There was nothing for her to say, nothing for her to do, except to keep in position, and yet she had a consciousness that she was fulfilling her obligations to the end; that she was aiding her husband, obediently, unquestioningly, as she had ever tried to do. That he was coolly planning to forsake her made no difference in her duty, — as Mrs. Floyd with her New England conscientiousness conceived her duty, — and the self-abnegation, for Floyd's unworthy sake, brought her a strange, sad pleasure. It was after eleven when the artist finally declared that she had done enough, took the kettle from her creased fingers, and unfastened the safety-pins which he had used in draping her skirts. Two or three times in the morning he had advised her to rest a little, but she had refused. Now as she straightened herself, and the blood coursed freely through her cramped limbs again, a sudden dizziness nearly made her fall. He saw it and put his arm around her, and then as she steadied herself, he kissed her, not without a certain embarrassment, upon the temple. She did not look up at him; if she had, he would have seen the quick tears well up from her eyes. She had been so happy once, when he had kissed her.

"You've done enough for all day, Phenie," he repeated, in good spirits at the progress made, and perhaps thinking more of that than of her. "I'll work at the background this afternoon."

After dinner, therefore, there being no whist that day, she took from the buttery a six-quart pail, and went off after red raspberries, leaving her husband painting away by himself, absorbedly. When she came back at supper-time, carrying slowly her full pail across the garden, which she had reached from a footpath that led out toward the high pasture around the Hollow, Floyd had stopped work. He had placed his easel in the kitchen, though, and she stood before it a minute or two, wondering, after all, at the great gift that Billy had. Perhaps there was a future before him yet — the future of which they both had dreamed, in those happy months after they were married. It might come yet, for him, — but for her?

She turned away, and lifted her pail of berries again, wearily. What could she do with them, now she had them? She had not thought any further than the amusement of picking them, and of playing she was a child once more. She did not want them, after all. There were plenty of berries in the kitchen of the hotel, and there was no use in giving them to Evans. She did not like the Welshman, anyway. Finally, she carried them across the street to Bill Trumbull's daughter.

"Perhaps your father would like to eat some berries," she said, timidly. "The first time I ever went red-raspberrying, he went with me. Ask him if he remembers it, will you, Mirandy?"

She came back to the cottage with her empty pail, in time to give a shy bow to Mr. Ellerton, who had just left Collins at the corner of the Broughton House. Then she washed the raspberry stains from her fingers, brushed her dark hair smooth, and tying round her throat a bit of lavender ribbon she had worn in her girlhood, went over to supper.

The next morning she posed again, and the next, and the day after. Strange hours they were for her; in which no new ideas came to her, and scarcely any new impressions, but a flood of old memories. Old things lay all about her there — the back yard with its thick, slippery grass; the flower-garden, whose yellow lilies, hollyhocks, and sunflowers were going to seed unheeded; the fruit orchard, where the Bough apples were rotting on the ground; the old well itself, whose mossy stones once seemed to her to stretch down so endlessly deep, and whose water lay there cool and dark, as she gazed down into it now, in the long hours of posing. She wondered how it could keep so dark and cool, being only a few feet from the blazing sunshine. Peace in the midst of trouble Mrs. Floyd did not understand; she understood only how to be calm.

It happened once or twice that Collins sauntered over to the cottage in the morning, and sat down beside the artist to watch him at his work. The manufacturer usually smoked in silence, with an occasional shrewd observation to Floyd about the picture. Tryphena did not mind his being there, and scarcely thought of him, except in the resting-time, when she occasionally seated herself by him on the grass, under the trellis, and was rather glad that some one was there to talk to. But as soon as she was in position again, looking away from the men, out over the garden idly, he went out of her mind, being a part of that present which seemed for the time like a blank to her, in comparison with all the figures and fancies of the past.

One thing only, in those days given to the Venetian girl, occurred to bring the quartette together, except at meal times. That was a drive, upon the manner of which Collins had set his heart. An ancient carryall of Bill Trumbull's, which had hitherto, during Evans's proprietorship, stood unused in the hotel stable, had just been repaired, in accordance with Collins's advice. The top had been removed, side-bar springs substituted for the original ones, and with new cushions and liberal coats of varnish, the vehicle assumed a tolerable degree of respectability, despite its somewhat anomalous character. It would hold four very comfortably, and a lank bay mare, belonging to Evans, was warranted of sufficient strength to pull the quartette over the Broughton hills as fast as they wished to travel.

Collins had a good deal of difficulty in arranging the time for the excursion, for both Floyd and Sonderby were somewhat obstinately bent on following their own concerns. But the manufacturer was accustomed to have his own way, and one afternoon, about four o'clock, they all started off for a drive around the Canuck Corner road. Collins held the reins, and Floyd, sitting beside him, flourished the whip. It was a perfect afternoon, and they rattled along gaily enough, up hill and down, for an hour or more. Then, not meaning to be late for supper, Floyd, who was driving by this time, turned the mare into an old road that led back to the village by a shorter way. The road had been badly washed out by successive spring rains since it had been last repaired, and the artist was as ignorant a driver as ever grasped the lines. Collins had admonished him once or twice. As they plunged down a little hill and the carryall struck sharply against the water-ridge at the foot of it, pitching them all forward in their seats amid a general explosion of laughter, the half-worn hold-backs broke. The carryall was thrown against the mare's hindquarters, but she stopped, though dancing in some alarm. Floyd did not understand what had happened, and, gathering the ends of the lines in his right hand, struck her across the loins. Then the mare flung her bony head straight out, with the bit in her teeth, and ran. Floyd, thoroughly scared, pulled impatiently at the reins: on seeing that the mare only ran the faster, he loosened them nervously and screamed, "Help!" Collins grabbed the lines and gave them a savage jerk, which brought the mare's head into the air for an instant, but for an instant only; he could not hold it, and she shook her neck and got it straight out before her again, and blindly galloped on. Collins, tugging in vain, half turned in his seat and shot a glance at Sonderby. The ex-oarsman rose upright, locking his knees into the back of the front seat, and, leaning far forward, wrapped the lines around his hands; then, drawing a long breath through his clenched teeth, he began to straighten, with a slow sidewise swaying that threw his weight now on one line and now on the other. Slow, terribly slow it seemed, for there was no chance for anything but pure muscle, man against horse. Slow, but steady, first one side, then the other. Slow, for John Sonderby's arms were not so big as they once were, though his legs and back and loins were like iron. Oh, so slow, with Canuck Hill sloping down ahead of them through the trees!

Yet, before they reach it, the mare tires under the cruel weight upon her jaw; lower sinks her stiffened tail; her ears are twitching, and — ha! up comes her head, with the foam flying from her lips; up and back over her trembling shoulders is it pulled now, as John Sonderby straightens himself at last, the quick breath hissing through his teeth, a victorious blue light in his eyes, the brown hair blown back from his bare temples, where the blue veins are corded.

Floyd jumped, as soon as the carryall slowed up. Collins followed him, a minute later, but only to get the mare by the head. When she was quieted, Sonderby dropped the reins, and got out, lifting Mrs. Floyd after him. Nobody said anything for a minute or two. The men busied themselves with the harness. Finally Collins muttered, as he drew out his penknife to cut a new hole in the broken strap:

"It was a close call, Sonderby."

That was all that was said. Floyd came up rather shamefacedly, and they got in, and walked the mare home. Tryphena did not speak. She had not felt so much frightened as she had always thought she would be, if run away with.

But as they turned into the village street, down at the academy end, Mrs. Floyd made one of those impulsive movements which she seemed unable to control. Whether in disgust at her husband's cowardice, or in admiration of the courage and strength of the man beside her, but at any rate, with a fierce swiftness, like the maternal caress of some animal, and yet with a shyness as of a girl, she laid her hand for an instant on Sonderby's arm.

XI.

One other thing distinguished that week, the last in July, from the ones which had preceded it. Collins seemed to be knitting a close intimacy with Floyd. As the picture of the Venetian girl grew upon the canvas, the longer and more frequent became the manufacturer's visits to the back yard of the cottage. In the late afternoon, when Floyd had finished work for the day, or in the evening, the two men sat in Collins's room, and played euchre. Floyd, who was a constant talker when in good-humor, found Collins a more attentive and respectful listener to his experiences and theories than had formerly been the case. As John Sonderby had noticed on the first day Floyd dined at the Broughton House, Collins had once taken scanty pains to conceal his tolerant contempt for the artist. But nowadays he cultivated Floyd assiduously, much to the elevation of the latter's opinion of himself.

The prosecution of this somewhat peculiar friendship was furthered by the fact that, as July came to a close, the quartette met less and less often for the whist and singing and random talk, which had filled up so much of the time earlier in the month. The responsibility for this change was generally flung upon Sonderby, who seemed to be more moody every day and more perverse in the disposition of his leisure. Taciturn always, his increasing silence at the table grew sometimes uncomfortable for the others; and Collins, who had from the first liked the fellow, did not hesitate to quiz him about the cause of his " blueness," watching him the while with an observant eye. Sonderby pretended to have at the laboratory of the academy some important work which demanded all his time; and he explained one day to Collins, incidentally, that he was fitting himself for his duties with the A. S. & F. Company. But it happened repeatedly, especially in the evening, when he went toward the academy, alleging that he had no time to spare, that he really did not go to the laboratory at all, but tramped off alone in the dusk, over the country roads, going at the top of his speed and tiring himself. Two days he spent in the hayfield of Bill Trumbull's son-in-law, offering his services with the explanation that he needed exercise, and that it would be an obligation to him if he were allowed to help the farm hands out in their late haying; and both nights he looked so white and tired at supper, that Mrs. Floyd timidly ordered the Irish waitress to bring him some tea, and Mr. Collins wanted to insist, afterward, on his taking a swallow of whiskey, which the school-teacher gratefully declined.

Floyd's new enthusiasm for work, too, did something to assist in the apparent disintegration of the quartette. The increasing number of strangers at the Broughton House made the four regular boarders less observed, and the red rocking-chairs along the piazza no longer made upon them any mute claim for occupancy. It made no particular difference, even to Evans, whether they stayed after dinner to play whist, or were sitting on the piazza when the afternoon stage lumbered in. Guests in plenty there were by this time to occupy all of the chairs, and to give an unwonted appearance of animation to the hotel. It certainly seemed as if the Welshman's luck had turned for good, and prosperity agreed with him. He no longer slid anxiously around the office and dining-room, watching pertinaciously the conversation of his boarders; but instead, stepped smartly through the hall or along the piazza, as if business pressed him hard, carrying his cunning, narrow head erect, while his bead eyes glistened with pleasure. He bought a new suit of clothes, paid off all his help, and began to settle with the farmers of the neighborhood for the butter, eggs, and other produce delivered during the preceding summer.

To be sure, the majority of the Broughton House guests did not remain many days, but new ones came infallibly to take their places, and to increase the Welshman's triumph. Evans was now indifferent whether the quartette remained with him; he begrudged Sonderby his second-floor front room, for which the school-teacher paid but half what it would bring now; he was anxious to keep on the right side of Collins, for various reasons; but as for the Floyds, he had taken them below cost originally, and Floyd was an enormous eater, while Mrs. Floyd was to him an uncongenial person. Now that the season was an assured success, he made no longer any particular effort to please the patrons with whom his prosperity had begun. His manner toward Trumbull grew steadily in insolence; and though he did not as yet dare to turn him out of the office, and was forced to satisfy himself by planning how he would do it when the time ever came, he succeeded in annoying his predecessor by outspoken criticisms of Bill's favorite newspaper, the *Springfield Republican*, and by removing the cushioned chair from the office, occasionally, when Bill was coming over for a tranquil smoke.

To Bill Trumbull, the fact that the quartette had for ten days or more fallen increasingly into the habit of separating soon after meal times, brought a good deal of mild disappointment. He liked to see the young folks together, enjoying themselves. Toward Tryphena he felt almost a fatherly affection, and indeed he was the nearest approach to a father she had ever known; for Abner Morton had gone to the war with Bill's brother, and the latter's dinted sword was all that had ever come back of either of them.

Bill had always felt a little uncertainty about Tryphena's husband; for however shiftless Trumbull might be, he shared in the New England suspicion of any one who got his living in irregular ways, ways not sanctified by orthodox New England traditions. He admitted, in confidential moments when the artist was the subject of discussion, that he couldn't "understand the critter." But with Collins and Sonderby, Bill's relations had been so genial that the diminution of the hours of intercourse with them made him feel rather lonesome. He disliked to have Collins and Floyd sit upstairs so much of late; if it was nothing but a game of cards and a glass of cider they wanted, there was no necessity of so much secrecy about it — although in the days of "Trumbull's," or rather of "Mis' Trumbull," not even the glass of cider could have been obtained at the hotel.

Perhaps more than all else, Bill missed the singing in the parlor. Without knowing anything more about music than the singing-schools of his boyhood had taught him, he grew constantly in fondness for it, as his contemplative life lengthened, and since the death of Mrs. Trumbull he was conscious of a mournful and quite indefinable pleasure in listening to certain tunes, especially some of those contained in Moody and Sankey's hymn-books. But the singing had grown less frequent, too, together with the whist, and Bill's ludicrous hints about the danger of the melodeon getting out of tune if it were not used, had apparently failed to have any effect upon Collins. It was greatly to the secret satisfaction of Bill Trumbull, therefore, that on that Friday evening when they returned from their drive around by Canuck Corner, the young people did not seem inclined to separate after supper. They had come back late, and had been the sole occupants of the dining-room; for Broughton air gave strangers a good appetite, and the guests of the hotel were very prompt at their meals. The supper was at first a silent one, like the latter part of the drive; but gradually, as they recovered from the nervous strain that had affected them all, more or less, they seemed on more intimate terms with one another than had recently been the case; and if the talk was less demonstrative than it had been during the first hour of their driving, it was more genuine. When they came out into the office, Bill Trumbull, who was the only person in the room, got up from his cushioned chair and made Tryphena take it. It was an act of gallantry so unusual for him, and so opposed to his ordinary chair-keeping, conversation-inviting method of hospitality, that it made an impression upon them all. On his inquiring about the drive, Collins gave a laconic account of what had happened, amid plenty of "Sho's" from

Bill, and a modest disclaimer from Sonderby. Then Trumbull, seeing they were gathered comfortably around him, began to draw upon his store of reminiscences of skittish horses, and told all the gruesome and ludicrous runaway accidents that had happened in Broughton for forty years. From uncontrollable steeds he passed gradually to trained ones, and gave an exhaustive account of an exhibition of trick-horses he had seen in Boston the second winter that he had been a member of the Legislature.

Seeing that his auditors were in an appreciative mood, he made a skilful transition to the subject of raising colts, and it was ten o'clock by the time he had finished telling about the marvellous colts he had reared, and how the fastest of them would have been entered for the 2.40 trotting race in the annual cattle show and fair at the county seat in 1876, had it not been for the unconquerable aversion of " Mis' Trumbull " to " hoss-racin'." In short, Bill's talk was of the most delightfully flavored character, and for once, as it happened, they were all content to listen to him, and sorry to break up at last. It had been like "old times" — the old times which were only a few days back, after all.

Saturday morning was spent much as usual. Collins drove off before daylight to a brook a dozen miles distant. Ellerton had arranged to accompany him, but had been obliged to give it up.

Mrs. Floyd posed again, though for a short time only, as the picture was making capital progress, and Floyd had almost reached the point where he could dispense with the services of his model. Sonderby came to the cottage for a while, shortly before dinner, and lounged on the grass, chatting leisurely with Tryphena, as if to take Collins's place. Just as the hotel dinner-bell was jangling, Collins returned, his six-pound basket more than half full of trout, small dark ones with yellow bellies, caught in the shadowy streamlets of a great alder swamp. At table he narrated his adventures, and finished by declaring that he had planned a fishing excursion for all four of them on the Tuesday following. That day, he explained, was the 31st of July, and the last available opportunity for fishing, for the game law prohibited the taking of trout after the first of August. So decidedly did the manufacturer seem to have set his heart upon the fishing party, that they all agreed to go, and spent most of the dinner hour in discussing the details of the project. When they came out upon the piazza, the other guests were mostly assembled at the western end, to watch a game of tennis upon the court which the elated Evans had recently been at the expense of constructing there. They looked on for a while, but finally betook themselves to the other end of the piazza, where they sat, aimlessly conversing, until the stage from the Center jolted up against the Broughton House steps.

Floyd and Sonderby looked at their watches, surprised that it was so late; and the artist, mumbling something about his picture, got up and stretched himself.

"Going to work any more?" asked Collins, compassionately.

Floyd nodded, squinting at him familiarly.

"Well, go ahead," Collins remarked. "I did my work this morning;" and he examined the mosquito and midge bites on his wrists, and thought, in satisfied retrospection, of the mud and the tangle of roots and branches in the swamp where he had crouched all that forenoon. Floyd lounged off, whistling the air of a German student song, his hands in his pockets, his shoulders stooping.

"Oh, say!" he cried, turning back at the corner of the piazza, where the new sign cast a strip of shadow over his face as he spoke, "Will you get my mail, Collins, if there is any?"

"Hm — humph," grunted Collins, affirmatively, being at that instant engaged in lighting a cigar.

Floyd disappeared, and before long Tryphena found the sun too hot upon the piazza and went over to the cottage, taking with her a magazine from the reading-room of the hotel. The two men sat for a quarter of an hour longer, exchanging an occasional remark, and then Collins said that he guessed he would go up to the office for his mail. Sonderby volunteered to accompany him; but when they were opposite Parkinson's, Collins noticed Meyer sitting disconsolately in front of his shop, and decided thereupon that he would have his hair cut.

"I'll get your mail," said Sonderby, a little at a loss what to do with himself.

"All right. Oh, if there's anything for Floyd, bring it along, will you?"

But when Sonderby reached the post-office, he found a letter for himself, and being a man with the slenderest correspondence, was surprised into forgetting his errand for Collins. He started back, reading his letter, which was from the A. S. & F. Company, courteously reminding him that the offered position could not be held for him much longer and requesting a reply at his earliest convenience. Sonderby read it through, and folded it, moodily. Of course the A. S. & F. people were right; he had not been business-like with them. Just then he remembered that he was to get Collins's mail, and he retraced his steps to the office. The postmistress gave him a whole handful of letters for the manufacturer, and then Sonderby asked if there was anything for Mr. Floyd.

"William J. Floyd," she repeated automatically, handing out a long envelope.

Sonderby glanced at it, almost unintentionally, as he turned away from the window. It was stamped in New York the day before, and on the upper left-hand corner was printed: *Hamburg Line.* Honest John Sonderby wondered for an instant why Floyd should have any correspondence with the steamship company, but his mind soon went back to his own letter. It was evident that a final answer could not be long delayed.

As the school-teacher crossed the road to the barber's shop, he was conscious of the old awkward balance, not perceptibly adjusted, so far as he could see, by his dogged work of the last ten days: upon the one hand, a life work for which he was fitted, upon the other — well, he could not exactly phrase to himself what was upon the other, but there was pity there, and sentiment and half-mastered passion, a chivalrous longing to be of help, as well as a sluggishness of will, and the treacherous force of the solitary, purposeless life he had led for three years — all these and more were heaped confusedly there, and he knew that in some fashion they must be swept away before he could leave Broughton. When he entered Meyer's, he found Collins enveloped up to his chin in the barber's apron, and Meyer indulging in one of his usual panegyrics upon "Mr. Floyt."

"Oh, he will not stay in America," the barber was saying. "See you, it is too *bourgeois*. He must go again to Germany, to the home of art." Meyer stopped as he saw Sonderby standing in the doorway.

"Here are a lot of letters for you," said Sonderby, tossing them into Collins's lap. "And there is one for Floyd," he added.

Collins extricated one hand from beneath the apron, and picked up the last one dropped. One glance at the envelope and he let it fall again, face downward. Then he turned over his own mail indifferently; but as he sat — his chin buried in the apron while Meyer was trimming the back of his neck — he rolled up his black eyes till they rested upon Sonderby with that quiet, searching scrutiny to which he had subjected the schoolteacher ever since he had seen the latter go over to the cottage, one rainy Sunday morning, holding an umbrella over Mrs. Floyd. But Sonderby did not notice the look, and sat down to wait for Collins, taking up the pink-tinted *Police Gazette* from the barber's table only to toss it away again in disgust. When the manufacturer was ready, the men walked slowly back toward the hotel; and when Collins turned in at the cottage, Sonderby followed him, unasked. They found Floyd in the back yard, engaged in touching up with sienna brown the shutters of his Venetian palace.

"Hullo!" he said, as they dropped beside him on the grass, but he did not stop work. They watched him for a while, in some admiration of the skill with which he was manipulating his tiniest brushes. Collins made no reference to the mail;

and Sonderby, thinking he had forgotten Floyd's letter, finally observed:

"There was a letter for you, Floyd."

The artist looked up quickly.

"Oh, yes," said Collins, taking it out of his pocket, with a slight air of embarrassment, and a peculiar smile, "Sure enough."

Floyd reached out his hand for it. He scowled involuntarily as he recognized the steamship company's stamp upon the corner, then remarked, with a feigned indifference — assumed for Sonderby's sake, for he suspected that the teacher might have noticed the envelope:

"Another advertisement. Those steamers have kept sending their sailing lists to me, ever since I went over on their line."

Nevertheless, Floyd carefully put the advertisement into his inside pocket, and Collins changed the subject abruptly.

XII.

That evening after supper Bill Trumbull began again, and with more hope than usual, to throw out hints about the melodeon. Collins indeed would have needed little urging, any of the time, and seeing that the others were lingering about the office just as they had done the evening before, he proposed that they honor Bill with some music. Accordingly the quartette gathered around the melodeon in the parlor, and Collins struck up "Old Black Joe," which was one of the first pieces they had ever attempted, and which by dint of practice they had succeeded in mastering. "Way down upon the Suwanee River" followed, and then came "In the Sweet By and By," which opened the way naturally for two or three specimens of sacred melody, in which Bill Trumbull, sitting in the office, took a melancholy comfort.

Little by little a group of the Broughton House guests gathered at the parlor door, and began to applaud at the end of each secular tune, and to nod the head, with commendatory sighs, at the close of the religious ones.

Collins rather enjoyed it, but the others were embarrassed. It was so different from the last of

June and the first of July, when they had had the parlor all to themselves, and could try as many musical experiments as they liked! As the crowd assembled at the piazza door, and finally even in the hall-way, shutting out Bill from view entirely, the singing grew more and more unsteady. At last Collins reached his favorite duet, and as he smoothed out the sheet of music upon the rack, Floyd whispered to Sonderby, "It's about time for us to get out of this, isn't it?"

Sonderby nodded assent, and his fancy catching at a double meaning in the artist's words, he was conscious of a humorous sort of transient liking for the fellow. Floyd, too, knew when he was superfluous! Two weeks before, he, John Sonderby, had listened to this duet with a vague pain and with strange, disordered thoughts; very well, perhaps the husband, too, read something into those battered concert-room lines! The two men, at any rate, sat down together in the corner.

> Kiss me to-day,
> Wait not the morrow;
> Waiting is sorrow,
> Love me to-day!

Collins was not nervous, certainly. He rolled out the magnificent bass notes, lifting his shoulders the while, and throwing back his head so that he gazed into Tryphena's face as he sang. Sonderby had never seen Collins look like that before; he took a sudden dislike to the thick lips, and to the eager, gleaming eyes, and to the whole dark, upturned, desirous face.

Tremblingly began the soprano:

> Love me to-morrow,
> Like me to-day;
> Kisses betray;
> Kiss me to-morrow!

And in John Sonderby, who was forgetful of himself now, instead of absorbed in himself, as he had been a fortnight before, there rose something which made his fist clench and the muscles stiffen along his arm, as the bass broke in with the sudden, passionate

> Kiss me to-day —

Ah! but Collins's touch on the keys was careless; he struck a false note, and there was such a discord that he stopped, involuntarily, an instant, leaving the soprano's frightened

> Kiss me to-morrow

to flutter alone, and as he impatiently struck the right key, she broke down altogether, and turned impulsively away.

The guests at the doors applauded encouragingly, and there were murmurs of "Go on"; but Mrs. Floyd shook her head and moved helplessly toward her husband.

"Let's go back," she whispered. The men rose; and Sonderby shouldered his way, somewhat impolitely, through the people in the hall, followed by Mrs. Floyd and the reluctant Collins.

"Wal," said Bill Trumbull, when they regained the office, "that was nice. Reel nice. Kind o' soothin'. Much obliged to ye. Sit down."

They sat down for a while, but the talk was rather constrained, and they broke up early.

Sunday morning was bright and hot. The mist rose slowly from the hills, like smoke, and the air was windless. The dog-days had begun. In the dining-room of the Broughton House, at breakfast-time, it was already close, and the flies settled unpleasantly upon the tables. The women guests wore their thinnest morning gowns when they came in to breakfast, and their husbands looked uncomfortable and sticky in the starched Sunday linen for which they had discarded their secular flannels and cheviots. In the costumes of the four persons at the head of the first table, however, there was not much that was peculiar to the day. Mrs. Floyd wore the black alpaca dress which she usually had on at breakfast, and the artist was arrayed in his negligently buttoned flannel shirt. Sonderby was the only one of the four who clung to the New England tradition of dressing up on Sunday morning, though the school-teacher's black cut-away, worn shiny long ago, was a somewhat ineffective tribute to the venerable custom. Collins noticed it, however, and took into his head the freak of going to church.

A month or so before he had without much difficulty persuaded the others to go with him, but to-day the artist positively refused, and Collins did not appear to urge him. Mrs. Floyd hesitated a long time, but finally agreed to go, and Sonderby thereupon decided to accompany the party. They started from the cottage when church-time came, leaving Floyd at work upon his picture. As they turned into Main Street, Bill Trumbull joined them. Attired in a neatly brushed blue suit, with a new straw hat bound with a black ribbon, Bill looked exceedingly respectable. He surveyed the trio with paternal interest.

"Goin' to church, be ye? That's right! Come and sit long o' me, won't ye? Mirandy's baby's got a leetle tetch of cholery morbis, and she's goin' to stay to home."

Collins accepted for the party the proffered invitation; and they all walked along together, Collins holding Tryphena's black parasol over her head, somewhat to her embarrassment, — for such a courtesy was unusual in Broughton, and would be noticed by every woman on the street, — while the school-teacher and Trumbull brought up the rear. Bill had not been much of a church-goer during his active days of proprietorship of the hotel, having always considered that the entertainment of his guests was his first duty; but since the death of Mrs. Trumbull he had been pretty regular in his attendance, and was regarded as being in a hopeful state of mind. He ushered his friends with commendable dignity into the Trumbull pew, which, though it had never during the memory of Samuel Parkinson, parish treasurer, paid a penny of rent, was always reserved, at the spring allotment of pews, for the genial hotel proprietor.

The faded green cushion was not uncomfortable, and the back, albeit a trifle too perpendicular, might easily have been worse. One of the big, tall side windows of the church was close to the end of the pew, and a breeze almost always found its way in; for the high white church on the knoll was in an airy place, from whatever quarter the wind might happen to be blowing. In short, Collins had not been wrong in declaring at the breakfast table that the Orthodox church was the coolest spot in town on a hot day.

Arthur Ellerton preached that morning an amiable, sensible, exhortatory discourse on the subject of "Family Religion." Bill Trumbull listened attentively, his blue eyes set encouragingly upon the young pastor, and growing moist, once or twice, at some allusion. John Sonderby, sitting next Trumbull, did not give any particular observance to what was said. His thoughts were far afield. When the minister announced the meeting of the Young People's Society of Christian Endeavor, and the topic, Sonderby wondered if Ruth Ellerton would be there, and what she could say upon it; and then he began to think over what she had said on that rainy Sunday evening in the lecture-room, and how he had walked home with her and listened to her grave, hesitating, anxious words to himself as they stood on the parsonage steps. But that was the nearest he came to any line of reflection connected with the church service.

Collins contemplated the bare white-painted interior, and the farmer and village people who nearly filled the pews, with a pleasurable sort of criticism. He had spent enough weeks in Broughton, during half a dozen years, to become fairly familiar with its types, and to get some amusement out of them. He listened good-naturedly to the efforts of the choir, and half wished he were one of them. Ellerton, standing up there in the high mahogany pulpit, with its quaint pillars and queer twisting stairs, was rather an interesting figure to Collins, and he thought of the parson's zeal for fishing and for other matters of this world, and at the same time was convinced that Ellerton, in the course of the thirty-minute sermon, was saying a good many practical things, which might very likely be true.

Tryphena looked out of the window more or less, not finding that the discourse upon "Family Religion" had any special helpfulness in its application to the Floyd family. She knew Aunt Tryphena would have been pleased by all that

Ellerton said, and then she looked across the road to the old burying-ground, with its thick rows of blackening, lichen-grown slabs, and tried to pick out Aunt Tryphena's grave.

Two or three pews behind Trumbull sat Ruth Ellerton, watching Sonderby and his companions with a kind of trouble in her heart. As the weeks had slipped away, her conviction had increased that this summer was forcing upon the schoolteacher a spiritual crisis, and that the influences surrounding him, in his life at the hotel, were not favorable. But she really knew little about him: he had not even called, after his invitation to tea at the parsonage. Neither had the Floyds returned the Ellertons' call, and with Ruth Ellerton's pity for the slender young woman before her, looking out of the window with idle eyes, there was mingled a quite feminine consolation in the fact that at any rate she had fulfilled her own social duty toward the artist's wife. Still, she wondered, as before, what sort of woman Mrs. Floyd was, and why Mr. Sonderby was so attracted by her, and what the manufacturer, Mr. Collins, found to interest him in these people whose pursuits were so unlike his own. Mrs. Ellerton saw, too, that Bill Trumbull was the only one of the four who was giving much regard to Arthur's sermon, and she felt vexed that her husband had happened to choose this special topic for that Sunday. If he had only been preaching about something else — something that might touch those indifferent people in that Trumbull pew! If she could only signal to Arthur in some way, and get him to make an excursus, or an application, or something or other that would catch the attention of these people and hold them and win them thereby to the Truth! And the time was going so fast! Paul's phrase about the "foolishness of preaching" Mrs. Ellerton had never been able to apply, least of all to the sermons of her husband.

When the benediction was pronounced, and the audience worked its way toward the front doors, Mrs. Ellerton, who remained to teach her Sunday-school class, stood at the end of her pew as the Broughton House people passed out. Collins bowed, and Sonderby nodded, with a friendly recognition in his face; but Mrs. Floyd happened to be looking in the other direction.

On the way back to the cottage, Bill took it upon himself to entertain the company, albeit in a decorously subdued fashion, by his opinion of the sermon, of the minister, and of ministers in general. The sermon he declared to be "Scripteral," and the minister a "likely one," a "dreadful smart man," — the more so when contrasted with the other clergymen of the conference, whom Bill described as "runnin' emptins," and "good enough for a lowery day," to the mystification of Collins and the amusement of the others.

The dinner hour was not very sociable. Perhaps

it was the hot weather. At any rate, the mutual intimacy of the quartette, which had seemed to thrive again since the runaway, appeared now to be diminishing once more. Floyd talked mostly with Collins. Mrs. Floyd and Sonderby found nothing to converse about which they had not already discussed two or three times. Yet Sonderby was never bored with her, nor annoyed into that sulky reticence whither he often withdrew when talking with persons who did not appeal to him; his principal feeling in these times of unprofitable intercourse with Mrs. Floyd was one of disappointment, because he knew how much they might say to each other — in the right time and place.

It was with this sentiment of disappointment, pathetic in its realization of the true things and the deep things which were crowded out by conventionality, by circumstances — by their set habit of trite talk, too, it must be said — that John Sonderby left Tryphena after dinner and went to his room. He spent there a restless, suspicious two hours. Once or twice he sat down at his desk and took a sheet of paper, in the pretence of writing to the A. S. & F. Company, but he knew that he was only creating for himself a deliberate illusion. He could not write them definitely. It was the old story. Fourteen days had slipped away since he had had any serious talk with her, since anything but commonplaces had passed between them.

True enough, she had laid her hand on his arm once, not so swiftly and shyly but that he had noticed it, and would almost have given the right arm itself to know just what she meant by it. Yet he did not know. The old story, with the same characters, the same plot, and the end not yet. Till something was cleared out of the way, something settled in himself,—and he knew well enough that this something, whatever it was, had to do with Tryphena Floyd,—he could not go to Boston. The fourteen days, with their alternation of severe mental application and benumbing manual labor, had, at least, made him less restless, forced him to think less of himself; but now in the leisure of Sunday, he seemed to have gained nothing by it all.

A noise of wheels outside, in the direction of the cottage, and Collins's deep, vibrant laugh made him go to the window and open the shutters, which had been tightly closed because of the heat. The hotel buggy stood in the driveway between the cottage and the Broughton House, and in it were Collins and Mrs. Floyd. Floyd stood by the horse's head.

Collins held the reins in his right hand and was leaning across her to tuck the duster around her knees. She was saying something to him, and Sonderby noticed, with a curious particularity of attention, that she wore a bonnet he had not seen before, and that her eyes were animated and her cheeks colored as she looked down at Collins, stooping across her, while she drew on a pair of dark brown lisle-thread gloves. Collins chirped to the horse, and off they went toward the east part of the town. Sonderby closed the shutter viciously and began to pace up and down the room again, with his hands in his pockets. He was more hurt by what he had seen than he would have owned to himself. He had no earthly objections to Mrs. Floyd's going driving with Bruce D. Collins if she wanted to; she probably knew Collins as well as he, John Sonderby, did. He was not over-scrupulous about social conventionalities, but he had, nevertheless, a sort of sentiment which protested against her going off with Collins in this way on Sunday afternoon.

Sunday driving was regarded by Broughton people as sacrilegious, fit only for persons who belonged in the Center, and for summer boarders, who brought with them to the country their Sabbathless ways. Now Mrs. Floyd knew the village opinion perfectly well, for it was the atmosphere in which she had grown up to womanhood. Her open disregard of it struck the school-teacher unpleasantly; it betrayed too much indifference to the standards of right and wrong that prevailed in the community, and Sonderby, though independent enough himself in such matters, shared the common masculine conviction that nice women should do just as other nice women do. He knew that Mrs. Floyd was in some sort of trouble, nay, a very definite kind of trouble, and he did not care to think of her driving off gaily on a Sabbath afternoon with a thorough worldling like Collins. It made her seem as much of a worldling as Collins himself.

Sonderby stopped suddenly in his walk, after a variety of reflections of this character, and said to himself, "Look here, my son, is the fact that she has gone driving with another man really what ails you?" He faced the question honestly, but for the life of him he could not answer; and then came a quick revulsion of feeling against all this introspection, and he felt smothered for some free air. What did he know about himself, about her, about anything?

He put on his walking-shoes and an old cap, and hurried out into the diffused glare of the dog-day sunshine. Unscrupulous about his own defiance of Broughton customs, he tramped off down the street at a racing pace, in front of the trim white houses where the Sabbath-keeping villagers sat on their front piazzas, with religious newspapers in their hands, discontented children around their feet, and upon their lips questions and guesses as to the passing teams. He left the academy on the right, and climbing one long hill after another, got rapidly out of sight of the village. The road was white with fine dust; the purple milkweed blossoms were ashy gray with it; it was thick upon the plantain leaves that pushed themselves out upon the side of the roadway. No birds sang; only the swallows circled low over the meadows, or twittered under the barnyard eaves of the deserted farmhouses, all along the desolate road. Hotter and hotter glared the sun, as it fell lower in the hazy west. But John Sonderby cared for neither the dust, nor the swallows, nor the sun. He threw himself desperately into physical exertion, letting his mind go out entirely — like a candle. He was conscious only of his rapid breathing, and of the play of his muscles. Nevertheless, at five o'clock, when he was seven or eight miles from Broughton, he felt thirsty and a trifle faint, and stopped at a farmhouse for a glass of milk. It was one of his own pupils — an awkward-looking boy — who came to the kitchen door; and then Sonderby remembered that the fellow lived out that way. He asked for some milk, and the boy summoned a bustling mother, who made the school-teacher come in; and although in some surprise at Sonderby's Sunday walk, she kept her curiosity to herself. The milk tasted good to him; there was a likable, homely flavor, too, to the conversation of these farming folks, to whom " the street " represented a world of civilization and culture to which they did not at all aspire, except in so far as they prized the academy. In chatting a half-hour with them, Sonderby forgot all about the Broughton House; and they were so evidently glad to see him, and the farmhouse seemed so hospitable and quiet, that he accepted their invitation to take supper. It was thick dusk when he started toward the village at last, and in trying to make a short cut through a wood-road he lost his landmarks, and was forced into a detour of two or three miles. When he finally got into the right road again, it was so dark that he could scarcely see the floury dust through which his feet were ploughing. By and by the stars became more radiant, though the night was thick and hot, like the day, and full of mist. At half-past nine he saw the lights of the village, and by a quarter of ten he was under the looming shadow of the academy, almost at home.

He sat down on the academy steps a moment to rest, leaning his back against one of the big hollow Doric pillars, with both hands clasped around his knee. The fluting of the pillar pressed sharply against his head, and he pushed his cap back till it served as a cushion. Then he sat motionless. The old academy steps! How many times he had come out upon this southeast corner of them, cracked school-bell in hand, to summon the boys and girls from their rough and silly games upon the playground! How many times had he shovelled them off, winter mornings, when they were drifted more than a foot deep with snow; and how cold it had been inside, when he had unlocked the door and kindled a fire in the stove, — a huge, bulging-sided, hippopotamus-looking affair, — and then had swept the room before he went back to his boarding-house for breakfast! Three winters! Three years! It was a long time; a solitary, and in some sense unfruitful period, yet not unlaborious. Perhaps, Sonderby thought to himself, he was after all as well fitted for school-teaching as for anything else. Not that he cared anything about it, really, except that it gave him a living, and kept him fairly busy; but what more could one expect? He might, too, have made more of his opportunities. There, for instance, was the young fellow at whose house he had taken supper that night; why could he not have gone there long before and learned to know the boy better and found out what was wisest for him to work at in the academy? There was the stoop-shouldered girl with whom he had walked to the Y. P. S. C. E. meeting; for three years she had been under him, and he had hardly ever spoken to her except in recitation time; it would have been so easy to give her a little pleasure. There was — Hark!

Down on the Center road, in the very outskirts of the village, some one was singing. Hark! Above the chirp of the crickets and the grating of the tree-toads, there came a clear, rich voice:

> And now whate'er befalls me.
> I go where honor calls me;
> Farewell, farewell,
> My own true love, farewell.

"It's Collins," Sonderby muttered, and listened again, while the academy and all connected thoughts were carried out of his mind by the rush of associations which that distant voice brought with it.

> Farewell, farewell,
> My own true love, farewell.

There was silence once more, except for the crickets. Three or four minutes passed. Then, startlingly near, this time, so quiet was the night, came the rollicking bass:

> Good night, ladies,
> Good night, ladies — good night, ladies,
> We're going to leave you now.
> Merrily we roll along, roll along, roll along,
> Merrily we roll along,
> O'er the dark blue sea.

Sonderby turned, and looked around from behind the pillar. The singer was still invisible, though only a hundred yards away, on the other side of the academy, apparently in front of one of the first houses on the Center road.

> Sweet dreams, ladies,
> Sweet dreams, ladies,
> Sweet dreams, ladies,
> We're going to leave you now.

There was no mistaking the voice. Sonderby thought of a foggy night in June, before the Floyds came, when Collins had made him go out for a walk on the North Broughton road, and had stopped at every farmhouse and insisted on singing a serenade. Collins had been in peculiarly high spirits that night, and the school-teacher had since suspected that he had been drinking a little. Sonderby wondered who was with the manufacturer now.

Farewell, ladies,
Farewell, ladies,
Farewell, ladies,
We're going to leave you now.

"Oh, shut up, Collins! Come along!" interrupted a hoarse voice. The school-teacher sat up straight and pulled his cap forward. Of course it was Floyd, Floyd and his friend Collins; one might have guessed it. The grumbling murmur of their voices drew nearer and nearer, up the fork of the road; they were not keeping step, and Sonderby seemed to hear the shuffle of many feet in the dust. In a moment more they were abreast of the academy, and Sonderby heard them halt, though he could scarcely make out their figures.

"Say, les' sit down," Floyd said. "It's so damned hot! Les' sit down."

"All right," chimed in Collins's voice, with jocund emphasis. "Mr. William J. Floyd, I will sit down to your health. 'How can I bear to leave thee?'" And clapping the artist on the shoulder, Collins dropped heavily on to the academy steps beside him, at the opposite end from

Sonderby, who sat motionless behind his pillar, feeling something like a thief.

"Say, don't sing any more," growled Floyd. "You'll wake up the whole town."

"What do you care for the town?" demanded Collins. "You profane old euchre-player! Much you care for the town of Broughton."

Floyd made no reply. He was trying to recall, as well as his somewhat fuddled brain would allow, just what he had said to Collins, confidentially, over that last glass of punch. There was some dispute about a jack of hearts, and they had quarrelled and stopped playing, and made up, and in the succeeding burst of friendship he had told Collins something about Munich, or Venice, or Watson, or Phenie, or something, — so much he could remember. Then it had grown so hot in Collins's room, and the lamp was so bright, — as bright as two, — and Collins was a good fellow, a damned reliable fellow, and they had come out to walk together, and Collins had been singing at every house on the Center road: Collins must have had too much punch.

"Collins," Floyd remarked, after this mental excursion, "you're a good fellow. You're a good friend of mine. Say, ain't you?" Floyd was struggling against an unusual thickness of speech.

Collins grunted affirmatively and waited.

"I'd like to 'splain something to you, Collins," Floyd continued, with gravity. "I don't want to have you get a wrong impression of me — of any such friend of yours, as you are a friend to me. Perhaps you misunderstood what I said about — that matter, you know. Now I want you to understand that I'm a gentleman; a gentleman and an artist. Did I say anything about going away?"

"Going away?" repeated Collins, in a feigned tone that struck Sonderby instantly as insincere, and made him think that the manufacturer was not so drunk as he pretended to be. "Going away?" Collins seemed to be searching in the dim recesses of his memory.

"Yes," said Floyd, anxiously. "Don't you know? To Munich — pretty soon."

"Oh!" Collins evidently recalled something of the sort.

"Say! I don't want to have you misunderstand me. It's going to be a square deal, you know — nothing underhanded about it. I want to have you understand that I'm a gentleman, Mr. Collins, Mr. Bruce D. Collins. If I am obliged to go to Munich — temp'rarily — temp'rarily — I shall support my wife — while I am over on the other side — a — a — temp'rarily, —"

"Of course," broke in Collins, soothingly.

"Oh, well, that's all right," Floyd went on, relieved by Collins's answer. "I didn't want to have you think there was to be any funny business — you know — leaving Phenie here — ah — 'bandoning her to th' elements, you know. I'm a gentleman, Mr. Collins; you're a gentleman. Say! you know my wife, don't you?"

"Oh, yes," assented Collins.

"That's all right, then. I wouldn't say this except to a friend — a friend of my family, Mr. Collins. You don't think it's anything d'rogatory, do you, for me to engage a single passage on the Ham — Ham —"

"Hammonia?" put in Collins.

"On the Hammonia. My wife can take care of herself, Mr. Collins, right here in Broughton. She's a property-holder. She's independent. But I'm not independent in 'Merica, Collins; it's a free country, but I'm not independent. Say! you don't think there would be anything d'rogatory, do you?"

"Derogatory? Hell, no!" The explosive emphasis of Collins's voice seemed to clear up the moral difficulty that bothered poor Floyd.

"Well, that's all right, then. This is between us, Mr. Collins, you being a friend of mine — 'n a friend of my family. Say! it's hot, ain't it? What time is it?"

Collins fumbled in his pocket, and then a parlor match spurted. Sonderby shrank close behind his pillar.

"Not much after ten," replied the manufacturer, consulting his watch. "It isn't late." And he began to whistle the air of "We won't go home till morning."

"No, les' go home now." A state of stupor was succeeding the mental effort to which the artist had subjected himself. He got up, rather noisily, and endeavored to pull Collins after him; but the manufacturer kept his seat, and Floyd fell over on to him, amid some laughter. Then this companionable pair rose simultaneously and started off with locked arms, Collins singing, but almost under breath, the chorus of "Good night, Ladies."

> Merrily we roll along, roll along, roll along,
> Merrily we roll along, o'er the dark blue sea.

"'The dark blue sea,'" repeated Floyd, in a hoarse murmur. "What do you know about the dark blue sea? Next week, Mr. Collins, Mr. Bruce D. Collins, next week, 'the dark'— 'O'er the dark '—"

And failing to complete his sentence, and failing equally to hit the proper key of the chorus, Floyd subsided into silence, as the two men went on up the road, which turned under the elm arches here, as if entering a huge black cavern.

John Sonderby leaped to his feet, and stood listening till the footsteps grew faint, and he could hear nothing but the pounding of his own heart. Then he dashed his fist into the palm of his other hand, with a smothered cry. How stupid he had been! Floyd not only did not love her, but he was going to leave her, to leave her there in Broughton alone. And he had blabbed his plan over a drunken game of euchre. The hound!

The blood rushed into Sonderby's temples till he was dizzy, and in the blackness of the misty night around him, he saw again the slim, white, rigid arms, and heard again the low, despairing words — words not of a dream, but of a real woman toward whom his heart had opened and who had sat all that summer by his side — "You cannot help me — no one can help me."

Not help her? Not be with her? Not give himself over to her? He sank back on the academy steps again, a strange elation in his heart. . . .

The next morning Arthur Ellerton, who had been recently chosen a member of the Broughton school committee, called upon Sonderby to learn whether he would continue at the academy for another year.

"I declare, that Sonderby is a queer fellow," the minister said to his wife, on his return.

Ruth Ellerton was in the sitting-room, wearing a big calico apron, and shelling peas for dinner. She put up her hand for her husband to kiss as he came in.

"I don't know what to make of him," he continued, dropping Mrs. Ellerton's hand, although very deliberately. "He was up in his room in the hotel, with his door locked, and if I hadn't known he was a perfectly straight fellow, I should have said he had been on a debauch. Appeared not to have slept; wouldn't look me in the face."

"Oh, Arthur!" remonstrated Mrs. Ellerton, a troubled look coming over her beautiful gray eyes.

"But he's going to stay."

"Is he?" she cried. "I am so glad! You're sure he isn't going to Boston?"

"He told me he had just written declining some offer there. I presume it was the one we heard about. I felt a trifle awkward about the possible reduction of the salary, though," added Ellerton, taking off his coat and sitting down to help shell the peas; "but I had to tell him that the committee thought it doubtful whether the same salary could be paid another winter. It seems that they all want to have him stay, even if he has shortened the devotional exercises and doesn't call upon the parents. They say that the scholars will do anything for the fellow. Still, nine hundred dollars is a good deal for us to raise, and I told him so."

"What did he say?"

"That was one of the queer things about it, for he must be poor; of course he's poor. He looked at me — it was almost the only time when he did look square at me — and said it wasn't a matter of salary with him."

"Oh, he is such a splendid fellow, Arthur!" she exclaimed, her eyes growing soft with enthusiasm. "He could do so much good here! We must ask him again to tea."

XIII.

Tuesday, the thirty-first of July, was the day decided on for that fishing-party upon which Collins had set his heart. All the afternoon before he had spent in the back yard of the cottage, with his rods and tackle spread around him on the grass, engaged in preparing a complete outfit for the other members of the quartette. Mrs. Floyd, as well as the men, had been made to promise to try her hand at throwing a fly, and Collins had planned to finish their sport at the meadows of Calvin Johnson's farm, where they could probably get permission to fish, as it was the last day upon which the game laws allowed the taking of trout. In this open ground Mrs. Floyd could easily make her maiden effort. She seemed a good deal interested in the prospective adventure, and plied Collins with many a droll, oddly phrased question as he fitted up for her use an old rod — so light that even her slender hand scarcely felt its weight — and repaired its tiny nickel reel, till it was in working order.

While the manufacturer and Tryphena were chatting about the fishing-tackle, and she was helping him now and then, by holding a thread tight while he knotted it, or handing him his pot of glue, Mr. Floyd sat diligently upon his painting-stool, a yard or two away, and worked on at his Venetian girl. A few lucky hours more and the picture would be finished, except for the varnishing and the last touches. Floyd had fished with Collins several times that summer, and was fond enough of the sport to listen to all the talk between Tryphena and the manufacturer, and occasionally to put in a word of his own.

John Sonderby was the only one of the four who betrayed no particular interest in trout and the expiration of the time allowed by the game laws. Nevertheless, he loitered all that Monday afternoon at the cottage, stretched out in the shade of the trellis, and resting on his elbow, sunk deep in the luxuriant grass. His old cap was pulled low down upon his forehead, to keep the glare out of his eyes. The school-teacher seemed to have plenty of time at his disposal and made no mention of any work at the laboratory. Once when Collins looked around for something with which to hammer a bit of wire straight, Sonderby pulled the big brass key of the academy out of his pocket and tossed it toward the manufacturer, as if the key were worth as much for a hammer as for anything else. None of them had seen anything of Sonderby during the morning, except for a moment, when he ran down, disorderly dressed, from his room at the hotel, to give to the stage-driver a letter for Boston, to be dropped into the mail-car at the Center. But if the school-teacher's morning had been somewhat unsociable, like so many of his mornings latterly, he evidently tried to make amends for it in the course of the afternoon. Not a word said by any of the three escaped him; from under the visor of his cap his eyes watched every motion, and he spoke, when at all, with a promptness and decision which were in curious contrast with the indolence of his attitude. When the artist laid down his brushes about half-past four, and started off round the corner of the cottage, Sonderby apparently disconcerted him a little by asking if he was not going to the post-office, and by volunteering to keep him company; whereat Floyd explained that he was only going to Meyer's. But when Sonderby said that he was going to the office anyway, and would bring back Floyd's mail, Floyd decided that he might as well go himself, after all. It was rather a clever piece of acting, on both sides, and Collins, who chose to be secretly amused at Floyd's changes of mind, understood but one-half the comedy. For John Sonderby, in his blunt, thorough way, was "shadowing" the artist.

The two men came back without any mail except Collins's *Republican*, and Sonderby, resuming his former position, tore open the wrapper, and read slowly to Collins the scores of the Saturday ball games, printed in an abridged form in the Monday issue. Sunday papers had not yet penetrated so far as Broughton. Floyd went on with his work rather peevishly. He suspected that Collins would laugh at him that night, if they two slipped off by themselves, about his anxiety for securing his own mail, and he wished that he had not told Collins so much about his plans, though he reflected, with some dissatisfaction, that he had only a vague remembrance of the extent to which he had confided in the manufacturer.

But after supper, when Floyd invited Collins to take a stroll, Sonderby impolitely proposed to accompany them. The stroll was not a long one. Collins smoked dispassionately, Floyd discontentedly, Sonderby not at all; but to make up for it the latter carried on most of the conversation. For the first time in his life, he was measuring himself against another man — perhaps against two men — in cunning, and there was an exhilaration in the struggle. When they reached the cottage, on the way back, Sonderby's quick eye detected Mrs. Floyd sitting alone, in the window by the lilac bushes. She had not lighted a lamp, though it was fast growing dark.

"Floyd," said Sonderby, "you'd better invite us in to play whist. There is too much of a crowd over at the hotel."

He turned up the path without waiting for an answer, and the other men followed him, Collins smiling slightly, all to himself. He had formed a theory of his own about Sonderby's attitude toward Tryphena, and was partly right, as a shrewd worldling is apt to be, and partly wrong, as a shrewd worldling is sure to be. Besides, he knew nothing about Sonderby's stopping to rest against the east pillar of the Doric-fronted academy, some twenty-four hours before.

Mrs. Floyd brought out from the parlor of the cottage — a room never used nowadays — a couple of high, queerly modelled brass lamps, and the quartette sat down to play. Sonderby held some remarkable hands, among them a trump-sequence from the eight-spot up, and he and Mrs. Floyd increased their lead, in the course of the evening, by more than thirty points.

The sky was cloudless on Tuesday morning, and the wind straight from the west. But there was no dew on the grass, and the air was singularly clear, as if it were late autumn. The summer boarders at the Broughton House were delighted by the change from the close, sticky atmosphere which the dog-days had brought, but Bill Trumbull remarked sagaciously that it was a "weather-breeder." In the course of the forenoon the wind fell, and the heat increased. Evans gave his four "regulars" an early dinner, and shortly after noon the carryall was waiting at the side door of the hotel.

Collins had planned to reach the head-waters of

the Johnson Brook in time to begin fishing by three o'clock, knowing that in the four or five hours of daylight that would remain, the fishing would probably grow steadily better, and that it would be lighter, after sunset, down in the open meadows by the farm, where the sport would close, than it could possibly be up in the woods. Just as Collins had helped Mrs. Floyd into the front seat of the carryall — which was to be drawn this time by a stout black farm-horse, instead of the bay mare — a buggy from the Center was pulled up at the corner of the hotel. The horse was lathery from his ten miles of uphill work, and three men got down from the narrow seat. Collins's face fell for an instant as he recognized them, but a sort of triumphant twinkle was in his eyes. It was a committee of the striking operatives in the Collins Mills. Advices from the treasurer of the company had warned Collins that the strikers' funds were nearly exhausted, and that a compromise could probably be effected. A telephone message that morning had informed him that he might be waited on by a committee, since he had sent word that he could not leave Broughton at present.

"We'll have to wait a minute," said Collins to his friends. and handing the lines to Mrs. Floyd he stepped forward to greet the newcomers.

"Hullo, George." he said, shaking hands with one of the men, who had grown up in the service of the company, and had played ball with Collins many a season in the old Collins Mills team.

"How d'ye do, Mr. Collins?" was the respectful answer. The manufacturer nodded to the other two, whom he did not know so well, and waited for them to announce their errand.

"You see, Mr. Collins," began George, the spokesman of the party, "we thought that seeing you couldn't come to the Mills just now, we'd come and see you."

"That's right," responded Collins. "Glad to see you."

"Can we have a bit of a talk?" inquired George, looking around uneasily at the various persons who were regarding the group.

"Well, George," was the deliberate reply, "I'm sorry to say that I have an engagement just now, but I shall be back by and by."

However strongly Collins might have set his desires on the fishing-party, he never believed in letting his pleasure interfere with business; but this time, confident that he could dictate his own terms to the strikers, he wanted to teach them what he considered a lesson. They had had him under the hammer long enough. They were ready to come to terms now; well, he would show them that he himself was not over-anxious.

"About what time, Mr. Collins?" asked George, taking a furtive glance at his shaky Waterbury watch.

"I really can't say," replied Collins, with an ugly kind of carelessness. There was for him a tyrannical delight in the situation. Relaxing a little, he turned to Evans, who was standing near by, on the piazza. "Evans, I wish you would give these gentlemen some dinner. Do as well by them as you can. Johnny, take that horse to the stable and rub him down." Collins was a generous fellow, when it did not derange his plans. Then, with a not unfriendly nod to George, and a "See you later," he turned to the carryall, where Floyd and Sonderby had by this time taken their places, and jumping in he took the reins from Mrs. Floyd, and the quartette started on their excursion.

The three operatives stood upon the end of the piazza and watched them drive by. From under the back seat protruded the ends of the fishing-rods. One of the committee jogged George with his elbow and pointed to them, muttering:

"Engagement! What d'ye think of that for an engagement? Fishin' engagement!"

George's only answer was a curse. Collins's action meant a day's delay; the funds of the Woollen Operatives' Union had been getting lower and lower, and were now quite gone; the strikers' pride had gone too, and they wanted bread for their wives and babies. The operatives were willing to come back at the old schedule of prices, rather than remain out longer. Collins's political economy was victorious: it had taken two to make a bargain; and now he had driven off on a pleasure party of his own, leaving the committee helplessly there on the Broughton House piazza, as if he meant to enforce a lesson that was already plain enough.

As Collins drove up Main Street past the parsonage, he checked the carryall suddenly as though an idea had occurred to him, but after a moment's hesitation he chirped to the horse again, and turned him into the road to East Part.

"What was the matter?" asked Mrs. Floyd.

"Oh, nothing," he answered, with a grim smile; "I had half a mind for a minute to give those fellows a letter of introduction to the parson's wife. She likes that sort of thing, — strikes — philanthropy — and drain-pipes — likes to fool with it. But I guess it wouldn't hardly do. Those fellows might destroy my reputation with the minister; eh, Floyd?"

Floyd made some humorous reply, and the strikers' committee was thenceforward forgotten.

The road to East Part, which, like the North Broughton road, came into the village street close by the meeting-house, had once been the most thickly settled highway in the town. For a mile or more after leaving the meeting-house the farms were still well kept up. But gradually the soil grew stonier, the hills increased in height, and unoccupied houses and half-tumbled-down barns began to come in sight on either hand. The East Part folks had had the Western fever back in 1830, and from almost every farm the youngest and best had emigrated to Ohio and settled on the Western Reserve. That section of Broughton township had never recovered from the loss, and in what had once been the village of East Part there were now but half a dozen houses, a churn factory, and a dilapidated Baptist church, never used. As the carryall rattled along past the decayed settlement, and a few old men and women stood in their woodhouse doors to peer at the conveyance, the forlornness of the place set Collins into some vigorous talk about the folly of going West, or even of drifting cityward, when there was plenty of good land all through New England to be had for a song. Sonderby joined in heartily. He admired, as always, Collins's practical common sense, and what the manufacturer was saying chimed completely with his own convictions. But the ten minutes of conversation about the decay of New England was the only serious talk there was upon the drive, and Mr. and Mrs. Floyd took no part even in that. By instinct all these four people, so singularly thrown together for a summer, chose desultory themes for a chance sentence or two, avoiding anything that might signify much of what was in their hearts. Each man had plans of his own, which he was bent on keeping secret from the others, although Floyd's plans were now for the most part clear, thanks to his fondness for Collins's society. Tryphena alone of the quartette had no plans, no future; she was merely waiting. For such a person, and indeed for any person, what better way to spend the time than in brisk driving along a country road? It satisfies the eye and gives some occupation to the mind; it may even, under the proper circumstances, do something for the heart.

The artist eye of Tryphena's husband caught every point of interest in the landscape, and, being fond of monologue, and having a sort of knack at describing natural objects, Floyd contributed decidedly to the entertainment of the party during their hot drive of more than two hours. It was he who explained how the male bobolinks changed their plumage before they wandered South; how the cicadas, piping shrilly in the elms in the pastures, had come up out of the ground as grubs, and had left their glistening empty skins, split neatly down the back, upon fences and tree-trunks; why the milkweed pods hung, as it were, upside down; why the line of hills they saw in every direction seemed higher than a photograph would show it, and lower than an artist must draw it; and why the sky was always of a paler blue at the zenith: common enough phenomena, all of them, but a source of enthusiasm to the tall, vagabond-like artist, and not without a certain attraction, when he described them, even to persons who had a thinly veiled contempt for the describer.

When the carryall had gotten well past East Part, a pair of marsh hawks started up from the meadow, and flew persistently along in advance of the quartette, skimming over the boggy ground and alighting until the carriage drew near again, when they would take wing once more. Floyd was in rapture over them, and indeed the graceful, powerful-winged creatures, so friendly, yet with such instantaneous possibilities of endless flight, fascinated the other occupants of the carryall as well, though none of them felt the peculiar analogy which made Floyd happy as he watched the birds. He could take wing, too, presently! The road became rougher and rougher, now climbing long, stony ascents, broken billow-like by rounding hillocks, and now diving steeply down into shady ravines, where mountain brooks were brawling, or singing quietly to themselves in the silence of the afternoon. There were long spaces, too, quite in the woodland, where the beech branches met over the roadway, which was so narrow here that one could sit in the carriage and pick the blackberries from the sloping bank above the road. Collins walked the horse very slowly through the woods, and none of the four were inclined to laugh so loudly as they had done out in the dusty sunshine. More than once they were all silent, and there was no noise except the crush of the wheels into the black, rich earth, and the squeaking of the whippletree. Then when they got out into the sudden glare of light, and Collins whipped up the horse, all four would begin suddenly to talk and laugh about nothing.

From the top of a hill, where they paused once to admire the view, caught in glimpses through the tangle of fox grapes overrunning wild cherry-trees, they could see the smoke that hung over the Center. So marvellously clear was the atmosphere that last day of July, that Floyd may have had reason to assert, as he did most stoutly, that he could see the telegraph-poles running over a bare hill towards the Center, though the hill was at least seven miles away. At any rate, the concentric circles of hilltops all round the horizon seemed to stretch out further than ever before, and to assume more subtle gradations of deep-toned blue, until it grew so pure and delicate, that Mrs. Floyd declared the color to be just that of Aunt Tryphena's old blue china, at which comparison the men were inclined to laugh, though Floyd supported his wife with more approval than he commonly exhibited. While they were looking off toward the northeast, Floyd called their attention to what seemed a thin, white mist coming over the blue. The mist thickened to a line of cloud, and almost while they watched, a row of pearl-white shining thunder-heads silently ranged themselves along the horizon. Collins wiped the perspiration from his forehead, and wished there were a little wind.

It was nearly three when they reached a long stretch of swampy ground, shut in on three sides by abrupt, closely wooded hills, where the Johnson brook had its source. The air was damp and heavy, here in the swamp, and the mosquitoes were vicious. The wheels sank deep into the rotten corduroy road, and Collins had difficulty in keeping the tired horse up to a trot. Finally there was a slight ascent, and the alders and hackmatack gave way to birches and hemlocks, while up through the woods at the right came the hollow sound of a cascade.

"All right!" cried Collins, triumphantly. "Here we are! Just on schedule time, too."

Jumping out, he took the horse by the head, and forced him into the bushes by the side of the road, so that the carryall might not block the way of any chance passing team. The others got out too, and while Collins was engaged in improvising a hitching-rein out of one of the lines, and fastening the steed securely to a birch sapling, he kept up a running explanation of the topography of the neighborhood. They were on a sort of watershed. The Johnson brook, gathering itself slowly from under the knotted alder roots, flowed sluggishly and aimlessly enough until it crossed the road, near where the carryall stood. Then it plunged downward through the woods, in many a long cascade, and after a couple of miles of headlong tumbling came out upon the broad Johnson meadows. Collins proposed that one of the three should fish down through the woods. He himself would try the swamp for an hour, and the third man, by walking up the road an eighth of a mile, would strike the upper branch of Bear brook, and could fish there for an hour or so likewise. Floyd chose the Bear brook, leaving to Sonderby the woods. Collins then went on to explain that after an hour, he and Floyd would meet again at the carryall, where Mrs. Floyd could in the meantime wait, and that they would then drive down around a spur of mountain and reach the Johnson farm. There they would leave the horse, and fish up through the meadows till they met Sonderby.

The plan, which Collins had evidently thought out with some care before leaving the Broughton House, seemed agreeable to everybody. Floyd drew on a pair of rubber boots, and slinging an old fish-basket of Bill Trumbull's over his shoulder, tramped off up the road toward Bear brook. Collins and Sonderby lifted the front seat out of the carryall, and taking it to a shady spot on the roadside, arranged a comfortable place for Mrs. Floyd. She declared that she was not at all afraid to wait alone, and would amuse herself by looking for blackberries, if she got tired of sitting still. Sonderby took off his coat and flung it over the back of the seat, saying that he would be more comfortable without it, and that it might make the iron back a trifle softer. Then the men bade her good by, and walking back a few rods over the road which they had come, separated: Collins, with a disgusted look at the crowds of mosquitoes around his head, pushing his way skilfully through the bushes on the edge of the swamp; and Sonderby striking straight down through the woods toward the cascades.

The mountain side was precipitous, and the school-teacher slipped every few steps upon the rotten leaves that slid away under his feet and left the stony ledges bare. But he was a fair woodsman, and by dint of swinging himself along from sapling to sapling, he descended rapidly, despite his awkward fishing-boots, and the borrowed rod, which he was forced to carry carefully. It was perfectly still in the woods, except for one or two scurrying chipmunks, and not a breath of air was stirring. Sonderby was hot and breathing hard when he reached the upper cascade, and paused a moment to watch the stream take its arching leap. Here the vibration of the shock of falling water made a sort of breeze that shook the leaves of the cushion-berry and the maidenhair ferns along the channelled rocks, and the air was deliciously cool from the spray. The school-teacher worked his way downward, over the wet rocks, till he stood at the bottom of the cascade, where the water struck unevenly against a quartzite shelf, and whirled on again into an oval pothole, four or five feet deep. Sonderby dabbled his fingers in it, disregarding the drenching spray that was falling around him, and was mightily tempted to strip off his clothes and take a plunge. But he gave up the idea as unworthy a fisherman in the first quarter of an hour of possible sport, and kept on down the shelving ledges where the moss grew so thick that the water swept over them almost silently, leaving shining bubbles in the moss along the under edge of each brink. The lower cascades were not so fine as the upper, being scarcely more than a succession of short plunges down a long, irregular incline, at the foot of which, Collins had said, the fishing began.

Sonderby got down to within a few yards of the bottom, and then reflected that he would better put his rod together, as at the bottom of the last cascade there would probably be trout that had run up stream as far as possible. He drew the rod from its case, and reached for the side-pocket where he had put line, reel, and bait-box. Confound it! He had left his coat on the carriage seat. Why had he not been bright enough to take those things from his pocket when he spread out his old coat for Mrs. Floyd to lean against?

Well, there was nothing for it but to go back. Slipping the rod out of sight under a rotting log, and taking a single glance at the chain of pools below him, over whose surfaces the midges were dancing and in whose depths, no doubt, the trout were lurking. Sonderby turned on his heel and started back on his stiff, upward climb. Bent almost on all fours, he clambered rapidly over the rocks by the lower cascade, and did not pause till he stood panting at the foot of the upper one, where he had waited an instant in coming down. The heat seemed to grow more oppressive every moment. Dropping his cap at the edge of the stream, and putting one knee on it to avoid wetting his trousers, he flung his weight forward on his hands, and stretched out to drink, swallowing the water in big gulps. He straightened up on one knee again, with a long, satisfied breath, and dashed away with his hand the drops that were falling from his brown beard. Then his brow contracted, his hand fell, and his eyes looked vacantly into the water.

Ah, sure enough! She would be there. She would be there all alone. It was so long since he had seen her alone, since he had had any real words with her; never, in fact, since that Sunday morning when they had been together in the sitting-room of the cottage. He had tried to avoid her, to keep down by dint of furious mental and bodily work his wild thoughts about her. Almost he had succeeded; then came the disclosure he had overheard at the academy, and for the first time he knew the truth about her trouble. His choice, then, had been instant: he had given up his prospects in Boston, he had given up trying to keep her out of his mind. He had devoted himself to her, scarcely knowing what he was doing, or what would probably come of it all — disregarding the right and wrong of the matter, if indeed there were any such things in the confusing tangle — resolved only to stay in Broughton by her side, to watch her husband like a hawk, and to show her, when the time came, that she might call on him for anything, anything. He had spent all Monday as near her as he could; nothing but accident had separated them this afternoon, and now accident was bringing him back up through the woods to the lonely road where she was waiting. He would find her sitting on the carriage seat which he had helped place for her, and leaning back against his own old coat. It was accident; but it seemed like fate.

Sonderby rose to his feet, knocked the wet sand off from his cap mechanically, and started for the top of the gorge. What should he say to her? "I have left my line and reel in my coat and had to come back for them. Good by again." Was that all?

Was that all, when he might not have another chance to tell her that he knew Floyd's cowardly plans, that he would do anything, everything, she wished — that his future was nothing to him, — that — no! it was not all, and it would not be all! A few minutes would bring him to the road; and he swung himself up from tree to tree with powerful pulls, ascending in swift, zigzag lines. But how hot it was! There was not air enough to breathe, and his heart thumped as if he were suffocating. The light of the clearing was just ahead of him; now he climbed up the last ledge of leaf-drifted rock, and pushed his way into the alders that fringed the roadside. There was another sound beside the pounding of his heart, and he stopped to listen. From behind rose the deep, trembling vibrations of the cascade; from the roadside by the carryall came the resonant murmur of a voice. He stepped out on to the road.

Aye, she was there. She sat on the carriage seat, leaning forward, poking at the ground with the tip of her sunshade; and sitting beside her, his right arm resting on the back of the seat so that it must have touched her, his dark, eager face turned as if in hope to catch her eyes at some word of that which he was rapidly saying, was Bruce D. Collins.

Poor John Sonderby! For a few long seconds he stood quiet, so helpless did that great surprise make him. Then he coughed awkwardly and came up the road, his eyes riveted on Collins. The latter's right hand changed position quick as lightning; then he rose deliberately with a cool "Hullo."

"Hullo!" Sonderby responded, and paused in embarrassment.

Mrs. Floyd said nothing, and seemed to be looking at the ground, as before.

"Did you get sick of fishing, so soon?" inquired Collins.

"I forgot my line and bait, and had to come back for them."

"Oh, well, you always need a line for fishing, Sonderby. You'll learn after a while." But the school-teacher did not smile at the mild sarcasm; he stood planted firmly before Collins, with an ugly look in his blue eyes.

"The mosquitoes drove me out of the swamp," continued Collins, stretching himself carelessly, "and I've come back for a pair of gloves." He sauntered over to the carryall, and after some fumbling under the remaining seat, returned with the gloves in his hand. He did it very well, but unfortunately for the impression which he sought to produce, Sonderby had seen him place the gloves in a pocket of his fishing-jacket when he started into the swamp a half-hour before. Collins had lied. He drew on the gloves and buttoned them.

"Well?" said he. He felt that Sonderby's eye was measuring him, as a boxer measures for a blow.

"Where is your line?" Collins continued, rather more hastily.

"I guess your things are here," spoke up Mrs. Floyd for the first time. She held out the coat, and Sonderby forgot his impulse to knock Collins down, and turning to Tryphena took it from her hand. With bungling fingers he got the desired articles from the side-pocket and dropped the coat upon the seat again.

"I'm real sorry you had the walk all for nothing." said Mrs. Floyd, compassionately. "Is it dreadful hot in the woods?"

"Rather," answered Sonderby, drily. Another awkward silence followed.

"I guess likely we'll have a shower by and by," hazarded Mrs. Floyd, still poking the black earth with the tip of her sunshade, and not glancing at Sonderby as she spoke.

"I shouldn't wonder."

"Well, here goes for the mosquitoes again," interrupted Collins, moving away. He made an upward motion of his hand, a sort of parting gesture, toward Mrs. Floyd; and she waved the sunshade slightly, in dumb rejoinder. That was enough for John Sonderby. It was no place for him.

"I'm off, too," he said huskily, and turning sharply, crushed his way through the bushes, and plunged down through the woods. Poor fellow! he had idealized her.

Down the gorge he stumbled, heedless of his footing, till he stood again at the bottom of the upper cascade. He had scarcely been gone a quarter of an hour. All was unchanged there; the water was beginning to ooze through into the hollow his knee had pressed in the sand; the water-spiders were skimming over the margin of the pool, just as he had left them. But in himself something was broken. The fantastic devotion, the reckless desire to let her know what was in his heart and to let her do with him as she would, was gone. She was not worthy of the devotion, and the desire had perished utterly at the sight of Collins's face. If she wished to have Collins near her, — as near her as that, — very well. Sonderby's pride in himself, in his power of influence over her, his belief in his own analysis of her character, was swept away. A dull shame had taken its place — shame at the unacknowledged amorous longing that had mixed itself with his unselfish pity for her, shame at her weakness and folly in allowing Collins's attentions. A crowd of black suspicions jostled against each other: he remembered Floyd's innuendoes against the manufacturer in the barber's shop; the start for the Sunday afternoon drive; the feigned tone of Collins when Floyd was boozily confidential on the academy porch; this very fishing excursion itself, so carefully planned. It all seemed drearily clear: Collins had been playing with his friends of the Broughton House as if they were pieces on a chessboard. But to honest John Sonderby, the worst of it was that Tryphena Floyd seemed light weight; not wicked indeed, but simply light weight.

Minute after minute he stood there, with the

deep silence of the woods all around him, the fine spray from the waterfall wetting his shoulders. Then he turned and kept on his way down stream, moving like a man who has risen from a sick-bed. The lust of the eye and the pride of life had left him. It was over; all that had so strongly stirred him, during these bygone weeks. It would not have been worth while, if he had known.

On getting down to the foot of the lower cascade he found his rod, and adjusted his line and reel. Why not? One might as well fish as do anything else. One thing was as good as another. The trout ran up into the woods that July in unusual numbers, and they leaped at the worms on Sonderby's hook more eagerly than they would have done at the most skilfully thrown fly. But he took no pains to fish carefully, nor did the sport rouse any zest in him. If he hooked them, well and good; if he failed, it was just as well. In vain did the strong-backed, orange-bellied trout dart out from along the sunken logs, snapping at his hook: no sparkle of enthusiasm came into the dull eyes of the school-teacher. He fished on heedlessly, standing half knee-deep in the foaming water, and letting part of the time the eddies play with his bait and suck it down into their white depths, forgetting even that he was fishing. The farther he went down stream, the quieter grew the water, until it lay mostly in long shallow pools shut in by underbrush. At the head of each one he would usually take a trout, and dropping it into the basket would splash on without caring to try for another, and then he would repeat the process at the next pool below. An hour thus passed. He did not notice that the woods were darkened by an increasing shadow, until he looked up on reaching a tiny clearing, and observed that the north, grown full of blue-black thunder clouds, was toppling them over upon the west, so that there came no longer any direct sunlight, but simply a dazzlingly bright reflection from the livid edge of the northern clouds. He saw that there would be a thunder storm, and then the fact went out of his mind under the benumbing pressure of that greater fact, and he strode wearily on into the woods. By and by it grew almost as dark as evening there in the shadow of the thick underbrush, along the sleeping water, but the trout leaped faster and faster, and Sonderby's basket was growing half full. As he climbed over the stump fence into the meadow, the first crash of thunder pealed from the northwest. Overhead there was only a patch of blue, and on this the round-edged clouds were mounting and closing in. A strong wind rose and sank, leaving a calm more oppressive than before. The others would probably get wet, Sonderby thought, putting on a fresh worm for the first of the meadow reaches.

"The others!" two hours ago it would have been "she will probably get wet"—now it was "the others": — she was one of the rest: they went naturally together. Sonderby scarcely glanced away from his hook as the first drops of rain fell, and the wind began to stir again. He turned up the collar of his flannel shirt around his throat, remembering obscurely, as he did so, that he had flung his coat down on the carriage seat, up there at the top of the gorge, and wondering what had become of it now. Thicker and heavier came the thunder crashes, and the rain-drifts began to march like swift-sweeping upright files of spearmen across the wide Johnson meadows. Then all grew gray; the farm buildings were lost to sight, great sheets of water streamed through the gloomy air, and a gale blew that whitened the willow-trees along the brook, flattened the blue iris flowers, and strewed the air with broken, flying leaves from the woodland. Sonderby could no longer see his line; he could scarcely keep his balance against the furious pushings of the wind, and the gusts of driving rain. He unjointed his rod deliberately, put the reel on top of his trout in the basket, tossed the contents of his bait-box into the brook, and tramped across the meadow in the direction of Calvin Johnson's. He was wet to the skin already, and the hail was beginning to sting his cheeks and forehead. But he was thinking of the idle summer; the vague, self-deceptive dreams; the useless and unwished sacrifice.

Rufus Johnson, standing in the wagon-shed to

watch the storm, caught sight of the stooping figure of the school-teacher, as it struggled forward toward the shelter, and recognized it.

"Hullo, Mr. Sonderby!" he shouted. "What, the land sakes! Did ye git ketched in the rain?"

"Hullo, Rufus!" was the quiet reply, as the school-teacher entered and put his wet hand into the calloused grip of the young farmer.

"Yes, I'm some wet, but it's no matter. Have you any hay out?"

Rufus was leaning on a pitchfork. "No, by Johnny!" he exclaimed, gratefully. "I pitched the last forkful over the great-beam just as that first clap came. 'Twas a big one, wa'n't it? Must 'a struck clost."

"I don't remember," answered Sonderby, squeezing the water out of his clothes. "Have they come yet?"

"Who?" said Rufus.

"Mr. Collins. At the hotel, you know. They were going to drive around here and fish up through the meadow."

"Were, eh? No, we ain't seen nothin' of 'em here. Won't ye come into the kitchen, 'n git dry? 'Twon't hold up yet awhile, t'ain't likely."

But just as Sonderby had been given a seat by the kitchen fire, where the boarders' supper was preparing, there was a noise of wheels outside, and Collins called out, "Whoa!"

"Drive right under the shed," shouted Rufus, running to the door. "Right in there!"

Sonderby stood in the kitchen doorway, and saw Floyd's tall form squirm out of the back seat of the carryall, followed by Tryphena, who was laughing vociferously. Collins was tying the horse. In a moment the three started for the kitchen, at the invitation of Rufus, who addressed Mrs. Floyd as "Phenie." She was the first to enter the kitchen, and paused in mock dismay, when scarcely over the threshold, to see the puddle that was already running from her clothes. Her thin dress clung to her. She was shivering, but was in the gayest spirits, and joked incessantly as they all crowded up to the stove. Mrs. Calvin Johnson emerged from the pantry, where she had been making pies, and bustled around with a shower of hospitable ejaculations: "Land sakes! Glad to see you. Don't say! Wet? Of course you be. Draw right up to the fire, sir. Make yourself to home." Then, in motherly solicitude at Tryphena's drenched clothing, she carried her off into her own bedroom, which opened out of the kitchen. A few minutes later Tryphena reappeared, attired in an old calico gown of the farmer's wife. Mrs. Johnson was a woman far from slender, and Tryphena had been obliged to gather the gown in at the waist and to turn it up at the sleeves. She looked like a mischievous child masquerading. She talked with everybody at once, danced around the stove, pretended to quarrel with Collins for the best place by the oven, and even won Mrs. Johnson, who had never quite liked her, into avowing mentally that "Phenie was getting to be quite like folks." Mrs. Johnson relished the free way in which the young woman ordered around her masculine associates. When down Mrs. Floyd's flushed cheeks the raindrops kept trickling from her wet hair, she put her hands to her head in pretty vexatiousness, and after a hesitating glance at the men, shook her hair loose. It uncoiled in dark, shining masses, and slid down over her shoulders, and wringing it dry, she twisted it into a low knot behind. The sleeves of the calico gown were still too long, bothering her as she tried to warm her hands over the fire, so she pushed them up above her elbows, and stretched out her bare, white arms eagerly to the warmth. Opposite her stood John Sonderby and Rufus Johnson.

Mrs. Johnson went off into renewed explosions of appreciative laughter over these evidences that Phenie was "making herself to home." The stout farmer's wife had had nothing but the vagaries of her summer boarders with which to amuse herself for several months past. More and more irrepressible grew Tryphena's hysterical exuberance, while Floyd growled at the weather, and Collins turned over Sonderby's basket of trout, surprised that there were so many there. As for John Sonderby, he gazed stupidly at the group around him, finding himself for the first time afraid of Mrs. Floyd, and shrinking from her merriment as from something unnatural. The whole noisy whirl there was meaningless to him, an indifferent matter. Rufus Johnson, standing by the school-teacher's side, watched Tryphena with eyes as undemonstrative as those of his own oxen, but he was thinking of the gay outbursts Phenie Morton used to break into, on a straw ride or at a husking frolic, long before she ever went to Brooklyn, and how like her girlish self she was now, yet somehow different, "sort o' different."

After a quarter of an hour, when the heat of the split hickory which Mrs. Johnson had crammed into the stove had, in some measure, dried the apparel of the visitors, there was talk of driving home. The rain had broken away. No one proposed any more fishing that evening. Mrs. Floyd's spirits were ebbing now, moment by moment. She was shivering again, and her fit of laughter left a sort of moodiness behind it. She said she did not want to go home; she would rather stay all night, just as Mrs. Johnson had hospitably proposed. Floyd gave vent to an impatient exclamation, and she yielded. While Collins and Rufus Johnson backed the horse out from the shed, and sopped up the water standing in the bottom of the carry-all, Calvin Johnson himself, a fine-looking man of sixty, drove into the yard, behind the iron-gray horses. He had been under some trees in the worst of the storm, and thought lightly of the wetting he had received. He told Collins that the roads would be badly washed, and tried, as his wife had done, to get the party to spend the night at the farmhouse. Mrs. Johnson, thus supported, began her urgings once more, and the whole discussion recommenced. But Tryphena cut it short by climbing into the carryall.

"Ain't ye rather hasty, Phenie?" Calvin Johnson asked, good-naturedly. Unlike his wife, he had always fancied Phenie Morton.

"No, I guess not," she answered. "You know I belong in town now, along with the hotel folks. Don't you see that this is the Broughton House carriage?"

Calvin Johnson and his wife laughed more than this remark in itself would warrant, for they felt she had meant to be jocose. Floyd was the only one who noticed the mockery in her tone, and it displeased him. He climbed into the carryall, too.

"Come on, Collins!" he cried. "We've got to get home before dark. Come on, Sonderby!"

Mrs. Floyd's teeth were chattering when she said "Good by," and as the horse turned, Rufus Johnson called out, "Hold on!" He went under the shed and returned with an old buffalo robe.

"I'm afraid you've ketched your death o' cold, Phenie," he said gravely, and wrapped the buffalo robe closely around her.

XIV.

THE three members of the strikers' committee, who were left unceremoniously upon the Broughton House piazza to await the pleasure of Mr. Collins, had no reason to complain of the treatment they received during the manufacturer's absence. They were clothed in their Sunday best, and Evans deemed them respectable enough to take the places of his "regulars" at the end of the first dining-table. After a much better dinner than they were in the habit of getting at Collins Mills Junction, they drifted into the office, and were there cordially entertained by Bill Trumbull. Bill had heard some particulars about the strike, early in the season, from the lips of Collins, and from time to time since then he had noticed a few lines about the situation at the Collins Mills on the local page of the *Republican*. He easily guessed, therefore, the nature of the committee's errand, and the answers of the men to his adroit indirect questions satisfied him that he was correct. Little inclined as they were to talk business with a stranger, there had been so much talking at Collins Mills Junction that summer that they all had caught the infection of the habit, and not one of them — even George, the clearest-headed but least open of the three — could keep a quiet tongue in his head under the irresistible attraction of Bill Trumbull's willingness to hear. But Bill was by no means in a hurry to make sure of the facts relating to the great strike; on the contrary, his manner was that of a person who had the whole afternoon at his disposal and was confident of securing his game whenever he wished. He told them his best stories, cross-examined them about the livery stable in the Center where they had hired their horse, exalted Collins's prowess as a fisherman. From a discussion of Collins as a sportsman it was not difficult to pass to the more practical subject of Collins as an employer of labor, and finally, in a private and more confidential fashion, — though there was no one in the Broughton House office to overhear them, — to the interesting and ultimate question of Collins's character "as a feller." Upon this point the members of the committee were not entirely agreed, but there was sufficient consensus of opinion to make Bill Trumbull open his vague blue eyes very wide indeed, and to set him uneasily wondering whether he had really found out so much about the world during the period when he had served in the Legislature as he had always thought he did.

Though the members of the committee were personally attracted to Bill, — else had they scarcely been so free in talk with him, — they were not entirely impressed with a sense of his important function in the community, until their discussion of Collins was interrupted by an urgent demand for Bill's presence in the back yard of Samuel Parkinson. The worthy storekeeper's Durham cow had been taken unaccountably sick that afternoon, and Parkinson himself appeared at the hotel, his anxiety breaking huskily through his smooth salesman voice, to see if Mr. Trumbull would not come to look at her. Bill rose instantly from his chair. He was prouder of his skill as a cow doctor than of anything else, and his judgment in veterinary matters was accepted as final by every one in the place. The deferential manner in which the bland but excited Parkinson requested Trumbull's expert opinion convinced the men from Collins Mills Junction that their after-dinner friend was something more than an ordinary hotel chairwarmer, and they accompanied him in his hasty march across the Floyd back yard to the storekeeper's premises. The cow lay there under a plum-tree, her legs disconsolately and awkwardly stretched out, her head flat on the ground. She had been in her usual high spirits when Parkinson's hopeful heir had tethered her by the plum-tree after dinner, and the sickness was alarmingly sudden. The women-folks had noticed that she was not chewing her cud; then they saw her fall to the ground, and they ran for Mr. Parkinson. Those were all the particulars Bill had to guide him in his diagnosis. But genius follows its own course. Without wasting a word upon the onlookers, who formed an interested ring around the prostrate Durham, Bill tried the temperature of her horns, passed his hand reflectively over her spine, and then held her tail in both hands, moving them up and down slowly, while one of the bystanders whispered approvingly that a cow's tail was her thermometer, every time. Taking out his jack-knife, Bill solemnly made an insertion at the tip of the aforesaid tail, and watched the thin trickling of bright red blood down upon the grass. The Durham flapped her ears in a discouraged manner. Then Bill turned to Samuel Parkinson, and announced oracularly:

"She's a pretty sick cow."

A great doctor of medicine was lost in William Trumbull.

"Pretty sick cow," he repeated. "Git some soft-soap."

He took off his coat and rolled up his shirt-sleeves, while they brought from the back kitchen a bucket of soap, — curiously enough, the soaps whose wondrous efficacy was advertised at the store did not find their way to the storekeeper's kitchen, — and with it a wide-mouthed quart bottle, which Trumbull straightway filled. Prying the cow's reluctant jaws apart, and cramming in the bottle, he lifted her head and poured the liquid soap into her innermost parts. Then everybody waited in respectful silence, two minutes — five — ten. But the Durham did not even flap her ears now. The case was evidently most serious.

"Pretty sick cow," reaffirmed Bill, poking her inquisitively in the region of the stomach. "Git some linseed oil."

Parkinson's boy started on a dead run toward the store, and the crowd, seeing that Bill's remedies had thus far proved unavailing, began to interchange theories and suggestions, and to emphasize in an ominous, post-mortem sort of way what an "awful good cow" she "had ben." Bill maintained a professional silence; but even he betrayed some agitation as he filled the quart-bottle with oil, and poured it down the Durham's unresisting throat. Her tail swung from side to side a little, in the grass. At this Bill filled the bottle a second time, and repeated the dose. After half a minute the cow shook her ears and pushed her nose into the grass; then she trembled, and gave two or three queer, hollow coughs, followed by a convulsive gulp, and behold, something seemed to slide up her throat. Then lifting her head and drawing in her legs decorously, she began to chew her cud as if nothing had happened, while from the circle of onlookers burst a whole volley of excited and commendatory ejaculations. Bill Trumbull, in a befitting calm, put on his coat, and then patting the cow gently he made her stand up, and felt once more of the temperature of her tail. He relinquished his hold, apparently satisfied, when Mr. Parkinson stepped briskly forward, and took the tail into his own fingers, pinching and pulling it as if to see that it was full measure.

"She'll git along," remarked Bill, in encouraging assurance. "She's ben a pretty sick cow, but —"

Just then the Durham lifted her horny, sprawling right hoof, and drove it viciously against Samuel Parkinson's irreproachable shin. There was a rapturous howl from the bystanders.

"But" — Bill concluded, the mildest twinkle in his eye, as he looked at the spot on Parkinson's linen trousers where the reddening storekeeper was frantically rubbing — "I guess she's all right now."

Thereupon, amid the renewed uproarious laughter and the sly appreciative nudges in the ribs with which the older neighbors conveyed to one another their secret delight at Parkinson's mishap, Bill Trumbull and his three companions walked back to the hotel. The trio were proud of the acquaintanceship, and as for Bill, he was happy to have such a retinue of the unemployed about him, and his only regret at the interruption was that it had interfered with some further questions he had intended to ask his new friends, as to the sort of man Mr. Collins was reputed to be at Collins Mills Junction. But unfortunately for the prosecution of his inquiries, in which he felt a somewhat uneasy interest, his daughter Miranda was shaking her apron at him from the other side of the street, and he was obliged to go over and help her take in the clothes from the line before the approaching thunder shower.

When he got back to the hotel after supper he found to his disappointment that Collins had returned and was closeted with the committee. Bill waited a long time for John Sonderby to show himself, and failing to get sight of him, learned from Evans that the school-teacher had gone to his room. Early the next morning the strikers' committee drove away, having without much difficulty accomplished their errand, and Bill did not see them again. When he went over to the Broughton House after breakfast, though he went more promptly than usual, he found that Sonderby, too, was gone.

An hour before Bill made his appearance, Calvin Johnson drove up to the hotel, and entering the office, asked for the school-teacher. Sonderby was finishing his breakfast, and, as it happened, alone; for Collins had taken an early repast with his re-instated operatives, and the Floyds had not yet come over. He came out of the dining-room at the stately old farmer's message, and found him in a heated dispute with Evans about some boarders who the Welshman claimed had been induced to leave the Broughton House and take up their quarters at Johnson's, through misrepresentations of the latter. Calvin Johnson, owner of the best farm in town and of another one in Ohio, selectman of the town, deacon of the church, was not the man to be browbeaten by the little Welshman, and Evans was already beginning to regret that he had opened the discussion, when Sonderby's appearance put an end to the quarrel.

"How d'ye do! How d'ye do!" Johnson cried, heartily, forgetting his valiant wrath at the hotel-keeper, who took advantage of the opportunity to slip away. "It *ain't* so very long sence I've seen ye; no. I suppose ye got home all right?"

"Yes," said Sonderby.

"Well, Mr. Sonderby, Rufus thought I'd better come up to see if ye didn't want to come down and help us for a couple of days with the tail-end of the hayin'. I'll tell ye how it is. Rufe was shuttin' the big door of the barn last night — 'bout an hour after you'd got away — when the wind was blowin', and I guess he must 'a pushed too hard — or somethin' — anyway he seems to have kind o' sprained his shoulder. Can't move it this mornin' without hollerin'. Mother's been rubbin' him down a little with St. Jacob's oil, and I dunno but that will help it some, and I dunno *as* it will."

"I'm sorry to hear it."

"Yes, yes! Oh, well, that ain't anythin' that's going to bother Rufe very long, only just now it don't seem very providential. Ye see we let our help go yesterday, last day of July, calculatin' that Rufe and I and the boys could finish everythin' up. There ain't much but the orchard, and that medder swamp, ye know, where you and Rufe was last summer."

"I know," interrupted Sonderby. "And Rufus wants me to come down and help you through?"

"Why, yes, that's the how of it," and his kindly face broke into a smile. "I told Rufe, says I, 'Mr. Sonderby is up there among those city folks, and he won't want to come down here hayin', the way he did last summer.' But Rufe, he would have it that you wan't naturally inclined to train with the city folks, no more than he is, and says he, 'I shouldn't wonder, now, if the school-teacher would be glad to come.' Thinks I, there ain't any harm in hitchin' up and drivin' in to the street and askin' him. — I had to git some skunk's oil at Parkinson's for Rufe's shoulder, anyhow, — and if he don't want to come, he can just say so. So here I be."

"Certainly," said Sonderby, slowly. "I can go just as well as not. Perhaps better. There's nothing for me to do here."

He took his hat from a peg in the hall, stepped into the wagon, and drove off behind the iron-grays. He stayed down at Calvin Johnson's two days. Most of the time he was mowing under the long rows of apple-trees in the hillside orchard, or out in the sunny swale. He no longer worked furiously, as in those two days on the farm of Bill

Trumbull's son-in-law, when he had tried to tire out and crush down something within him. There was no need of that now. That was all over. But he mowed steadily and quietly, up and down the peaceful orchard rows, or in the wet bottoms where the Johnson brook streamed noiselessly through the sedges; and the familiar employment, and the homely life, and nature's midsummer restfulness were all ministering to him. Hour after hour Rufus Johnson, his arm in a sling and right shoulder bandaged, walked along beside the schoolteacher, for the mere sake of having his company; and though neither of the young fellows said much, Sonderby was glad to have him there. Unsuspected by himself, these two uneventful days were the turning-point of John Sonderby's life.

Late on Thursday afternoon, Calvin Johnson, who had driven up to the street to get the mail for his boarders, came down into the meadow with a couple of letters in his hand. Sonderby was in the middle of the swale, throwing the green hay with a fork out toward the firm ground, for curing. Rufus sat near by on a willow stump, nursing his lame arm in his left hand.

"Here y'are, Mr. Sonderby!" called old Johnson, cheerily. "Well, it does beat all how you git along. Never mind cockin' this up to-night; we shan't git any more rain right away."

He handed over the letters, and picking up Sonderby's rake, began to pull the grass into windrows along the edge of the swale. Sonderby broke open the notes. The first one was from Mrs. Ellerton, dated the day before.

"DEAR MR. SONDERBY: I can scarcely tell you how delighted we are to learn that you expect to remain in Broughton another winter. It is a great pleasure to us personally to know that you are to be here, and certainly every one who is acquainted with the academy would have regretted that you saw fit to relinquish your work there.

"For some time I have been thinking how we might make some of the evenings in the coming winter more attractive and helpful to the young people, and some photographs which have just been sent to us have made me wonder if we could not arrange a course of 'travel evenings,' or something of that sort, at the academy, or in the lecture-room of the church. What do you think of the plan? Would you be willing to help? Won't you, at any rate, come to take tea with us to-morrow evening, at six, and talk it over?

"Very sincerely,
"RUTH ELLERTON.

"BROUGHTON, Wednesday, August 1, 188–."

He ran his eye twice over the strong, almost masculine handwriting, and then pushed the note back into the square envelope, glancing at the sun meantime. It was almost six then. To accept

Mrs. Ellerton's invitation was an impossibility. The second note was brief, and was scrawled stiffly in lead-pencil on a half-sheet of Broughton House paper.

"JOHN SONDERBY, Esq.:
"*Respected Sir*, — I want to see you particular.
"Y'rs, WILLIAM TRUMBULL."

There was no date, but the envelope had been stamped at the village post-office that afternoon.

"Mr. Johnson," called out the school-teacher, "do you suppose one of the boys could drive me up to the street?"

"To be sure" — and noticing the seriousness of Sonderby's tone, he added, "There ain't any bad news, is there?"

"Oh, no," replied Sonderby, "I'm invited to tea, for one thing."

"Ain't that bad news for you?" put in Rufus, who dared to twit the schoolmaster on his reputation for social shortcomings.

"Well, we won't settle it," Sonderby answered. "It's too late to go, anyway. But I think I shall have to drive up to the village."

"Let one of the boys take ye in the buckboard," said Rufus. "Hitch on the old horse; he'll get ye there now as quick as the span. I allers tell father so, but he hates to drive single."

"How will it be about to-morrow?" asked Sonderby, hesitatingly.

"Jest as ye like," answered old Johnson. "The boys and I can turn this over and cock it up, easy enough. And I guess we can git it in without ye if you'd rather do anythin' else. Rufe, here, can ride a horse-rake by day after to-morrow, it's likely."

"No, there ain't any use in your coming down again, unless ye want to," chimed in Rufus. "But ye know we're awful glad to have ye here, Mr. Sonderby, whether there's any hayin' or not."

"I guess we be!" affirmed the elder man.

"Well, we'll leave it this way, then," Sonderby decided. "I won't come to-morrow, for you don't need me, and when you drive up for the mail to-morrow afternoon, we can see how it will be for Saturday."

"All right, all right! You've helped us out of quite a hole, in these two days. Tell the boys to hitch right up. I'll finish this little spell of work here." Johnson went back to his rake, and Sonderby and Rufus crossed the meadow to the farm-house.

It was nearly seven o'clock, in spite of the activity of the old horse, when the buckboard deposited Sonderby in front of the Broughton House. The piazza was gay with people, just from the dining-room; but Sonderby knew scarcely any of them, even by sight. He went up to his room and put on his black suit, meaning to call at the parsonage after he had seen Bill Trumbull, and explain why he had failed to accept Mrs. Ellerton's invitation. Calvin Johnson's wife had made him eat some supper while the horse was being harnessed, and he did not therefore stop at the hotel dining-room when he came down stairs. The parlor was full of newly arrived guests, and some young ladies were trying merrily to waltz to the discordant strains of the melodeon. At the office door Sonderby found Bill Trumbull waiting for him. The ex-hotel-keeper looked very much relieved when he caught sight of the stocky figure of the young fellow coming toward him, and he drew Sonderby's arm into his — an entirely unusual proceeding — and walked him across the office to the most retired corner. They sat down there, underneath the mouldy lithograph of Daniel Webster. Bill Trumbull was nervous; his straw-colored eyebrows were crumpled toward each other, and his smooth-shaven upper lip was twitching just perceptibly.

"I'm glad to see you," he said, in a husky whisper. "I'm gosh darned glad to see you."

"I got your letter this afternoon," said Sonderby, wondering what was coming.

"Yes. You ain't heard nothin'?"

"Why, no."

"Well, I dunno's you would. Come to think on't, I dunno's there's anythin' *to* hear. But I'm mistrustful, Mr. Sonderby. I don't exactly know what to think, and I wanted to see you. You always seemed a square kind of a feller, and I dunno but you know more about young folks than I do. Say."

The stable-boy was lighting a kerosene lamp above the fireplace, and Bill lowered his voice still more, so as not to be heard. Sonderby drew his chair a trifle closer.

"It's about Collins. You know those fellers that were up here the other day to see him?"

"From the mills?"

"Yes. Pretty likely kind of fellers, too. I talked with 'em a good while. And by and by we got to talkin' about Collins himself. Say, they know more about him down there than we do up here."

"I shouldn't wonder," was the dry rejoinder.

"There ain't no doubt of it. He's one of the pleasantest fellers that ever came up here fishin', but in some ways, they told me, he ain't a nice man, not at all. I didn't ask them all I wanted to, but there wan't no doubt about what they had in mind."

Sonderby was silent.

"Now that's all right for you and me," Bill went on, his innocent old heart making an awkward pretence of worldliness; "it don't make much difference to us whether he's just the right sort of man or not; he don't trouble us any. But it's a different thing, when you come to the women folks — when you come, for instance, to Trypheny."

Sonderby's eyes were on the floor. The stable-boy looked curiously at the two men whispering in the corner, and then went reluctantly out of the office.

"Now she don't know anythin' about him. If she knew what kind of a feller he was, she wouldn't have nothin' to do with him. And that's what I want to see you about. It looks kind of queer to have me pokin' myself into other folks's business, but I set a big store by that little girl — she ain't nothin' more than a girl, you know — and it would be a darned shame if folks got to talkin' about her. They do a'ready, though, Mirandy says. Now I shouldn't dast say anythin' to Trypheny. I'd be too ashamed, you know — old as I am — but I didn't know but perhaps you, bein' more 'round with her — and bein' the school-teacher — could kind o' drop a word — sort o' — " Bill stopped helplessly.

"But she is a married woman, Trumbull," said Sonderby, slowly, as if he were patiently explaining an intricate matter to a child. "It is the place of her husband — "

"Exactly," broke in Bill. "That's jest the trouble. If Floyd was here, I dunno as there would have been any need of my writin' to you. But now he's gone — "

"Gone?" cried Sonderby, starting up in his chair. Then he sank back. What less could he have expected?

"Yes, gone to New York — didn't I tell you?

Why, when you was all off fishin'. — it was that same afternoon I had the talk with these fellers, — a telegram come to Floyd from Chicago, and another one yesterday morning from New York. I heard tell he had to meet somebody in New York; guess likely it was that feller he was paintin' the picture for, for he had the picture all boxed up to take away with him. He told Evans here, that he might have to be away a couple of weeks."

"A couple of weeks," repeated Sonderby, in a tone that Trumbull did not understand.

"Yes; Trypheny's goin' to keep house by herself while he's gone. She ain't comin' over to the hotel. And now I'll tell you what I don't like."

Just then a couple of the young ladies who had been all this time waltzing in the parlor whirled out of the door and across the hall into the office, where they made the circuit of the room once — with delighted little cries at the new-found space. Their flying skirts brushed against the knees of Bill Trumbull and Sonderby, as they circled past, and then they danced out of the office again, as gaily and suddenly as they had entered.

"I'll tell you what I don't like," repeated Bill. "Collins was over there yesterday afternoon, after Floyd went off. And last night he took her to drive — I guess out towards East Part. Now she probably don't know any better, not suspectin' anything against Collins. But it ain't the right thing, Mr. Sonderby. It ain't the right thing."

Bill drew a long breath, having at last relieved his mind of what he wanted to say.

"Where is Collins?" demanded Sonderby, in a hard voice.

"Well, that's somethin' else that p'raps I'd ought to have said. He went away this mornin', to see about the startin' up of the mills, and he told Evans that he was comin' back to-morrow afternoon — yes, Friday, to-morrow — to get his things. Now if that's all there is to it, if he's really goin' away, I dunno but I've made a great bark over a little woodchuck. But if he's goin' to stay along here at the hotel, and Trypheny not knowin' anything about him more'n he's a good-lookin' feller and a rich feller, and in good society, — knows the minister's folks, you see, — why, it ain't the right thing."

Sonderby got up and paced the floor once or twice. He was more touched by what the pure-hearted old gossip had said than he cared to show.

"Bill," said he, coming back and laying his hand on Trumbull's shoulder, "you're quite right, sir. I'm glad we've had the talk. I don't know that there's anything for you or for me to do in the matter," — and his words seemed to the older man thick and strange, — "but if there is, we'll do it."

Bill rose too. There were two or three other persons in the office now, by the fireplace, Evans among them.

"Good night, sir, if I don't see you again." said Sonderby. "I'm going up to the parsonage for a while."

"Good night, good night! I tell you, I'm much obliged to you;" and Bill shuffled over towards his accustomed seat with a lighter heart than he had had for twenty-four hours.

Sonderby went out at the side door, to avoid brushing his way through the crowd of people in the hall. Bill's anxiety for the motherless and solitary Tryphena had affected him profoundly. There were other elements in the problem, however, of which Bill was apparently ignorant; but the school-teacher did not have it in his heart to reveal them, even had he thought it wise. His disappointment in Tryphena herself had been so personal and so bitter, that there was something sacred to him about it. It was not something to be spoken of. Yet he did speak of it in less than ten minutes, and to Mrs. Floyd herself.

As he walked up the driveway towards the end of the hotel piazza, his eyes bent on the ground, he heard some one on the left call his name. He turned, and saw her advancing from the lilacs, the same thin red shawl around her shoulders that she had worn when posing for the picture. Sonderby halted, making rather an awkward bow. She came right up to him and put out her hand. He held it a moment, and remembered afterward how very small it seemed, and cold. Indeed, she was shivering a little, for there was a heavy dew on the grass, and it always grew cool in Broughton after sundown.

"I've been waiting for you," she said, glancing at him with that shy frankness which had charmed him with her at first. "I saw Johnson's team stop at the hotel, and guessed likely you had come; but I dursn't go over alone for you among all those folks."

He stood looking at her, not knowing what to say.

"I can't stay here," she added. "It's awful damp," and she stretched out one foot and looked ruefully at the thin wet shoe.

"Yes," he blurted out, "you'll catch cold. Rufus was afraid you had the other night." It was the first word he had spoken to her since the fishing-party.

"Oh, Rufus," she replied. "He was always worrying about me." She took a step or two back toward the cottage, and then turned her head as if she were not sure that Sonderby was following her. "Come on in," she cried, tightening the folds of the shawl across her narrow little shoulders, and seeing he had not started, she added in a lower voice, "Do you mind, Mr. Sonderby? Were you going anywhere else?"

He shook his head and strode after her, as she stepped daintily and swiftly over the long tangled grass. In the sitting-room one of the lamps was already lighted. Tryphena threw off her shawl, and sat down in the low rocking-chair by the window. It was getting dark outside. The young ladies at the Broughton House were still dancing to the sound of the old melodeon, and Mrs. Floyd shut the window. "I get kind o' sick of one sort of tune after a while, don't you?" she asked.

"I don't notice them much," he said, absently. "One tune is a good deal like another to me, most of the time. You know I wasn't any great help in our quartette." He was thinking that she and Collins had done most of the singing.

"Oh, the quartette!" she cried. "Well, it wasn't much of a quartette, was it? No great shakes. But it was as good as anything else to make the time go."

"The time is gone, at any rate," said Sonderby. He did not know what he could say to her, nor why she had called him in. What could Mrs. Floyd want of him?

"Yes," she replied, shrugging her shoulders.

There was a long pause.

"Did Bill Trumbull tell you anything?" she suddenly asked.

"Bill Trumbull?" he repeated, startled into feigning ignorance of the drift of her question. But John Sonderby made unskilful work of any such artifices, and she offered no reply except to look him in the eyes.

"What do you mean?" he said, resolved to make her speak first.

"About my hus — about Mr. Floyd."

"Bill said he had gone to New York, to be away two or three weeks."

"Oh, yes," she exclaimed, hastily. "Then he did tell you!" She seemed relieved.

"But I know better," said blunt John Sonderby.

"You — know — better?" she repeated, with a long, slow breath, as if each word hurt her. "What do you know?"

She thought there were but three persons in the world who knew her husband's plans, — her husband and Collins and herself.

"What do you know?" she demanded, pitifully. "Tell me."

He flung himself out of his chair and paced the room twice, as if it were his own. How could he tell her the bare truth overheard by him in all its ugliness? Yet of course she knew it, had known it all the time, had known it when she made that gesture with her parasol at Collins, up in the woods above the cascade.

"Mrs. Floyd," he said, hoarsely, stopping in front of her. "I knew that he was going away to be gone — a good while. I have known it since last Sunday night — I overheard him say so."

"You — overheard — him?" She lifted her face, and it hardened into scornful lines, but she was not thinking of Sonderby's eavesdropping.

"I could not help it," he said, simply, believing that it was he whom she despised so. "I could not help listening, for I thought I might do you a service."

"Oh, don't — I don't mean that," she cried, wistfully; "I wan't blaming you." Then something in his attitude, as he stood looking down at her, seemed to remind her of that other time when they two had been in that same room together. "Do me a service?" she repeated the words almost tenderly. "Don't you remember I told you once, right here, that you couldn't help me, that nobody could help me?"

He stood staring at her, struggling within himself. Hers seemed like an honest woman's voice: if he could only believe it was! She made a strong effort, apparently, to control herself, and motioned to him to sit down.

"Perhaps I oughtn't to have said that, Mr. Sonderby, but I was kind of desperate. I knew this was coming. I knew it pretty near a month ago — and sometimes I haven't known just what I was saying or doing." She spoke quietly, only with a sort of girlish pleading.

"Ah, yes," he said. "I may have misunderstood you. May God forgive me if I have; but I have thought — I have had to think — that there was no help for matters; — that you did not care, any longer —"

He stopped entirely, not knowing how he could put delicately to her the words that were on his lips.

She waited for him, and then said, gently as his mother might have done, "Hadn't you better say it right out — all of it? It'll make us both feel better."

That last sentence conquered his heart, although his brain was still confused in the tangle of the evidence against her.

"Mrs. Floyd," he cried, "I can't understand it. It is too much for me. What have you meant, when you let Collins — go on so? Tuesday — when he was — talking with you on the carriage seat? You drive with him — Great Heavens, what a botch I make of it! But can't you see? Don't you care?"

"Oh," she said, without lifting her eyes from the carpet. "I guess I understand, Mr. Sonderby. I suppose you think I haven't let my moderation be known, — as Aunt Tryphena used to tell me to do whenever we went on straw-rides. 'Let your moderation be known, Phenie.' And I don't know as I have." Her tone was very girlish. It made him think of having one of his pupils at the academy on the front seat, and lecturing her for some slight misdemeanor.

"No," she continued, seeing that he was not inclined to speak, "I don't know but I have given you some chance to think I didn't mind much what people said. I guess I've acted sort of queer. Men don't understand those things very well; none of them do. They think some little thing means too much; or else that it doesn't mean enough. And I didn't want to make Mr. Collins mad. I'm sort of afraid of him."

"But —" broke in Sonderby, hesitatingly.

"Yes, I know. You're particular. You're more particular than Broughton folks are, even if you don't say anything. You didn't like to see him sit there with his arm on the back of the seat. You didn't like to have me go off to drive with him. I knew you didn't, all the time. Neither would Aunt Tryphena. She would have had conniptions over it. But I was only fooling. I was kind of desperate, and had to do something." She looked up in his face as she finished, as if waiting for the decision of a moral judgment superior to her own. She met his scrutiny without wavering; she seemed to be blushing a little, but that was all. John Sonderby gazed into her shadowy eyes, so fully open to him now, and he believed her. She was only a girl, — an ignorant country girl, — who had had, perhaps, some excuse for "fooling," as she certainly had had cause for feeling "desperate." Poor girl! The old pity for her came back: but it brought nothing else with it now, for in those terrible two hours in the woods on Tuesday, and in the quiet two days in orchard and swale, John Sonderby had worked his way, irretraceably, through a certain part of the experience allotted to him.

"Yes," he said softly. "God knows you have had a hard time. And I have misjudged you."

She dropped her eyes, and trembled slightly; then reached for her shawl, and drew it around her, as if she were cold.

"Shan't I build a fire for you, Mrs. Floyd?" asked the school-teacher.

"No, it isn't worth while," she answered. "Thank you."

The words "Mrs. Floyd" seemed to recall him to the real situation, and the sense of her girlishness passed away. He felt that in some way he must offer to help her, to let her know, too, that Trumbull had been caring about her. But it was she who spoke first.

"It's all right now. There won't be any more trouble, Mr. Sonderby. You won't have to worry any more."

He looked at her inquiringly.

"Don't you see?" she said. "It's all over, now. Billy has gone away; he wasn't happy up here in Broughton. It wasn't anybody's fault; he was made different from other people. He'll come back by and by; he won't be contented over there either, always." This defence of her husband was delivered in a rapid, even voice.

"And you?" said John Sonderby, simply.

"Oh, I? I shall stay here, right here in Broughton, where I was brought up and where I belong. And what other place is there for me?"

He was silent.

"I own this house. Didn't you know it?" She

was trying hard to make light of the matter, as if it were only an ordinary domestic expedient that was occupying her mind. "You needn't trouble. It will be all right."

He still sat looking at her.

"Don't you miss me at the hotel?" persisted Mrs. Floyd. "Oh, I forgot; you have been down at Calvin Johnson's. Bill is the only one of us left at the Broughton House, now, isn't he?" She laughed, but rather nervously.

"Collins's things are there," he said.

Her manner changed. "I know. He is coming back for them to-morrow."

"Bill Trumbull said that Collins might stay a while longer."

"Oh, no," she cried, excitedly. "He won't. He — told me so."

"You are sure?"

She nodded at him with a curious look in her eyes, for answer. He could not understand the expression, but he believed her implicitly, and the worst of the weight that had been on his mind rolled off. There was nothing between her and Collins, after all. She had been wrong and foolish, but there was nothing back of that, and there would be no chance for further mischief.

"And you are going too, Mr. Sonderby," she said reflectively.

"I?"

"Why, yes! To Boston. They all told me

you were going — to be with the electric company."

"I did think of it," he remarked. There was no use in telling her that he had abandoned all that for her sake.

"You *did* think of it? Don't you think of it now? Why, they told me it was a splendid place, just what you wanted."

"I have reason to think that they have given that position to some one else."

"But there must be plenty more," she cried, with an agitation that puzzled him. "Aren't there a great many electric companies nowadays? There must be ever so many places in Boston where they would be glad to have you. You know so much about those things, you are so strong and — faithful — so —"

"Thank you," he broke in clumsily, with a sort of embarrassed bow, and a half pretence of taking her words as a compliment merely.

"Oh, but I mean it!" exclaimed Mrs. Floyd. "I mean it! You ought not to stay here in Broughton any longer. You can do so much more for yourself in Boston. I know it. I have heard the others talking about it — weeks ago. It is a pity to have you stay here — way up here — kind of out of the world, when you want to be in a big laboratory, and to have books and to invent things."

She spoke eagerly, firmly, and he felt a sort of

conviction that she was right. There was a strange sensation within him, as if the oscillations of purpose that had carried him back and forth all summer were ceasing now, and his will was coming to rest at a fixed point. A few days before he had resolved to give up all this new life which she had just marked out for him, to give it up that he might stay in Broughton and be near her. But now it was she who was telling him to go.

"You seem to want to have me go," he said, trying to smile.

"Yes," she replied, straightening up in her rocking-chair and leaning forward toward him, with clasped hands and eyes dilated; he had never seen them so deep. "Yes, I do. I wish — you would, Mr. Sonderby. I should — feel — easier." She sunk back, at these last words, as if finishing a confession.

He hesitated. "There's the academy; I told Mr. Ellerton I would stay another year." It was only an attempt to gain time for a moment's more thought.

"There are a dozen others who want the place," she said, quickly; "there always are. You can resign — if you wish to." She lay back in her chair, her breath coming quickly, her eyes fastened on his honest, troubled face.

"I will," he said, rising slowly to his feet. "I will go to-morrow. I have been all summer making up my mind, Mrs. Floyd, but I could never

know quite what to do. It was first one thing
and then another. I am going now, because you
tell me to. If anything comes of it down there —
oh, I shall work hard and I can make a place for
myself! — I shall thank you for sending me."

"To-morrow?" she cried, with a curious eager-
ness. "You will really go to-morrow? Oh, I am
so glad!" She rose too, but she rested one hand
on the table, and she was shivering again. His
eye swept over the barely furnished and low-ceiled
room, with its rag carpet, battered soapstone stove,
rickety furniture, and its oval-framed pictures of
Aunt Tryphena and Aunt Tryphosa on the wall.

"Ought you to try to stay here, Mrs. Floyd?"
he asked, in a low voice. "It will be very lonely.
Wouldn't you better go to your aunt?"

"My aunt? Oh! Aunt Tryphosa?" she asked.
"No; I don't like Brooklyn. I shall get along. It
will be all right."

John Sonderby put out his hand, admiring her
bravery. "You have lots of pluck," he exclaimed.
"I don't understand it."

She took his brown hand in both her trembling
ones, but she did not look him in the face.

"Oh," he cried, "I go out so much happier
than when I came in! It is all clear to me now —
what I ought to do, I mean; and how brave you
are!"

"Oh, don't, don't!" she said. "I haven't done
right. But I was kind of desperate."

"I know," he murmured. "It has been too bad; I know how hard it has been."

She stopped him with a convulsive pressure of her hands and a great effort of self-control. "Never mind. That's all past now, Mr. Sonderby. You would have done anything for me — I knew it all the time. But it just couldn't be helped. Good night. And you will surely go to-morrow?"

"To-morrow; yes. Good night, Mrs. Floyd. We won't say good by now."

"No, not good by. Oh, no! Good night." And woman-like she had strength enough to stand there and smile gently at him till he had closed the door and gone out.

But John Sonderby strode back over the wet grass of the cottage yard, and through the noisy, bustling hall of the Broughton House, and up to his room, with a great happiness in his heart. The world seemed sane and sweet to him. She was a brave woman and a true woman, and if she had given him cause for misjudging her, there was plenty of excuse for her. But all that was past, as she had said. The long weeks of uncertainty, of temptation, of idling, of crazy dreams, of irresolution, the days of black suspicion and self-shame; those terrible minutes when his life had seemed to stop and then slowly start again; — it was all behind him now. He had pulled through. There was clear water ahead of him. What had done it? Was it his own staying-power? He felt too much shame at himself to think that. Was it then simply a happening, a kind of luck? Down in his secret soul he knew better than that; and there in his dimly lighted room, while people were waltzing underneath, and Bill Trumbull sat wondering why he did not come down, John Sonderby dropped upon his knees, for the first time in many a year, and what was left of his pride and selfishness went out of his heart, and a peace, deeper than any he had guessed at in orchard and swale, flowed into it. It was a long time before he rose, and the dancing had ceased underneath; Bill Trumbull had gone home, and the lights were out in the office. The divine peace was in the young fellow's breast, and it lay all about and around his human purpose, enfolding it. To make a man of himself, to go where human life was thick and the push was keen and strong, to earn a place there by using the talent that had been given him, to work with hope and courage and belief, with a heart open to his humankind, — that was what John Sonderby with God's help meant to do.

While he lay awake that night, — for things so new and beautiful and far-reaching were in his mind that he could not easily fall to sleep, — he remembered that he had not carried out his intention of calling at the parsonage, and he began to think about Mrs. Ellerton, and what she said to him one rainy evening. He believed she must have meant the same things that were now in his own will to do, and he wondered if she had been thinking about him sometimes in all this interval. and if, when he went to say good by to her on the morrow, he would dare tell her in what new spirit he was going away.

When the morrow came, the bright, clear morrow, and John Sonderby had packed his books and his scanty wardrobe, and paid his bill at the Broughton House. and had bidden his friends in the village good by, — there were far more of them than he had ever realized, — he went up to the parsonage and found Ruth Ellerton there alone. He left his resignation as academy teacher, to be given to her husband. and he told her, albeit a little shyly — he, the stout, brown-bearded fellow — that he hoped his days of purposeless work were over.

It was easier than he thought it would be; for she seemed to understand him almost before he spoke, and the beautiful gray eyes were soft and bright as she bade him good by, and she said nothing of her own and her husband's disappointment in not having him longer in Broughton, for she saw clearly enough that it would be better for him to go.

There was one more farewell for the schoolteacher to leave; but when he stopped at the cottage, the door was locked, and he found that Mrs. Floyd had persuaded Bill Trumbull to go berrying with her. He did not perceive that she had done it to avoid saying good by, and persisted in waiting till the last minute in hope of their return. But the berry-pickers were very deliberate that day, and finally Sonderby had to get into the wagon, in front of his box of books and his old hair trunk, and drive off for the Center, without waiting longer for them. On the way he met Collins, who was driving up to Broughton, and Sonderby had to stop and explain briefly that he was going to Boston, after all, though probably he would not be with the A. S. & F. people. Collins expressed gratification at the decision, and sincerely, for he drove on smiling, after Sonderby had disappeared. This delay was a brief one, but it was enough to make Sonderby miss the express, and he was obliged to stay over night in the Center.

XV.

"There will be another month," Floyd had muttered on that hot July morning when the sparrow was twittering in the lilacs outside the cottage window, and the artist and his wife were looking at each other over old Watson's letter, as it lay between them on the floor. It was August now. The month had slipped away, as all months will. The crisis in the married life of Mr. and Mrs. Floyd had passed, and its ending was a mean and pitiful one: Floyd had slunk away without facing her at the last, though he had thus spared himself and her the ignominy of making and listening to excuses. Yet the fact itself was enough. Their experiment, as Mrs. Floyd had surmised in those mornings when she posed for him by the well-curb, their three years' experiment, was indeed over. Other things, too, had those serene and silent July days seen change. The reticent, brown-bearded schoolmaster, with his irresolute eyes, had learned a harder lesson than ever he had set, and had turned his back on Broughton forever, but with no bitterness of heart; rather with the joyous power of one who has just come to his own.

Collins, that triumphant fisherman and idler,

had finished his summer's fishing and his summer's amusement — almost. As for the other people whom chance had thrown in the way of the four persons above mentioned, there was no particular reason why the first days of August should find them very different from what they were in the first days of July. Human nature, like the great Mother Nature herself, is averse to violent change. Mother Nature deceives us, to be sure, by crooning us to sleep and bandaging our eyes; and we open them again to find that she has tricked us and made very sudden changes indeed while we were not watching. If we are vexed at it, and press her for the secret, all she whispers to us is that what seems so sudden has been long preparing, if we could but have known it. Perhaps human nature may have caught this trick from the old Mother, and might answer, if pressed close, that everything which showed itself during that month, in the four "regulars" at the Broughton House, had been long preparing; that the real causes were far back of those idle weeks of summer.

But Mr. and Mrs. Ellerton, for instance, seemed to be just what they were when John Sonderby went there to tea. They had been busy all the time with a hundred solicitudes and responsibilities whose extent the Broughton people never guessed, and of which the minister and his wife did not often talk, except to each other. They had been happy, too, as well as busy, but that was their own affair. They did not know much more at the end of the month about John Sonderby and their other acquaintances in the Broughton House group than they did at the beginning, to tell the truth, though Sonderby's brief parting call at the parsonage left Ruth Ellerton mystically happy. She tried to communicate her happiness to Arthur, but his vexation at the man's leaving the academy in the lurch made him for the moment sympathize less warmly than he ought with her rapturous announcement that Mr. Sonderby had gone to Boston, with a "real purpose — the best purpose, Arthur." Yes, the atmosphere of the parsonage remained much what it was when Arthur Ellerton joked his enthusiastic wife about the "germ" that she professed to discover in the school-teacher.

As for Bill Trumbull, he had had one of the pleasantest summers in his long list, long actually. — for Bill was nearer sixty than fifty — but marvellously extended if any one undertook to compute the length of time necessary for the occurrence of those manifold events of which Bill preserved such a remarkable recollection. There had been but two drawbacks to his enjoyment of the past month: Evans had been increasingly disrespectful; and secondly, what the committee from Collins Mills Junction had told him about the sport-loving manufacturer had given Trumbull's tolerant faith in human nature a decided jar. But he kept his chair in the Broughton House office, nevertheless, smoking his pipe and stroking reflectively his yellow beard, and by dint of turning his benevolent blue eyes invitingly upon all recent arrivals at the hotel, he succeeded in making many a new acquaintance wherewith to solace himself for the absence or deterioration of the old ones.

It was the best month's business that Evans had ever seen, and for the first time since he had bought out "Trumbull's," he was sure of his venture. The Broughton House justified itself. The little Welshman could thrust his hands deep into the trousers pockets of his new suit and jingle the loose change there, while he paced his new piazza. He no longer had any lingering doubt as to the paint, nor the plumbing, nor the piazza chairs, nor the name of the hotel. The smoking-room had been well patronized, and *Harper's Weekly* had often grown quite tattered with use, before the next week's number came. Best of all, the prosperous month seemed likely to merge into one of still greater prosperity; for August ought by rights to bring even more guests to Broughton than July had done. Evans looked at Parkinson and Meyer, his sole rivals in the business world of Broughton, with that friendly pity which is born of conscious superiority. Ah, there was money in a hotel, with the right man to run it!

Meyer and Parkinson contemplated the Welshman's success from different standpoints. Meyer had known Evans in the Center, and found in the rapid rise of the fellow to an important position in the Broughton community an inherent injustice, which he did not fail to point out to his customers, in the course of those socialistic diatribes with which the barber was in the habit of astounding the persons who sat in his chair. Samuel Parkinson considered the prosperity of the Broughton House in a more philosophic light. Had he not seen " Trumbull's " go under, in his time? "Let the Welshman have his turn," reflected the astute Samuel, as he looked across the street, in those July afternoons, and saw the stage unloading passengers at the hotel. The next season might not be so successful. Nevertheless in the meantime Mr. Parkinson added a new candy counter to the attractions of his store, — or his Emporium, as the advertising-boards on barns and fences for a radius of ten miles around called it — Parkinson's Emporium, — and the more children and young people there were at the hotel, the more did the treasurer of the parish rejoice in the good fortune of his neighbor.

But the people of the village, excepting that small faction of them who believed in the future of Broughton as a summer resort, and wanted to purchase a public watering-cart and to have the houses numbered, the plain people of Broughton village did not trouble themselves very much about the hotel nor the summer visitors who came there.

Broughton folks were occupied enough, that July, in looking out for their own interests and the affairs of their next-door neighbors. Quietly had the days of the month gone by in the white houses up and down Main Street, under the shadow of the elms. Sleepily had the little village drawn its breath, waking each afternoon at mail-time to a weak pretence of life, only to relapse into somnolence. Out upon the farms, scattered over the surrounding hills, there was the unchanged, uneventful existence, the same round of tranquil days, which left when the month was over only the general impression that the season was, on the whole, late and rather cold. Over hotel and village, farms and hills, had swept each day the steady sun, careless whether its rays warmed to life or parched to death, or whether they were chilled and hidden altogether in the storms of rain. Oh, the impartial sun and the unknowing rain, that poured down upon this upland country when there was nothing but primeval forest there and no human cheeks to be warmed or wet, that will ages hence pour down, impartial and unknowing, when mayhap every trace of human life shall have vanished and all is savagery again, how much do they survive!

The month was over, and Tryphena Morton Floyd had endured to the end. It had been a hard time, and lonely. In the innermost chambers of her heart, where the struggle had taken place, there was no one by to help her. She had made no effort to retain her husband, nor had she ever referred, in talking with him, to the possible event of his going away. She had taken it for granted that he would leave her when the time came. Reasoning from his standpoint, as she had once or twice tried to do, she could find no very great obstacle to his going, since it was obvious that it did not lie within her power to make him happy. Obligations which she felt were binding upon herself, she knew instinctively were not recognized by her artist husband. Billy was different from other folks. He had to be satisfied, or to think he was satisfied, with his surroundings, before he could do any work. She had failed to satisfy him. It was humiliating, for the country girl was in her own way proud. It was heart-breaking, for she had loved him. She was too clear-headed to underestimate her own loss, or to make herself believe that there was anything left for her when she felt well enough that there was nothing. Nevertheless, to the very last, she had tried to do her duty by him. Was not her own figure, in the picture Floyd had painted to earn his deliverance, the seal of her wifely obedience?

There had been, indeed, especially in the closing days of her probation, certain times when an inner revolt against what seemed her fate would manifest itself, and carry her actions almost beyond her control. For instance, there was John Sonderby.

She had liked him from the very first; by and by, after the morning they had spent in her cottage, she began to suspect that he cared for her, and she pitied him. She did not mean to lay her hand on his arm, the day of the runaway; she cried over it afterward, but she could not help it at the time. Afterwards she grew to think she had been mistaken in imagining he had cared for her at all, and it made her ashamed and angry with herself to reflect what her thoughts had been, and perhaps, too, it made her a little out of temper with the school-teacher. It was just at this time that Collins began to pay her increased attention, and she had permitted it, partly out of ignorance, partly out of desperation, and perhaps out of a strange defiance of what she felt to be Sonderby's yearning respect for her. But she had never meant to let matters go so far. Collins had treated her with a kindness and politeness such as she was unused to; he was much older than the rest of them, and had his own way; he treated her half like a child and half like a great lady. She had felt, on that Sunday when he asked her to drive, as if she must do something or she would die, and so she had gone with him, though she knew perfectly well that neither Trumbull nor Sonderby would exactly approve of it. Then had come that day of the fishing excursion, when Mr. Collins had come back unexpectedly from the swamp, seated himself beside her, and had talked so strangely that he had frightened her a little.

She had felt his arm on the back of the seat behind her; she had been afraid to speak out, she had thought of a dozen excuses to make in order to get up; and then John Sonderby had marched up the lonely road with his eyes on them, and she was mortified and provoked, and had waved her parasol to Mr. Collins on purpose, to show John Sonderby that she should do as she liked.

The very next day Billy had gone. He had not even said good by to her. Oh, the terrible day! Yet she had not shed a tear, she said no word to herself; she had no thoughts, no mind at all. It was as if she had been under an enchantment, where all things about her moved, and she only was without motion, without will. It was so pitiful to have it all end that way, — all her dreams, her hopes, her brief happiness. Yet there was nothing to be done. She had borne her burden, and at last the end had come. In the evening Mr. Collins had taken her to drive. She did not remember his asking her to go, nor why she went. She seemed to have no voice in the matter. It was the enchanted country again. But she was awakened rudely. Somewhere, out on the moonlit road, she became conscious of what he was saying, of the shameful plan he was rapidly rehearsing, with his face turned toward her. Her mind came back at the shock; she saw his whole plot in an instant, and with the cunning instinct of helplessness she had wits enough for deception; she whispered a shuddering assent; and she got him to take her back to the cottage and promise not to see her again until the time came. He went away, believing she would keep her whispered word; and Mrs. Floyd, her mind beginning to lose its hold again, and her body worn out by sleepless nights, flung herself upon the bed in what had become once more Aunt Tryphena's chamber, and slept like an exhausted child.

When she woke the next morning, Thursday, there was the least touch of autumn in the air, though it was only early August. A spray of golden-rod, in the back yard of the cottage, by the fence, was beginning to turn yellow. Tryphena noticed it when she went out to the well to draw water with which to prepare her solitary breakfast, for she was not able any longer to go to the hotel for meals. She might meet Collins. She was afraid to go alone, knowing what had become of her husband, — and then, she had no money. "Autumn is coming," she thought, as the golden-rod caught her eye. Autumn already! Why not? It was just as well. Mrs. Floyd was entirely composed that morning, and looked upon her life as if it lay behind her like a clear, gray, autumnal landscape. She was no longer a part of it. She had travelled over it indeed, but had now passed beyond it. She had walked faithfully to the very end, as faithfully as she could. But she was tired now; she had no desire to enter upon any new road, to cross any novel tract of country. She did not feel strong enough to go on, nor could she see any use in trying. She remembered perfectly well, now, what Collins had said the night before. Words whose utterance had seemed to make no impression upon her senses at the time, recalled themselves exactly. How quietly and skilfully the sportsman had drawn the network of his plans! He was in possession of her promise. But was life worth having upon those terms? Tryphena shuddered; not with the insane terror she had felt the night before, but with the shame of an honest woman, bred in the moral traditions of a New England ancestry. As girl and woman, she had always been scrupulous of her name, until in the desperation of these last weeks she had possibly compromised herself. There was one person more than any other by whom she dreaded to be misunderstood, and her strongest desire, throughout that slow-dragging day, was to see John Sonderby, to make herself right in his eyes while there was yet time.

When evening came and she spied Calvin Johnson's buckboard bringing the school-teacher back to the Broughton House, she summoned up all her resolution, as one gathers and blows upon embers that have already served too long, and went out to watch for him. It was a hard thing to do, to call him into the cottage and tell him what she did, but it was an expiation of all her folly. She saw too that Sonderby believed in her, that he was still ready to be influenced by her, and this gave her audacity to try to accomplish that for which she had scarcely dared to hope. She had longed all day to have the school-teacher leave Broughton, as soon as she had seen him and made that pitiful intercession for herself. She had always read him well, and knew that his future would be richer if he went to his own proper work; but it was not for that simply that she now wished to have him go. It was for something else, — for her own sake and for his. When she watched him hesitate, and pushed her entreaty, and finally saw him yield and heard him say that he would go, — and that upon the morrow, — her heart, which had never claimed very much as its own portion in the world, was satisfied. It was too late for anything to bring her happiness, but John Sonderby's belief in her and obedience to her wishes brought her a kind of peace.

Strong as she was in many ways, she could not bid him good by, and partly for that reason she persuaded Bill Trumbull to go berrying with her, Friday morning, an hour before the time when she knew Mr. Sonderby would be starting for the Center. Trumbull never needed much persuasion to accompany Tryphena, and they wandered through the pastures above the Hollow for two or three hours, picking some early blackberries, and a few late raspberries. Bill kept putting the largest ones into her pail, just as he had done often when she was a girl. She smiled her thanks to him each time, though she was so silent during the whole ramble that Bill decided that she was missing her husband more than he had "callated," and he tried in his fatherly fashion to impress upon her that two weeks would go quickly. Trumbull could not imagine what should keep the artist so long in New York, but he regretfully abstained from making any inquisitive remarks. The old hotel-keeper's kindly, simple chatter was soothing to her; it reminded her of such far-away things, of the time when he used to bring her home from berrying, upon his shoulder, while her chubby fingers were twisting his yellow beard. The air was sweet and cool, and the pastures were still, solitary. The year, in the full burden of its bearing season, seemed to drowse, in prevision of its time of rest. Yet if anything could have won Mrs. Floyd back, it would seem that the gentleness of that bright day, and the companionship of her sympathetic, garrulous old friend, might have done so. Bill Trumbull was so human, so much a part of the world that now is!

It was an hour after noon when they returned. Mrs. Floyd yielded to Bill's invitation, and went over with him to Mirandy's for dinner. The presence of Mrs. Floyd saved Bill from the scolding his punctual daughter had in store for him, and Mirandy thought that Tryphena seemed very friendly and natural, and that perhaps she herself had been too sharp-tongued in criticising the way Mrs. Floyd had "gone on with that Collins man." Trypheny Morton always had her queer streaks, but she wan't any worse than other folks, after all. Such was the considerate conclusion of Mirandy. After dinner Mrs. Floyd went back to the cottage, and locking the front door behind her, sat down in her rocking-chair by the window. She was strong, though not strong enough for life; brave, though not brave enough for life. Yet once, in that long, lonely afternoon, her heart almost failed her. But just then there was the grating of wheels on the hotel driveway; she peered out and saw Collins's dark, smiling face, and strength and bravery came back to her, sufficiently.

Mr. Bruce D. Collins, having had the satisfaction of seeing the spindles start again at the Collins Mills, had come back to Broughton to get — what belonged to him. He spent an hour or so in his room, packing, and elaborating a brief explanation which he proposed to make to Evans. This latter task had given him some trouble for a couple of days; but Collins felt that something of the sort was, on the whole, necessary, and that Evans would feel it was his own interest to believe what was told him. The plan was a trifle daring, but perhaps none the less likely to succeed on that account.

"Evans," said Collins, gravely, when the chambermaid had summoned the Welshman to Collins's room, "I want the buggy hitched up at ten-thirty, to-night."

The hotel proprietor bowed.

"I've got a telegram from Mr. Floyd," the manufacturer continued. "He is obliged to sail for Hamburg — for Europe — to-morrow, at nine o'clock. It's a sudden matter, you perceive, and he wants to have Mrs. Floyd get there to see him off. If she can hit the twelve-three express to-night, she can make it, and I'm going to drive her to the Center, and shall go down with her to New York. It wouldn't do to have her start off like that alone."

The Welshman nodded. "Is Mr. Floyd to be gone long?" he asked, respectfully.

"Yes; he may be. It's important business — some painting to be done, or something of that sort."

"There is a little matter of a board bill. Thirteen days' board — excuse my —"

"Oh, put it in with mine," interrupted Collins, tersely. "I'll settle with him. He went off in a hurry."

"Very well, Mr. Collins," said Evans, smoothly. "At ten-thirty, you said? I'll speak to Johnny."

"All right — Say!" Evans closed the door again, and waited. Collins had not finished his speech. It was more awkward than he had anticipated. There was no other way, though; the bolder he was, the better the chances.

"If Mr. Floyd doesn't come back pretty soon,

she may have to do something for a living in the meantime. I shouldn't wonder if she would go into my mills, as a typewriter, or — book-keeper."

The little black eyes of the Welshman were cocked astutely, but he made no reply.

"That's all, Evans," remarked Mr. Collins, with the slightest expression of relief. "And — you've taken pretty good care of me this summer," and he pushed a roll of bills into the fingers of the surprised Welshman, who kept the money, nevertheless, and backed out of the door, bowing deeply. He ran his thumb through the bills as he crept down stairs. Collins had never feed him before. Why this time? As he passed noiselessly through the smoking-room, he caught sight of a New York paper, and had a sudden curiosity, which it took but a moment to satisfy. The Hamburg steamer was advertised to sail, not at nine in the morning, but at three in the afternoon. Collins had been lying to him. The knowing little Welshman thrust his hand into his trousers pocket again, and grasped the bills as if to assure himself of the reality of the experience through which he had passed, and then with a shrug of his shoulders and a weasel glance around the empty smoking-room, he gave vent to his opinion in a single sarcastic ejaculation: "Book-keeper!"

It was four o'clock. In spite of the hot sunshine that now flooded the western end of the hotel piazza, a crowd of guests were huddled there, watching a tennis match upon the court below them. The playing was spirited, and there was frequent spatting of hands and quick cries of excitement, at the more brilliant strokes. The Broughton House had lost altogether the air of emptiness, of pretence, which it had worn earlier in the season. Everything was going very well there, very well indeed. Even the arrival of the stage this afternoon failed to attract interest away from the game, and the only persons who paid any attention to it were Evans, who assigned Sonderby's room to a newcomer, and Collins, who came down to the piazza to give the driver explicit directions about taking his trunks to the Center in the morning. The driver was repeating these directions to himself so assiduously, as he drove up the sleepy street, that he forgot to take off his hat to Mrs. Ellerton, who had once shaken hands with him after a Young People's Society of Christian Endeavor meeting into which he had strayed, and who now bowed so friendly to him from the sidewalk, as almost to make him vow to go to the meeting again.

Mrs. Ellerton had come out to make a call. Arrayed in her gray Henrietta and her best bonnet, carrying her ivory card-case in one hand and her parasol in the other, she was a very attractive-looking parson's wife, and the stage-driver might well turn to look at her as her tall figure wound in and out among the elm-trees that encroached upon the narrow sidewalk. She was very happy and contented that afternoon, albeit her face was graver than usual. She had been reading since dinner the concluding article of a series upon "Divorce," in one of her favorite Reviews, and the statistics as to the moral life of her beloved New England had shocked her, accustomed even as she was to the consideration of social questions. It was inexpressibly painful to think that there was such selfishness and animalism left in the world, even here in the beautiful old New England towns, where truth had been taught so constantly. But no shadow could rest very long upon Ruth Ellerton's pure, strong face, and more than one thing happened, as she went down the street, to recall her from painful thoughts to her own happy work here in Broughton. There was the sight of the stage-driver, for instance; how little did the lanky fellow suspect that behind that charming bow there lurked a plot for his moral amelioration! There was Samuel Parkinson's boy, who ran across the street to speak to her; a precociously pious youth who had been designated by candid Arthur Ellerton — in temporary forgetfulness of ministerial prudence and simply in the presence of his wife — as "a thorough little ass," but a boy nevertheless whose real virtues were appreciated, and whose high lights were being gradually toned down, by this wise and loving woman. Above all, there was the call she expected to make, one requiring all her tact and cheery spirits and sympathy; for she was going down to the Floyd cottage.

From certain words dropped by Sonderby when he called at the parsonage that morning, she had inferred that Mrs. Floyd was in some kind of trouble and was left much to herself. It seemed that the artist had gone away for a while, and that his wife was living all alone at the cottage. Sonderby had even gone so far as to suggest, bashfully, that if Mrs. Ellerton could get better acquainted with Mrs. Floyd, it would be well worth while — it might do a great deal of good. At such negotiations the inventor of the telephone-switch was particularly inexpert, but Ruth Ellerton needed no urging when her sympathy was touched. Mrs. Floyd had never returned her call; but the minister's wife could not stop for that, if there was a chance of reaching this slender, dark-haired young woman, with black clothes and shy, melancholy eyes. To fancy her living all alone in that old house of her aunt! Mrs. Ellerton stepped faster as she thought of it; she framed some excuse already "for running in without waiting for formalities." She opened the creaking gate, at the cottage, and walked swiftly up the neglected path to the front door. Upon the left was the bench upon which she had sat when she and Arthur had made their call; but rain-water was standing in the hollow of the seat, and a spider had flung his web across one end. At the door there was neither bell nor knocker. Mrs. Ellerton rapped, and then waited. There was no response. She rapped louder, bruising her dainty glove against the cracked paint. Still no answer. She looked regretfully at the knuckles of her gloves, and stooping, picked up a little stone that lay by the low, rotting steps, and rapped sharply with that. She was almost ashamed to make so much noise. Yet no one came. She hesitated. Perhaps she had misunderstood Mr. Sonderby, after all; possibly Mrs. Floyd had gone away too. She tried the door softly; it was locked. How very unfortunate! There was no use in waiting longer. She took one of her cards from the ivory case, and slipped it under the door, in the hollow of the worn threshold. Then she looked round her a moment, before she turned away. The lilac leaves had grown thick and leathery, and there seemed to be a dampness in their shade. The last pink-edged petals had long before fallen from the Smith roses, and the green rose-apples were forming there instead. It seemed as if such a long time had elapsed since she and Arthur called upon the Floyds; and the dooryard had such an abandoned air! She was not sorry to escape from the shadow of the lilacs into the sunshine again, and yet she was vexed at not having found Mrs. Floyd in, greatly vexed and disappointed. She had had a sort of intuition that she was needed at the cottage.

It was true. It was a pity that the door was

locked, and that Mrs. Floyd, who had seen her coming, sat quite still in the rocking-chair, and did not rise to let her in. That gracious presence, with its loving gentleness, its yearning desire to be of help, its strong vitality, might not have come into the lonely sitting-room too late to bring hope, sweet hope and endurance and faith for the things of life. But the heavy door was locked, and Tryphena Floyd sat with fixed and awestruck eyes, hardly hearing Mrs. Ellerton's rapping; for in her ears was the soft rustle and before her eyes the dusky wings of another hope, the shadowy, all-encompassing hope that broods sooner or later over every mortal soul. . . .

Evening came. The lamps were lit in the Broughton House. Collins came downstairs, having at last finished his packing. The sound of the melodeon in the parlor made him think of his music, however, and he went in and gathered that up, taking it to his room and unstrapping a trunk to put it away. There was no use in leaving anything behind: he might not come up to Broughton again the next summer; perhaps not for some time. With these reflections still in his head, he descended to the office, and sat down by the fireplace, smoking cigar after cigar. He was rather ill at ease. Perhaps, he thought, it had been foolish in him to say so much to Evans; but then the thing was bound to get out, in some shape or other, and his own version would stand the best chance of being considered authoritative. The whole scheme was pretty bold; somewhat worse than anything he had ever done before; but then, whose business was it except his own — and hers? Everything, too, had worked to favor him. He was glad Sonderby was out of the way: Sonderby was a good enough fellow, but queer; there might have been some kind of a row. Yes, she had been right in getting a promise not to see her again until she was all ready, at ten-thirty; it was a good deal safer and less likely to make talk in the village; he would hardly have thought that she had so much head as that, with only a minute to think it over in, that night in the buggy. She was deep, though, like all of them! Well, in two hours they would be off. Not a soul in the village would be awake to see them drive away. It was the simplest thing in the world.

Nevertheless, Mr. Collins kept getting more and more restless. He could not sit still by the fireplace any longer, and took to pacing the floor of the office, and looking furtively at his watch from time to time. Bill Trumbull tried to start one or two topics of conversation, but in vain. Suddenly Collins's eye fell upon the fish-spear that was hung along one of the huge ceiling beams, and he had an idea. There was but one thing he had planned this summer which had not turned out to suit him: he had failed to capture the big trout down in the Hollow. He had half a mind to go down to-night and spear him. There was time enough, and there would be some fun in it. Why not drive away with the trout under the buggy seat — under their buggy seat — and make a complete thing of the summer? He went to the side door of the office and called to the stable-boy, who was drumming with his heels on the side piazza, waiting till it was time to hitch up.

"Johnny, have you got anything to do?"

"Not yet awhile, sir," said the boy.

"Well, put some oil into that torch you had in the stable the other day. I want to have you come down to the Hollow with me, to see if we can't get that trout."

Collins climbed up on a chair, and pulled down the dusty spear from the hooks on which it rested.

"Why, say," interrupted Bill Trumbull, benevolently, "I thought you said that when you'd sunk so low as to spear that trout —"

"Is it any of your damned business, Bill Trumbull, what I do?" cried Collins, glaring down from his eminence. The astonished Trumbull made no reply, while the stable-boy grinned, and ran off for the torch. The sportsman in Collins had, indeed, degenerated, too. The boy came back in a few moments with his plaything, a tin can swinging on the end of a stick, a relic of the last presidential campaign, when Broughton had had the first torchlight parade in her history. Collins got his hat, and they started out, Trumbull looking at them wonderingly. Evans had sidled into the office in time to hear Collins's outburst against the ex-proprietor of the hotel. He could not resist the temptation to add to Trumbull's discomfiture by showing that he, Evans, was now the one who enjoyed the manufacturer's intimacy. Then, too, he felt a sly curiosity to see how Trumbull would take the news that Mrs. Floyd was going to New York with the manufacturer. There would be no harm in telling Trumbull; indeed Evans had rightly suspected that Collins had wished him to repeat the facts in the case, just as they had been presented to him.

"Mr. Collins is going to New York," said Evans, indifferently. "What do you think of the news from Floyd?"

"I don't know any," replied Bill, sulkily.

"Aha? Oh, yes. Mrs. Floyd is going down with Collins to-night to see him off for Europe."

"With Collins — to-night?" gasped Bill, taking his pipe out of his mouth.

"You didn't know it, eh? You don't keep up with the times very well. I thought you knew everything that was going on." The Welshman's sneer was lost upon the excited old man.

"I've got to see her!" he exclaimed, rising from his chair, and rapping the tobacco out of his pipe. "I've kind o' got to send a message by her — a little matter — " and he hurried out of the side door, jumped from the piazza and was gone, leaving the Welshman in terror lest Collins's wrath should descend in turn upon himself, for letting out the plan too soon. Across the back yard of the Floyd cottage, under the Seckel pear-trees, hastened Bill Trumbull, with the activity of a man thirty years younger. He knocked at the back door with agitated fingers, and entered the kitchen without waiting for a reply. Was it possible that Sonderby had been deceived, in what he had declared before leaving town that morning? Had not Tryphena said that she did not expect to see Collins again? Half-way across the dark kitchen Trumbull stopped, and lest he should frighten her by bursting in like that, he called out her name —

"Trypheny!"

The cottage was still.

"Trypheny!" His voice trembled this time. Then he stumbled forward and flung open the sitting-room door. There was no one there. Upon the rocking-chair by the window lay Mrs. Floyd's shawl. The lamp was lighted, and a whole troop of little moths, entering through the open window, were fluttering about the flame, singeing themselves to death against the chimney; and the flapping of their tiny, feathered wings was all the sound the alarmed old man could hear, though he strained his ears to listen through a long, anxious minute, before he turned and hurried out.

But meanwhile Collins and the boy had picked their way down through the lane, and had climbed over into the meadow. It was barely nine o'clock, and the night was not very dark, though the sky was partially overcast and the stars were few and languid. The meadow grass was drenched with dew, and Collins stopped to turn up his trousers. The boy had on his stable boots, and did not mind the wet. He carried his unlighted torch in an eager hand, and was proud to be asked to accompany Mr. Collins upon such an expedition, though once when a belated sparrow started up in the tangle of golden-rod to the left of their narrow path, the boy jumped, and kept close behind his companion after that. Johnny envied the fearless way in which Collins strode along, cigar in mouth, not seeming to be startled at all by the sparrow. Over the moist meadow, where the rowan was already started, fireflies were wandering, gleaming softly for a minute and then going out. It was so quiet there in the meadow: no sound at all except the brushing of the fisherman's feet upon the wet rowan, and the rattle of the oil-can of the torch. They climbed rather noisily over the stone wall, and wound up the path through the pasture, along by the dark, fragrant clumps of sweet-fern, which wet Collins's legs to the knees, as he brushed past them. Up they pressed, panting a little till they reached the level, and saw the pasture bars standing out huge against the sky. Here they stopped to rest a moment; behind them were the straggling lights of the village, on either side the wide sweep of pasture and meadow, lying indistinct now in the murky light, except where the valleys and the strips of woodland made dark patches. The horizon was narrowed to a few hundred yards, and the quiet, cloudy sky hung down close to the earth. From in front, louder than by day, rose the noise of water, and the Hollow broke away at their feet like a black abyss. Across it they could see the hemlocks, dimly towering, and beyond their gloomy branches, at the eastern end of the ledge, there was a yellowish tinge in the clouds, as if the moon were behind them.

"Well, come on, Johnny!" cried Collins, starting down into the Hollow. He had a keen zest for the business: his blood was hot and high: he was bent on having his own will, this silent night. As they descended, the hill kept rising dark behind them, between them and the village, isolating them. The air throbbed with the plunging of the water. When they got within a few yards of the pool, Collins stopped, and scrutinized the length of the torch. It was a very long one.

"Look here," said Collins, "you stay on this side, close up there, by the stump. I'll get on the other side, just over the ledge, and then if he comes out to look at your light, I'll be right on top of him. Don't light up till I get over there."

He went down below the lower end of the pool, and the boy heard him splash through the brook, over the loose stepping-stones. Then his figure, a black shadow, came in sight again, creeping cautiously along the narrow rock, just above the water. Nearer and nearer he crawled, till he was opposite the stable-boy.

"All right!" he hissed across the water. "Light up." He half rose to his feet, and the shaft of his spear rattled against the ledge as he got it well in hand and made ready to poise it. The boy struck a match, and touched it to the wick of his torch. There was a red, smoky flame.

"Now shove it out toward me," whispered Collins. "That's it. Now steady. Farther! Farther! — *Hold on! What's that!*"

But the boy had seen it too, in the same instant. The torch dropped into the pool from his frightened hands, and he turned and ran up the black pasture-side for the village, screaming, "Help! — Help!" in a paroxysm of fear, "Help! Help!" in his clear, boyish voice, while on the ledge, close by the water, crouched the cowering sensualist, and the moon, peering from under the hemlock boughs like a huge eye, gazed down at him omnisciently.

XVI.

Down at the Center Saturday morning broke clear and sunshiny, though the night had been cloudy and a little rain had fallen. The pavements were wet and steaming when John Sonderby walked out of the Central Hotel and down the street to the station, whither the hotel hack had just carried his trunk and box of books. He squared his shoulders, inhaling long draughts of the fresh air. His room at the Central Hotel had been rather close, and the electric light had shone in through the transom enough to keep him awake awhile during the first part of the night. At five o'clock the chorus of bells and whistles from the factories had wakened him again, and, as the Boston express left at six, he rose at once, and having succeeded in getting a tolerable breakfast, had ten or fifteen minutes in which to catch his train. The walk to the station cleared his head, and he passed with a springy step through the crowds of workmen on their way to the factories. Erect, vigorous, with enthusiastic new hopes and purposes, John Sonderby was a happy man that morning. The world was before him. It made his breath quicken to hear the cry, "Here she comes!" as the heavy express swung around the curve and rolled into the station. He got aboard, finding a seat in the first car behind the sleepers. There were not many persons there, and most of them looked frowzy and tired from the night's ride. "All aboard!" cried the conductor; the grimy brakeman slammed the door of Sonderby's car, and the train resumed its scarcely interrupted motion. Away from the smoky Center, from the clattering noises of mill and factory, off down the wooded valley it sped, on its tireless way to Boston.

But it did not move any too fast for John Sonderby. He was already planning what he would do that afternoon. Perhaps Harry Duffield would meet him at the train; at any rate, he had telegraphed that he was coming. It was queer that Harry might do him a good turn in Boston, after all, even if it were nothing more than to secure him a place at a boarding-house. He thought it would be best to call upon the A. S. & F. people, just to make their acquaintance, even if the position they had once offered him had now been filled. Very likely there might be an opening there later. But it was no matter if there should be none; there were plenty of places in the world, and he knew well enough the stuff he had in him. Oh, to get to work again! And he thought of his books in the baggage car, and wished he had one with him, that he might not waste the time. He tried to work out some equations in physics in his head, and then smiled at himself for being so eager. There would be time enough for all that. He might better look out of the window now and gaze his last at the green hill country; there was no knowing when he would see it again.

Through the narrow valley down which the express was thundering ran a river, and Sonderby watched a long time the brown, shallow water and the white, up-curving heaps of foam where the rocks protruded. The foam seemed trying to climb up stream; and though it always slipped back, it never lost patience, and Sonderby amused himself by watching the ever-repeated struggle, as curve after curve of the river brought new rapids into view. It occurred to him suddenly that this was the stream which turned the Center factories, and which took its rise up in Broughton. Sure enough, the very stream! He retraced, in his fancy, its course, and with his turn for mathematics tried to calculate its velocity, and the length of time required for a given particle of water to be carried, say, from the Hollow behind the village, which was as far up as Sonderby had ever followed the brook, down through the meadows and long pasture slopes to the Center, past the black wheels of the factories, and so on down the river till it was opposite him, and made a part of one of those white spurts of foam. Then he began to think about Broughton, and it seemed as if he had already been away from the village a good while.

He wondered if he would ever go back, after a time, to see the old acquaintances, made in the course of those three dormant years. Yes, he thought he would. But he did not intend to wait so long as that before he learned news of some people up in the village. He meant to write to her — to Mrs. Floyd — as soon as he was settled; she undoubtedly would be willing to answer, just a few words, from time to time, to let him know how it was going with her. There would be no harm in it. Poor little woman! She was brave, though, and he had cruelly misjudged her. Still, if it had not been for that, — he thought with a sort of tremble at the heart, — if it had not been for his thinking ill of her, he might not have been cured of his own folly, he might be up there in Broughton still, waiting to throw himself away, if she ever had given him the word. Instead of this, it was she who had urged him to go, to win for himself the place in the world that belonged to him, and it was really in obedience to her wish that he was here now, on his way to his life work. Strange that he had not thought of it in that way before! Ah, how much he owed her! more than any one could ever know. The brave, silent woman, with her own great trouble.

The express train rumbled out of the valley, and slowed up again at another town. A few passengers came into the car, among them a fresh-faced girl of twenty, with her mother. They took the seat in front of Sonderby; and when the girl dropped one of her bundles into the aisle, in seating herself, Sonderby handed it to her, and thought she thanked him prettily. He watched the two for a while, wondering where they were going, and admired the way in which the girl made her mother comfortable, and the business-like air with which she handed their tickets to the conductor. People seemed wonderfully interesting to him that morning; it was as if he were beginning his human experience all over again, and could look at everything with new eyes. So the train rushed along, in the cool morning hours, crossing fertile valleys and barren scrub-oak ridges, leaving the foaming river far behind as it bore John Sonderby toward Boston, and the fellow was strong in purpose, and had hope and tenderness of heart.

Over the Broughton uplands, that afternoon, a gentle west wind was blowing. Mr. and Mrs. Ellerton felt it upon their faces, as they drove slowly along a hill road, on their way home from Canuck Corner. They would scarcely have gone on this day, had it not been that a case of extreme poverty and threatening illness had left the pastor no alternative, and Ruth would not let him go alone. The minister and his wife were very silent, and Ellerton was grave. The horror of the last night had scarcely had time to disappear from their faces, and even now, Mrs. Ellerton cried a little, from time to time, as the phaeton carried them through the lonely outskirts of their parish. In all the excitement that had wakened the village the night before, in the unavailing efforts, the awful sense of impotency, these two persons had had a share. She had been one of those who in the early morning had rendered that last loving service which only women understand. It was the first time she had ever helped to do it. Arthur had been telegraphing, arranging, driving hastily to the Center, doing whatever was necessary. There was no one else to take the responsibility. Aunt Tryphosa had replied to his message, and expected to reach Broughton that evening; but he could get no trace of Floyd. It had been a strange morning; unlike anything else in the cheery young minister's experience. He was sobered, haunted with a feeling that he had underrated the terrible forces that were playing all about him. At dinner-time he and his wife had sat for the most part speechless, looking at each other. It was so sudden! Only the day before Mrs. Ellerton had slipped her correctly engraved card under the locked door of the cottage. But when the afternoon brought the summons to Canuck Corner, Ellerton collected himself, and drove off to do his work. Mrs. Ellerton, too, found that she was needed in the French Canadian hovel, and in the effort to bring cleanliness and comfort and a little heart of grace into the squalid house, both the minister and his wife forgot something of the other — the nightmare. As they left the Corner behind them, at last, and made their way homeward over the hill road, walking the horse, and letting the west wind cool their heavy eyelids, something of the accustomed composure came back to them. The tears might creep up, now and then, into Ruth Ellerton's gray eyes, but she could not help that.

"Oh, Arthur," she cried once, as the horse stopped of his own accord at the summit of a long hill, "we must try harder! We must not let them slip away." Her voice trembled in its intensity.

"Yes, my dear," he answered, seriously, understanding her. No other word was needed. Different as these two were, and differently as they had received that day's experience, they had a common aspiration and a common peace. There are shores many; there is but one inflowing tide.

Lower sank the sun in the clear August sky. Shadows began to fill the hollows of the pastures, though mile after mile of sunlit lonely hilltops were spread all around. It was a beautiful world they beheld, a beautiful world to live in and to work in. The wind blew cooler, but still they sat there on the hilltop, gazing, wondering.

Out on the Atlantic the wind blew cooler, too, and the Hamburg steamer quivered slightly as she caught the long rollers of the open sea. The blue waste was roughening, and the horizon, which had appeared so distant when she left Sandy Hook, seemed narrowing in on every side. Floyd, leaning contentedly against the rail, cigarette in mouth, noted with an artist's interest the change, and tried to explain it in German to his companion, an affable Jewish wine-merchant from Wiesbaden, who had been informing him about the prospects for that year's vintage. They watched the water a while longer, chatting together, and then as the wind grew chillier, they lounged into the smoking-room, to see if any one was organizing a pool upon the first day's run.

But on the Broughton hilltop the horizon widened as the sun sank lower and the wind blew keener. Infinitely remote seemed those farthest lines and crests, but clear, and suffused with the same light that turned the bleached grass of the nearest pastures to a sudden gold.

www.ingramcontent.com/pod-product-compliance
Lightning Source LLC
Chambersburg PA
CBHW032045220426
43664CB00008B/871